Advanced Praise for...
My Obit: Daddy Holding Me

"Powerful. Honest. Heartwarming. A courageous examination of the secret nooks in the soul that expose to the self who we truly are...and why. Atchity's memoir is riveting, reflective, and revealing. A MUST read!"

—Tracy Price-Thompson, bestselling novelist

"*My Obit: Daddy Holding Me* by Kenneth Atchity is a compelling autobiography worthy of the analogy of Sisyphus discovering the burdens and pleasures of each push of the rock up the hill of his extraordinary life. And he gives the readers the powerful encouragement to explore their own journeys, coming to terms with family misunderstandings, life changes both imposed and embraced, and the courage to make each day an opportunity to compound and expand your own dreams and ambitions, as well as bond with loved ones and friends. I doubt that any reader would not have analogous stories in their lives, whether it's watching your grandmother make stuffed grape leaves in the tradition of her Lebanese upbringing, or as I did, helping my Czech maternal grandmother make fried pastries that I finished off with sprinkles of powdered sugar... Read this biography and, as Kenneth Atchity shares his life with you, including favorite family recipes and jokes told by friends, you will explore details of your own life, both distant and recent."

—Norman Stephens, producer,
former head of Warner Brothers television

"This memoir is as proactive, witty, and engaging as its title. A compulsively readable tale of a journey through and beyond the American Century."

—Robert M. Shrum, Director of the Center for the Political Future and the Unruh Institute of Politics, University of Southern California

"Ken Atchity is a rarity in this modern world—a true Renaissance man. Noted author, scholar and Hollywood producer, his memoir is a funny, moving, and compelling journey through a fascinating life."

—Dennis Palumbo, psychotherapist, screenwriter, and novelist

"Autobiography is the source for all narrative genres, especially a fine one like Atchity's. For, it not only illuminates what we already know about him—his brilliance, his productivity, his ability to work on five projects at a time—but also reveals new dimensions we didn't suspect—his cross-dressing, his sensitivity to names, and his desire for taking big risks."

—Marsha Kinder, Professor Emeritus of Cinematic Arts at USC and director of The Labyrinth Project, a research initiative and art collective on database narrative

"Ken Atchity's *My Obit: Daddy Holding Me* engages the reader with a narrative that is amusing and thought provoking in its universality. Peppered with literary references, it is reminiscent of John Irving's *Cider House Rules.* An orphan must make a personal journey to understand his own meaning of life regardless of the rules. In *My Obit,* Ken Atchity is emotional orphaned by a distant father but able to find purpose living life his way."

—Mai-Ding Wong

"My *Obit* is a delightful journey of an examined life and accumulated wisdom, told with perception, humor and heart."

—Charles Matthau, filmmaker

"This fascinating book captures with intimate detail the heart, soul, and spirit of a remarkable man."

—Michael A. Simpson, author, and producer

"I finished reading Vol. 1 of *My Obit*. If I had been holding a copy of the book, I couldn't have put it down. As it was, I read it in two sittings on my computer with the use of one eye.

"I really did enjoy the read. When can I expect volumes 2 and 3?"

—Tom DeCoursey, Rockhurst High School classmate

"This wonderful book tells it all about a life well lived. A truly inspiring read."

—Laurence O'Bryan, author and founder of the Dublin Writers Conference

My Obit 1:

Daddy Holding Me

Kenneth Atchity

STORY MERCHANT BOOKS
LOS ANGELES • 2021

ISBN-13: 978-1-970157-27-7

Story Merchant Books
400 S. Burnside Ave., #11B
Los Angeles, CA 90036
www.storymerchantbooks.com

kenatchity.blogspot.com
storymerchant.com
kenatchitydoortodoor.blogspot.com

www.529bookdesign.com
Body text is set in Goudy Old Style, titles in HelpUsGiambattista

Other Works by Kenneth Atchity

Japanese In-Law: Words and Phrases for Living Day to Day (with Keisaku Mitsumatsu)

Your VIP Biography: How to Write Your Autobiography to Land a Hollywood Deal (with Alinka Rutkowska)

Tell Your Story to the World & Sell It for Millions (with Lisa Cerasoli)

The Meander Tile of Lisa Greco (as Andrea Aguillard)

The Twaesum Aik of Brae Mackenzie (as Andrea Aguillard)

Sell Your Story to Hollywood: Writer's Pocket Guide to the Business of Show Business

The Messiah Matrix

Seven Ways to Die (with William Diehl)

How to Quit Your Day Job and Live Out Your Dreams

How to Publish Your Novel

Writing Treatments That Sell (with Chi-Li Wong)

Cajun Household Wisdom

The Classical Roman Reader

The Classical Greek Reader

The Renaissance Reader

Sleeping with an Elephant

A Writer's Time: A Guide to the Creative Process from Vision through Revision

Italian Literature: Roots & Branches

Homer: Critical Essays

Homer's Iliad: The Shield of Memory

In Praise of Love (premiered at Lincoln Center)

Eterne in Mutabilitie: The Unity of the Faerie Queene

My Obit 1:

Daddy Holding Me

Kenneth Atchity

To Frederick J. Atchity, my father, to settle accounts between us. And to Vincent and Rosemary—and granddaughter Meggie and grandsons Teddy, Oliver, Eliot, and Louis Ignatius. Live *your* stories to the max and share them joyfully with the ones you love.

"Where is home? Most of us are born with the answer. Others have to sift through the pieces."

—Anthony Bourdain

"The unexamined life is not worth living."

—Socrates

Foreword from Writer to Reader

As someone that has been writing all my life, someone who's never experienced writer's block, it bothers me to think that another writer might scribe my obituary. It just doesn't feel *right*. Besides, I'm way too much a control freak to wait around until someone else scrawls "the end" and decides how to summarize me.

So I am telling you this story myself, in my own sweet time, hoping it will inspire you to take charge of and report your own story someday.

Since the morning at the breakfast table at age nine when my mother egged me on to finish a dreadful short story about an African American God surprising a racist white man at the gates of Heaven, I've been not only a *story merchant* finding, polishing, selling, and producing stories but an inveterate *storyteller.* Learning Homeric Greek in Jesuit high school so I could read *The Iliad* and *The Odyssey* in the original, I marveled to learn that in the heroic world Homer describes, the word for the storyteller was *teknos.* In the oral tradition, where all stories were *spoken* instead of *written,* the peripatetic *teknos* enjoyed honor and status equal to that accorded to kings. Eagerly welcomed from his endless journeys with food and drink, the singer of tales wove the human community together by bearing news and stories from hearth to hearth, port to port. In the tradition of my distant ancestors, the ancient Phoenicians, I would dedicate my life to the story trade.

Only *you* should fashion meaning from the things that happen to you. It's your life, after all. If you can't do it now, you *will* do it someday—if you keep track of things that happen, store the evidence, and hang around long enough to figure out the pattern the pieces form: the pattern of your life. The ancient dramatist Sophocles said, "Count no one happy until he is dead. The ending tells all." I beg to disagree. "I'm not dead yet," to quote *Monty Python and the Holy Grail*, but I am here to tell you joyously about my oddly-estranged, often exhilarating, intellectually insatiable, and relentlessly schizoid journey *toward*, not *to*, Ithaka (that island from which Odysseus set sail to discover who he was, and to which he returned only decades later as somebody else—the somebody he'd *become*). Along the way, I learned to commune with pleasant people and pretend to be happy and clear. I experienced the great people I encountered. But that doesn't mean I *was* happy and clear. I missed much of the greatness of those moments until I realized that the condition I felt myself to be in as I pretended wasn't one to be avoided or even understood, but one to be sought and relished. Happiness can come from being with pleasant people and pretending you're happy.

Egocentrism aside, I'm telling my own story about where this eccentric mind that inhabits my body and soul came from and what it struggled with to become what it came to be—that is, how I ended up as what Albert Camus would call absurdly happy. Through constant revising—"Writing *is* rewriting," as I chant to clients and students—I've done my best here to get my story straight and deliver it to you, learning along the way that everything that happens to a person ends up being back story to his present state of mind. As my dear friend, the late Charles Champlin at the *LA Times* said when someone asked him what it took to write a good review, "It takes everything that's happened to you until the moment you write it." After living through fifteen US presidents, I think enough has happened for it to be high time.

In Act 1 of my *curriculum vitae*, which ended at age 17 when I drove away from Kansas City (KC) for Georgetown in Washington, DC, in someone else's car, my guiding light was that ultimate Female Authority Figure, my mother. Because of the estrangement she wove between me and my father, me and my brother, even in Act 1, I, more or less unconsciously, began my determined search for Male Authority Figures to help me grope my way toward independence and manhood.

Act 2 was my life as an academic. At Georgetown and Yale, I found mentors who, while gently showing me my inadequacies, yet instilled in me the self-confidence that I could achieve whatever I set my mind to—confirming what my mother told me, but in a way I found credible and grounded.

Act 2 ended when I flew from Los Angeles to Montreal to begin my producing and literary management career and relinquished my tenured faculty position at Occidental College, where I'd discovered other Male Authority Figures to inspire me, counsel me, and cheer me on as I pushed my rock of the moment up the hill of life.

In Act 3, I came to realize that, as so many of my MAFS passed on to their reward, they've left me to become, by default, my own MAF—though, God knows, I still consult them as "my saints" that populate mind and memory. Their photographs, reduced to postage-stamp size, stare at me from the wood panels of my desk.

Looking back as I piece my life-puzzle together, I realize I'd been wrong—misled—about my father; and blinded-wrong about my mother; unfairly wrong about my adopted midwestern hometown and about my birthplace in the deep south. Growing up with mixed signals and loyalties, I was confused about money vs self-realization, evils of the city vs virtues of the country, guilt vs redemption, protective introspection vs businesslike gregariousness, South vs North, rice vs potatoes, loving to stay home vs needing to see the world, living vs writing about it, and God knows what all else. Now, well into Act 3, I'm no doubt still confused by a few things. But I offer to you here the things I've managed to sort out in hopes they might help you in sorting as you go.

For writing is meaningless without readers. Maybe the Greek orator Demosthenes enjoyed giving speeches with rocks in his mouth against the roar of the waves, but to me, a story is only meaningful if someone is there to hear it. Can you imagine sitting on an empty front porch and telling a joke—alone? At the end of his epic novel *Moby Dick*, the story's narrator, Ishmael, tells us, quoting the Book of Job: "I only have escaped alone to tell thee." We either must believe Ishmael's incredible story and its massively implausible, dramatically allegorical, ending—or not; and that, after investing our attention span for nearly six hundred pages. Like Odysseus returned from twenty years of adventure, Ishmael spins a whale of a tale about a damaged man working through challenges to find his compass center, his North Star. Odysseus can only hope that his long-suffering wife Penelope believes the tale of his adventures. Human consciousness doesn't die with the body when it's passed along to family, friends, associates, clients, audiences, students—and readers. Dear reader, the final judgment resides with you. Read it in *your* sweet time, which I appreciate you are spending on my pages. I will be satisfied if you find anything in these pages to internalize.

My Obit 1

Act 1

Inferno: Prometheus bound in the land of the Cyclops

In which the author moves from the idylls of south Louisiana to the Cyclops' island of Kansas City and progresses from his rapt awe of well-told stories to learning to tell, first, jokes, then his own stories; then stories he can control by publishing his own parish newspaper and advancing up the ranks to editor in chief of his high school newspaper; then reviews for The Kansas City Star. *He receives recognition for his writing and scholarship enough to propel him free of the Cyclops' kingdom and into the wide, wide world where he becomes a master juggler of stories in many languages.*

"Let Your Brother Win"

In the game of life, we're all handicapped by always having to play against ourselves. I gained that insight, like many others, from my life-long love for tennis. Tennis, pursued long enough, forces insight; it reveals all the secrets of the mind. For the first few years I played, it was mostly physical: trying to learn the right moves and angles, frustrated that they look so easy and seem so hard to get right under the pressure of the game. It only takes a microsecond for the ball to hit my racket—or not—but that's not only the most important microsecond in which to practice focus, it's also the most elusive. Somehow my almighty brain, which has cooperated in "keeping my eye on the ball" from the moment it leaves the opponent's racket to that crucial instant when it approaches mine, suddenly wants to be anywhere else: crossing Park Avenue in Manhattan, waving for the *Kibbeh* Man on Ipanema Beach, waiting for a prescription at the drugstore, ogling the bleached blonde on the next court, my recent altercation with a meter maid—the list is infinite.

I blow the point.

Year after year of playing, I learned a few things about myself. I learn in point scores how my unconscious and my conscious mind interact, vying for control of my body—or my ego taunting my calmly competent deeper self.

I can be playing against Hilton, who's in his late eighties, on gorgeous, blue-surfaced Beverly Hills courts. I know I can beat him, but to do that, I have to play normally and *not* blow my shots. Why Hilton's age and my doublethink are even factors:

How important is it to beat an eighty-six-year-old man?

On the other hand, why should I let him beat me?

I am having this exact dialogue as the ball approaches me, with the predictable result that, as easy as this shot should be—I blow it.

Before long, the score is 15-40, and again I need to concentrate on not blowing the next shot.

I am, I think, fully aware and in control.

He hits a surprise, I do blow it, and he wins the game. Sometimes even the set.

What is going on here?

What's my story?

Who's running my show?

I've often observed that I play better when I'm behind—not only behind, but way behind: Love-40 is "my favorite score." If I blow the next point, I lose. Time after time, year after year, the same pattern repeats itself: I let myself fall to Love-40, or 5-40, make a heroic comeback but, just as often as not, lose one more point and lose the game. Even when I became fully aware of this pattern years ago, I couldn't seem to overcome it. The same thing kept happening on the court.

One particularly frustrating Saturday, as my doubles partner David and I were losing the second set this way (by "coming from behind" too late), I swear I heard my mother's voice from the heavens—and she was still alive then:

"Let your brother win!"

I stopped short, asked for a minute to retie my shoelaces.

Another childhood scene flashed before my eyes:

My brother Freddy, Jr. and I are playing "War" (my Cajun grandmother, Mamère, taught us this game that she knew as "*Bataille!*") at the kitchen table in our 75th Street home. My stack of cards was higher than my brother's stack, and a first-class Freddy tantrum was brewing; he'd inherited *his* temper from Dad's Lebanese side of the family, while I'd adopted the brooding Gallic nature of Mom's Aguillard family (she was born Myrza Marie Aguillard).

If Freddy lost, he would throw himself on the floor screaming until he was placated by rewards (culinary, monetary, or both).

My mother's face, over my brother's shoulder, came into focus. She was mouthing the words sotto voce, "Let your brother win," and winking.

My scowl displayed my protest at the unfairness. Mom's shrug was her way of asking me to keep my perspective: What was more important, winning or helping her keep the peace? Winning or being my beautiful mother's secret ally in the game of pacification?

So, I would slip a card and lose to please my mom and avert the brat squall. It became such an adroitly practiced move on the part of my unconscious it would stalk me on tennis courts for much of the rest of my life.

Until becoming aware of it, that sunny day, enabled me to overcome it.

So brainwashed had I been that losing began to *feel normal.* If I won, I lost Mom's respect. If I lost, I retained it: She rewarded me with approval and affection in the form of the first piece of fried chicken. Losers are lovable, I learned from her.

Brother Freddy walked away, crowing because he'd won. I walked away, confused.

Did he ever realize I was cheating to let him win? The thing about my brother is that it didn't matter *how* he won or even whether he knew how he won or not. All that mattered to him was winning—whether in liar's dice, gin rummy, craps, or business, or bragging.

Meanwhile, the whole issue of winning and losing had become mightily conflicted for me, a question of self-worth. Dang it.

Did I *have* to win to prove my self-worth? Wasn't it okay to let the other person win?

What if my singles opponent is eighty-six years old? Is it really important to beat him? Mom was whispering in my memory, "What if his beating you might make his day?"

But if I let him win, consciously or not, what was the purpose of the game? Why play it at all?

My answer, by the way, is yes, it *is* important to win. In my Atchity family, the only point in playing any game is to win. Not so much in my mother's Aguillard family, where playing meant simply hanging, talking, cooking, and eating together.

Though I could feel the frustration of losing on the court, I didn't even know how to define the tug of sadness that came when I was winning—except to say that it was even more potent. I became sad for all those who were not winning—who were trying to win, not realizing that their trying was not directly connected with whether they would or could win or not.

As life went on, the sadness turned into counterproductive nonchalance. I hesitated to take credit for, or even acknowledge, a great shot of my own. I took my next position and either said nothing or congratulated my partner instead. A shrink told me I manifested "severely impaired sensitivity to reward."

Gee whiz.

No wonder I blew shots. No wonder I didn't celebrate, or even rejoice internally, when a newly published book of mine arrived in the mail or my latest film was premiered.

But my father's life lesson kept rising in my mind to counter Mom's reverse programming: Keep trying anyway because the trying itself is enough to give you a feeling of control and self-respect. Doing our best is the best we can do.

And self-respect is the most solid foundation for hope.

Hope keeps us going. As comedian George Burns said, "the secret of longevity is falling in love with your future." Amen!

So went the do-loop in my brain, to the point of absurdity, ad nauseam, ad infinitum, and beyond.

All of which explained my violent reaction to the phrase, "It's only a game."

Only a game!? Give me a break! I'm an Atchity. No, it's a major fucking existential crisis, thank you: a test of self. It's the meaning of life played out on a green-painted game board.

The exact kind of existential dilemma I'm absolutely sure my father, not for one second in his life, ever had to face. Dad was Lebanese on both sides, I, half Lebanese, half Cajun.

What it came down to, as I eventually came to see clearly, was that my mother's self-worth depended upon her success in convincing young me, her overly sensitive confidant, that *she* was the winner, my father the *loser* in the biggest game of all.

The game of life.

My father was the straight arrow, going after what he wanted and working hard to get it. He didn't have time or need to be any other way.

My mother was more the superficially benevolent side-winder, a classic passive-aggressive "old-fashioned gal," arranging what she wanted through indirection, manipulation, triangulation. "Could you call Ken," she'd ask my sister Andrea, "and tell him I'm thinking of coming to California, see what he says?"

Even what she wanted was not what it appeared to be. On the surface, she wanted attention, recognition, and respect for her power, vision, and intelligence. Beneath it all, she wanted exactly what my father wanted: the security that they both believed only money brings. She wanted Lebanese.

Despite their decades of bickering and out and out fighting, my parents were, after all, birds of a feather. My father cut a dashing figure in his officer's uniform that he'd earned at officers training in Camp Shelby, Mississippi. In the mind of this farm-girl nurse from south Louisiana who'd fled her father's ten-acre plot of land to study *En Ville*—as the big city of New Orleans was called in Cajun French—he'd saved her from returning home to her father's humble farm to pick cotton. Her mother, my grandmother Mezille Latiolais Aguillard, as a wedding present from her husband's family, had received an acre of cotton for her to work with her own hands so that she could sell her harvest and "buy her a sewing machine"!

From the comfort of her Kansas City kitchen, in a house of stone incomparably grander than the white wood-frame houses she'd grown up in the South Louisiana countryside, Mom could well afford to whisper to her older and closer son (me) that winning wasn't important, that money wasn't everything.

Thank God I got over it.

Now I have no trouble with winning, on the court or otherwise. Now I know that though making money isn't everything, it's a pretty damned useful marker in the game of life. Dad used to repeat, in his joke-fumbling way, Jack Benny's crack: "I never said money was the only important thing in life. I just said it's a helluva lot more important than whatever's in second place."

For me, what was in first place wasn't money.

It was figuring all this out.

It was, I see in retrospect, becoming myself.

It was spinning tales, including this one.

The Seed Planted

By the way, despite all else I might say about the sparks that flew between Mom and Dad, I gratefully recognize that those sparks caused my existence.

I'm happily grateful for being born—grateful I didn't have the power to stop it all from happening.

Dad met Mom in 1942 on her weekend nurses' school outing to cheer up the boys in uniform at Officers Training School at Camp Shelby, Mississippi. She was completing her nursing studies at Charity Hospital in New Orleans. They met at a USO dance. It was love at first sight, catalyzed by the romantic urgency of war.

Dad loved to dance. She was Cajun, and gorgeous, and light-years from Prairie des Chiens where her father farmed cotton,

9

watermelon, and corn on his ten acres. For the duration of their stormy marriage, dancing was the one place where I could witness my parents being compatible.

Later, Dad refused to let me take dancing lessons. "Boys don't need to," he said. I learned years later from Tata (pronounced TAY-tay), my father's mother, that all her boys, including Dad, took dancing lessons. Dad's declaration had nothing to do with gender. It was just another instance of applied frugality which I mistook as cruelty. I wish he'd said, "We can't afford them," instead of adding to my gender confusion.

Θ

Mom and Dad were married on March 5, 1943, at St. Aloysius Church in KC. He was twenty-four, she twenty-one. She had graduated from nursing school the Fall of 1942.

They spent their honeymoon in Washington, DC, where Dad was stationed at the Pentagon, perfecting his accounting skills for two and a half months. That's when I was conceived.

He was then shipped out to London with the Quartermaster Corps, where he was assigned to the Department of Transport staff of General Dwight Eisenhower, Supreme Commander of the Allied Expeditionary Forces. SHAEF Headquarters is memorialized today with a plaque near London's Teddington Gate. After Dad died, my oldest sister Mary let me lift Dad's *The Officer's Guide* from its forlorn and leaning position on her basement bookshelf. I remember reading the stern volume from cover to cover when I was a kid (to sign it, "approved readable," as I did with all the books in the house). I eventually passed the guide on to my son Vincent, hoping he will pass it along to his sons.

I opened the book to find Dad's military record written in his unique calligraphy on the flyleaf. Looking at the way he made his "k" at the end of "Frederick" and the "E" in "Embarkation" tells you everything you need to know about my father at his best: Dad was an artist of the neat, with precise handwriting to die for. Quite the opposite of my garrulous mother and, therefore, of me.

My father was also somewhat of a career prodigy—moving from rank to rank with

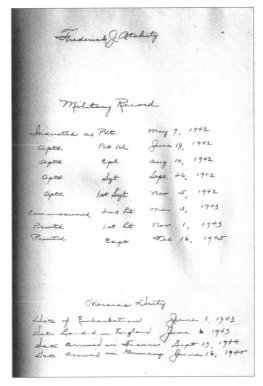

the speed possible only when wartime need meets native genius. What strikes me about his record is its humility. Not a single exclamation point, no sign of pride except, perhaps, the very, allowable act of recording.

Dad's assignment in Eisenhower's Department of Transport was to locate and assemble non-military light naval craft, thousands of which his team enlisted for the invasion. When, after the Invasion of Normandy's success, SHAEF moved to Paris, headquartered in Versailles, Dad moved along with Generals Eisenhower and Bradley.

By the time they made it to Berlin, Dad had been promoted to captain and offered a position in the post-wartime army. He declined the offer, opting to return to his family in KC. Later, to ease the transition from military to civilian life, he joined the VFW (Veterans of Foreign Wars) and the American Legion.

Dad said nearly nothing to us kids about all the action he must have seen. I didn't ask, even when I ran across his military gear here and there—his uniform smelling of mothballs, his captain's hat with its scrambled eggs, his medals, and his SHAEF badge. My asking Dad anything wasn't popular with Mom. But the accouterments of war were all visible when we lived on Benton Boulevard. By the time we moved to Virginia Avenue, they had begun to vanish from sight. War was in the past, its equipage obsolete and stashed away. Like others of his generation, Dad didn't make much of his service. He went over to Europe to do what had to be done and then returned to do his best to make a living for his family.

Defining Event Number One: The Naming

The inciting incident that constructed my father's mythic view of me, mine of him—and my automatic estrangement from my younger brother Freddy, Jr. who felt entitled by his name to play the older brother role—lay in my mother's passive-aggressive defiance of patriarchal demands for submissiveness.

Her rebellious decision was duly memorialized in my "baby book," which my sister Andrea handed me after going through my mother's things:

"Kenneth John Atchity."

If ever a name could change its recipient's life course, here it was: My mother made up her proto-feminist mind to name me "Kenneth." With this "Defining Event Number One," my psychological development was sealed.

Why she named me Kenneth, no one ever found out. When interrogated, even by me, she would shrug her shoulders and say, "I thought it was a nice name." According to Wikipedia, the name means "handsome" in some ancient and esoteric Scots-Celtic nomenclature I'm certain Mom knew nothing about. It's an Anglicized form of two entirely different Gaelic personal names: Cainnech and Cináed or Cinoed ("born of fire"). The modern Gaelic form is Cainnech, or Coinneach. The name reached its zenith of popularity around the year I was born. Hmmm. All this, to quote *Don Quixote*, "is of but little importance to our tale," so long as in "the telling of it, it will be enough not to stray a hair's breadth from the truth."

Mom did have the heart of a poet.

I clung to reasons to be proud of my name and absolutely hated being called "Kenny" by Dad, my parents' friends, relatives, and even Mom. "Ken" was the only diminutive I could tolerate growing up, and it wasn't until a few years ago that I could stop from cringing when someone called me "Kenny."

All my Aguillard relatives (Mom's family) called me "Kenneth." That felt right, reinforcing my split allegiance between KC and South Louisiana. That schizophrenic divide would perpetuate itself in every subsequent adult "trip home" that began with my internal debate on whether to visit Louisiana or Missouri. Sometimes, when I had enough time available, I'd finesse the whole dilemma. I'd fly to KC and drive from there to Louisiana, down old familiar Highway 71/171, hauling along any family member eager to exchange the high-stress northern environment for the laid-back Louisiana lifestyle, if only for a few days.

Being split became my defining characteristic: between Mom and Dad; mind and heart; between north and south; east coast and west coast; the driven urbanity of coat-and-tie-garbed New York and laid-back intensity of sunny, polo-shirted Los Angeles; between creativity and business; between writing and producing; between proper Georgetown-enforced no-accent diction and the unique patois of bayou country; between LSU and Yale; between rice and potatoes; between popular and esoteric; between *In Praise of Love*, my sinfonia-cantata premiered at Lincoln Center in 1974, and my blockbuster monster movie *The Meg*; between academic esoterica like *litotes* and *zeugma* and down-home country wisdom, like "Don't get in a pissing contest with a skunk"; and later between Europe and Asia (I married Tokyo-born Kayoko, though my foreign cultural loyalties lay in Italy, France, Spain, England, and Lebanon).

Once split, the mind gets used to it. Even—when the stress doesn't get the best of me—thrives on it. It learns to operate like a spinning laser disc, its cursor pointing to one compartment after another. The faster it spins, the more the energy from one groove spills into another.

The idea that Mom came up with "Kenneth" on her own, lying on her post-partum bed in the tiny bayou town of Eunice, Louisiana, doesn't look quite so strange when you consider that *her* mother, "Mezille," named my mother "Myrza." *Those two* names no one came close to ever figuring out—although once in Old Delhi, by sheer accident, I stumbled across the tomb of an ancient Persian/Urdu poet named "Mirza."

"How about that?" as Mom liked to say.

Θ

The act of my naming might have been innocent enough of consequences if it weren't for Dad evoking what he told her was the "Atchity Family Tradition of naming the first-born after the father." According to that "tradition," my name should have been Frederick John, not Kenneth John. That's what my father, allegedly, had instructed Mom before he went off to win the war. While he was busy liberating the northern French coast, my mother on the southern French coast of Louisiana was tweaking *his* internal mythology and mine. She sent a telegram to his desk at Supreme Headquarters Allied Expeditionary Force informing Lieutenant Fred Atchity of his son's birth and of my name. While, on a macro level, all hell was breaking loose on Omaha Beach, on a micro-personal level, marital discord invaded the banks of Bayou Teche and the Missouri River.

Dad wasn't pleased.

Minor skirmish by comparison with world events, but major for my father, my mother, my future brother, and me. He raged at Mom, she later told me, that he was embarrassed, that he wouldn't be able to face his father and brothers. My Uncle Anthony, Dad's oldest brother, had named his first son, my oldest cousin, Tony (we called him "Junior"). His second oldest brother, Uncle Eddy, named his son Edward– "Little Eddy." Mom shattered the family tradition–though, she argued, she *had* stuck with the middle name "John."

Feeling betrayed and disenfranchised, Dad ranted from afar. Mom shrugged.

So profoundly were Mom and I both made to believe in the primal sin of a son involuntarily betraying his father, it wasn't until years had gone by, and primal scars had become permanent, that I came to realize something: My grandfather's first name was James, his second name was Anthony. Yet he named his oldest son Anthony, not James. It wasn't until my youngest uncle came along–the youngest of my grandfather's seven children, to be precise–that Jede got around to naming a son after himself: James A. Atchity, Jr. Jede (pronounced *JZHOO-dee*) is Lebanese for grandfather.

Which meant it had to be Uncle Anthony, the oldest of Jede's sons who'd started the so-called "Atchity tradition," by naming his first son (my favorite cousin) Tony, Jr.

Suddenly "the Atchity family tradition" sounded more like (a) a fraternal pact, with dubious existential, much less paternal, import; or (b) a self-constructed myth in my father's mind.

My father's estranging rage had more to do with male chauvinistic shock at Mom's conjugal disobedience than with family tradition and expectation. The warrior felt emasculated by the bullheaded farm girl.

Not that I was any less split between them.

The day my father received word of my existence, and my name, my emotional patrimony ceased to exist in his mind. He was forced to wait until he could plant the seed of a proper namesake.

Defining Event Number Two: The Cyclops' Voice

I was a journeyer from the start, wrenched from my blissful birth nest in warm Louisiana to the windy winter chill of Kansas City, land of the raging Cyclops. I lurked around the house in fear of my angry father, whose piercing glare withered my spirit, stifling my love for anyone but my mother. Fleeting memories of being four years old still roll around the cellar of my mind: tart cherry pie from the sour cherries Mom and I picked from the tree behind our sprawling bungalow at 3637 Benton Boulevard, KCMO; Mom cooking her first (and last) goose for Christmas dinner during a visit from Uncle Anthony Prince—and we end up eating hot dogs instead—and a house filled with black smoke; Dad destroying with a hose the bayou paradise I'd constructed from the mud of our side yard; and, most confusing of all, the day my baby brother Freddy arrived from the hospital in swaddling clothes.

But by far, my most vivid memory of age four, was the day my father came home from work at the end of what had so far been for me a joyful afternoon.

The Cyclops, that fateful day, was wearing a straw fedora, so it must have been summer. That would mean it was a few months *after* my brother moved in with us in April, "the cruelest month."

I recall with cinematic clarity my father's hat sailing casually into the living room armchair at the same moment that my boisterous, "Dad!" greeting was shattered by my father's words to my mother:

"Can't you get that little foghorn to shut up?"

Looking back, I see this as my Defining Event Number Two— the first defining event I was conscious of. It's also my first memory of my father, the moment he died as my father and became the feared Cyclops.

Maybe if Mom hadn't constructed my psyche to be the understudy of her hypersensitivity, I could have taken my father's comment in stride. My brother wouldn't have paused enough even to shrug it off. Freddy had a way of turning barbs into power positions. When his Rockhurst High classmates started calling him "camel jockey," he repainted his first car camel-tan and named it "Clyde," after Ray Stevens' goofy song "Ahab the Arab."

I, by contrast, faced with my father's insensitivity, retreated, ego tucked between my legs, to my bedroom cave. I crawled under the bed—and remained there, as much as possible, in a state of silent introversion, until the age of ten. There was, I realized, a lot to sort out. Maybe too much for a young brain whose sensitivities had grown more rapidly than its knowledge base.

The incident redefined the Eden of my childhood as my native Louisiana, defining me an unwanted immigrant in my father's Kansas City. Which became the island of the Cyclops, where my life was in danger, bound to the implacable rock of my very identity as surely as Prometheus was.

While some might classify my behavior as incipient passive-aggression, I see it in retrospect as the first step of my survivalist evolution, of my dual nature as journeyman storyteller.

Θ

Some years later, I was finally cajoled out from my under-bed retreat by family friend and childhood nemesis, Betty Lafferty. The Laffertys were the bosses at Lafferty & O'Gara Pabst Blue Ribbon Distributorship, where Dad was employed as bookkeeper. Bill Lafferty's red-haired, goggle-eyed, freckle-faced wife Betty squatted at my bedside and chanted vaguely sexual innuendoes about what I might be doing under there: "Kenny's under the bed sleeping with turtles; Kenny's sleeping with little girls!"

I had no idea why I'd be sleeping with girls though it seemed a pleasant enough prospect, but the very thought of sleeping with turtles horrified me.

Mom had given Bully Betty the challenge: "Every time we have company, he hides under his bed. It's been that way for years now. We try and try, but he won't come out." I could visualize the shit-eating grin that Betty transported from the living room to my cell in response to a challenge she couldn't turn down. To Betty's dying day, I had a hard time *not* seeing that exact grin when I encountered her at family weddings and funerals where both of us circled each other with fake smiles.

By the time of Betty's callous intervention, we'd moved from Benton Boulevard south to the house on Virginia Avenue, so my hyperbolic memory and imagination had me making the move without emerging from under my bed.

Θ

That sweltering foghorn afternoon, my developing mind registered clearly:

Bad enough that he didn't accept my name.

My father did not see me as his son.

Freddy, Jr. had just been born, the namesake Dad had been waiting for. Dad was Darth Vader, Freddy his designated heir.

My father saw me only as an object. An impediment. An irritating one at that.

A foghorn.

The man who should have been my Primary Male Authority Figure became, in a moment, my tormentor, my warden, my antagonist—the angry Cyclops.

Whence I became introverted, sullen, quiet, withdrawn, a reader, an ex-pat, a writer, a behind-the-scenes producer playing bit parts in my own movies.

Poor me!

Lilacs and Shoelaces

A single happy memory can light up any amount of darkness. One of the few pleasant images I retained of our Benton Boulevard bungalow was the heavenly fragrant lilac bush between our side of the house and the next-door neighbors'. The scent of lilacs in full bloom, the buzz of honeybees—and Virginia Fuller, who lived in the house next door with her sister Maureen, bending down beneath the lilac bush to show me how to tie my shoelace. From that day forward, I've loved looking down at a woman tying my laces. Something about how she smelled against the lilac made an impression on me that turned shoelace tying into a proto-erotic experience.

Meanwhile, I was being challenged by Mrs. Pearl C. Miller, my kindergarten teacher who represented another strong and kindly Female Authority Figure without the subtle perfume of erotic attraction or the suffocating emotional quilt I came to associate with Mom. Mrs. Miller presided over my first classroom, in the four-story elegant brick Sanford B. Ladd Elementary School across Benton Boulevard. Between the excellent group rug-naps she allowed us in the afternoon, Mrs. Miller insisted that I learn to walk the wooden bar that stood in for a tightrope and showed me how to use a balance. Considering that the bar was no more than six inches from the floor, I thought the whole thing was a bit silly. But somehow, it, too, proved to be a defining, symbolic experience. I liked the feeling of balancing so much I didn't fall off even once. A life walking tightropes was off to a promising start.

Because we both carried Atchity blood, Freddy and I tried to be in business together even in our first home. Witness this letter from "House Cleaners, Inc." dated January 22, 1954 when I was ten and he was seven:

Dear Mrs. Atchity,

Would you like to have five percent of your housework done for you? for 10¢ per week we do all of the following. 1 We shine all the Shoes in your house once a week 2 We clean your bathroom every other day 3 We dust your furniture every other day 4 We would sharpen all your pencils once a week. 5 We would feed your fish. 6 We would clean Mr. Atchity's desk. 7 We should set our table. 8 We would mark your special calendar dates. 9 We would replace your broken pencils. 10 We would scrub & clean your kitchen do the dishes etc. 11 We would empty your trash & Garbage 12 We would be sure you had a number of scratch pads handy. 13 We would clean your bookcases. 14 We would have writing and scrap paper handy. 15 We would make your beds and hang your clothes. If you want to no [sic] all the other advantages just put a note on the mail box please sign your name.

Name   *Name*

*Yes*_____ *No*_____

Sincerely yours,
Kenneth Atchity Pre.
Frederick Atchity Vice Pre.

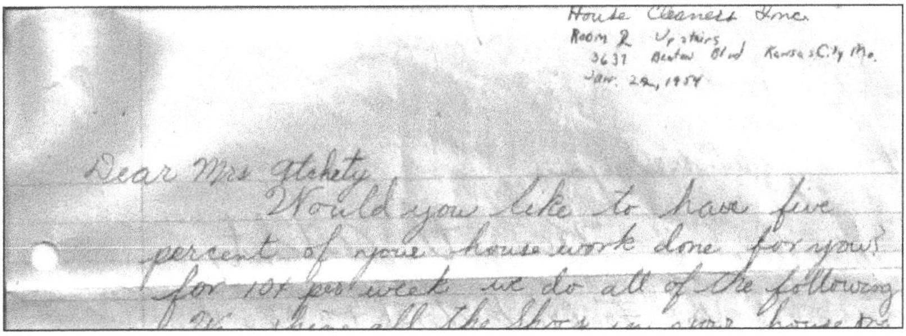

It ends with the official notation:

First Class Mail
Return to
K.A.J.J.F.A.J.J.
3637 Benton Blvd
Kansas City 3 Mo

I have no memory of Mom signing up for our service, but somehow can't imagine her signing above the NO. Encouraging industriousness—work for pay—was the official party line in any self-respecting Atchity household.

When we moved to our next home, at 5741 Virginia Avenue, Freddy and I progressed to running a grocery store in our basement. When no one was watching us, we were playing at working together. When the parents were around, we enacted our bellicose birthrights—and went for each other's throats.

Θ

By the age of five, I adored cherries of all kinds. Even sickly-sweet fake-bright red maraschino cherries. When Mom asked me what I wanted for my birthday cake, I told her I wanted a cherry cake.

"A cherry pie, you mean?" she asked. She and I had often worked together to pick enough sour cherries from the backyard tree to make a pie.

I shook my head. "No," I insisted. "Cherry cake!" Besides, there were no fresh cherries in January.

She ground up several bottles' worth of maraschino cherries into a Betty Crocker cake mix and constructed three layers of cherry-flavored interior. Then she ground another bottle of maraschinos into the Crisco to make cherry-flavored icing for the lining of the cake and red-dye-2 cherry-colored icing for the top. Finally, she covered the top of the cake with whole maraschinos— which I started picking off one by one before the guests arrived. I was thrilled to see this festive monstrosity on the dining room table on Benton Boulevard, where, on that cold January day, my neighborhood friends gathered—to witness me eating three enormous pieces.

And then, dreadfully, throwing up. Miserably and repeatedly.

I still have an almost physical reaction to the sight of maraschino cherries.

Cross Dressing

Our white garage behind the house on Benton Boulevard was memorable for rock fights, illicit climbs to the tar roof with neighbor Ronny Lilly—and an ill-fated christening dress. It was a four-car white-frame building, with doors that never quite hung square on their hinges. Since we had only one car, and Dad drove it to work each day, most of the time, the garage was empty: the perfect corral for cardboard forts and rock fight showdowns between Freddy and me. The backyard was filled with loose white granite gravel from the driveway, a quarry for perfect projectiles. Discarded cardboard boxes provided shields and forts. Unresolved sibling rivalry unleashed more than enough blind rage to keep the rocks flying—until one of us, usually Freddy, ran into the house screaming. Leaving me in triumph to savor the heavy smell of settling gravel-dust. We're lucky neither of us lost an eye in the process, though we both sport hairline scars on our skulls that came from hurling each other off our twin beds onto the old-fashioned sharp-ridged steel radiators in our joint bedroom.

Behind the garage was an alley that seemed like an escape corridor to me, and from the alley, a path led to the Happy family house on College Avenue. Paul Happy was my playmate when I couldn't roust out Ron Lilly. As far as the neighborhood was concerned, we were "Paulie," "Ronny," and "Kenny."

One afternoon I let myself be dressed by Ronny in Jeanie Crow's First Communion gown, only to face the Cyclops' wrath when he returned to see photographs of his misnamed oldest son, a vision of voile and lace. No one could tell me how I got elected to play the belle to Ronny Lilly's beau. Was it a stage in my mother's conjugal development in which she, having experienced the disillusionments of intimacy with a man, wished that her beloved eldest child had been born a female?

Alas, Mom is no longer available to prompt my memory. That is another of life's ironies. Ask questions while you can, or you may never otherwise get answers except for the ones you spin for yourself. I posed hand in hand with Ronny in front of those slightly askew white-frame doors, holding a doll to my voile dress as though I'd been born to the manner. I was quietly delighted to appear like my heroic Mom instead of my villainous Dad. Although his rage that day was primarily directed at my mother, I, of course, internalized it. I'd been conditioned by her to internalize her suffering.

After the Communion dress incident, rather than reacting to my father's outrage with affirmations of masculinity, I was only glad that Dad never found out about my nighttime dalliance with further transgender behavior. Until he forced me into pajamas at the age of eight, I preferred the nightgowns Mom liked me to wear. I would roll up my socks at bedtime and tuck them underneath my gown to create bosoms. Once configured, I'd stand on my bed, then fall down. Stand again, and then fall down until I was exhausted. I know, hunh? Then as I fell asleep, I'd cup the sock breasts in both hands, giving me a feeling of superiority over my brother in the bed next to mine in our radiator-warmed bedroom. Oblivious to my trans gendering, Freddy was lost in happy dreams of flying rock victories against a brother who commanded his mother's priority attention.

My favorite novel in those days was *Heidi*: an exiled girl living on top of a mountain with an elderly Male Authority Figure, who fed her wholesome country food and built her character with gentle discipline.

My later teenage obsession with becoming a priest was maybe my unconscious' way of finding a legitimate reason to wear those cool black robes. Becoming an altar boy was a sartorial step forward. It wasn't far to daydreams of cardinals' red robes and the ultimate papal white. Dressing up as an old-fashioned cleric, Roman collar and all, was long into adulthood my preferred Halloween costume. Once I wore cassock and collar to a writer client's costume party in Beverly Hills, quickly attracting an alluring Asian flight attendant wearing a bright red skintight devil's outfit. Within minutes, as I solemnly egged her on, the satin siren was confessing sins Satan would blush to contemplate. Later in the party, the little devil came up to me and slapped me.

"What was that for?" I thanked her, my masochism igniting.

"Why didn't you tell me you weren't really a priest?"

Why Dad cared about the sexual orientation of a non-son he couldn't bring himself to acknowledge, I never quite figured out.

Was it his absolute prohibition of cross-dressing that set me onto the heterosexual straight and narrow? Could I have gone another way?

Cats & Dogs

Many evenings, sitting at the top of the cherrywood staircase on Benton Boulevard, I eavesdropped on fierce battles between Dad and Mom—almost always over household finances. "All you care about is money," I heard my mother screaming. Words she often repeated to me: "All your father cares about is money."

Mom was raised in a sharecropper's family where money was rarely the issue, and somehow there was always enough to eat. She told me the only things they had to buy on Papère's farm were matches and coffee. Everything else they needed, including cotton for cloth, they grew for themselves.

I don't recall what the Cyclops screamed back at Mom that particular night, but it was nasty and enhanced by that deep masculine voice that quaked me to my roots. I recited to myself a poem I'd memorized at school about a spatting gingham dog and calico cat, Eugene Fielding's "The Duel":

Next morning, where the two had sat
They found no trace of dog or cat.
And some folks think unto this day
That burglars stole that pair away!
But the truth about that cat and pup
Is this: they ate each other up!

I sat in tears in the darkness, watching him reach the front door and declare he was "leaving." He had his suitcase with him—the beige plaid-like one, with the dark brown stripe. Mom didn't stop him. She didn't care. He walked out the door.

I prayed: "I hope he never comes back. I hate him."

It was such a remarkable and immediate change when he left the house. I breathed easier. Mom started singing. The atmosphere lifted. My entire being transformed, I was so happy with the Cyclops gone—filled with joy.

But he always returned to reclaim his island.

The joy evaporated.

She took him back. I didn't understand.

I never witnessed their reconciliation. Mom made sure she never showed me that side of the bedroom door. She was bent on making me think the worst of him.

In the city where Dad was born and raised, it took money to buy the things a family had to have. So, yes, he was focused on money. As a son of the Great Depression, he certainly was not alone.

But, at the time, sitting in the dark at the top of the stairs, I hadn't figured much out.

Going to Hell

I am standing at my Benton Boulevard bedroom window, listening to my mother and my Uncle Wib, her youngest brother, down below in the backyard where Wib's 1947 Plymouth was parked. Uncle Wib is furious; I can tell by the way he articulates between puffs on his pipe and tries to remain calm. "He's an angry man," Uncle Wib says—this from the eventually angriest of all my uncles.

"I'm so sorry, Wib," Mom is saying. They are speaking French, so my father won't understand them. "I don't know how you can live with that man," Wib is responding as he climbs in behind the wheel.

My father hates it when Mom and I speak French, tells me only "the poor and ignorant farmers" speak that language. Thank you, Dad, for giving me a lifelong tongue-tiedness in speaking not only French but any foreign language except Italian.

Tears in my eyes, I shudder to recall what I'd witnessed at the dining room table a few minutes earlier. My father, no doubt because he had one Pabst too many, declared that my uncle "is going straight to Hell." And he means it.

Uncle Wib had driven the 900-some miles up from South Louisiana to report that he'd gotten divorced, from a woman named Freddy (is that hilarious, or what?), a woman he'd been married to only a few months and that none of us had even met. His mission was to tell Mom, his closest sister, the news, to explain himself and get her blessing. I can still hear the agony in his voice as he explained his mistake to Dad and Mom, trolling for understanding.

Instead, he got blasted with my father's curse.

Roman Catholics, at least in those days, were taught that divorce was a sin that forever excommunicated its adherents from the Holy Catholic Church; and condemned them forever to Hell. I later learned that if divorce were the only road to earthly happiness, kick that road for luck and move forward. Watching Mom and Dad stay married was enough to convince me of that, along with my first father-in-law confiding in me, as we took an after-dinner walk to get out of the house, that his philosophy had become, "Peace at any price."

"I won't have someone who is going to Hell staying in my house," my father declared that night. Pope Francis would not have approved.

As I stood at my upstairs window witnessing the farewell conversation in the backyard and feeling like someone was choking me to death. I couldn't imagine my beloved Uncle Wib—who'd changed my diapers when I was still an infant and still living happily in Louisiana—going to Hell for *any* reason.

Now I couldn't believe my eyes: Wib turned his car around and headed down the driveway to return alone to Sugartown only hours after he'd arrived.

Wasn't the sacrament of Penance, forgiving us our sins, good enough for Dad? It seemed to work well enough for the Mafia.

I wanted to jump out the window and flee south with my uncle.

Bloody Nose & Stars

My memories of Blessed Sacrament Grade School, where I attended first through fourth grade, are few but sharp:

I am on my knees in the sanctuary of our magnificent Italian Renaissance-Romanesque parish church, in altar boy's black robe and white surplice, blurring my eyes to make the gold mosaic tiles behind the altar glisten magically through clouds of incense. I'm serving Sunday High Mass for Monsignor McCaffrey, the liturgy of which he recited in an Irish brogue so thick that Uncle Anthony Prince, visiting from Oregon, was convinced the good monsignor had preached the sermon in Latin, too.

No doubt seeing me eyeing monsignor's chasuble as I knelt happily in my flowing altar boy's cassock, Dad decided that I should sign up for boxing. He was going to break me of these cross-dressing tendencies once and for all.

On one of the most painful nights of my childhood, Dad came to watch my first—and last—grade school fight. I was pitted against a kid named Bud, who outweighed me by twenty pounds and was a good five inches taller. Those few seconds in the boxing ring seemed to last an eternity each. To the words, "That's enough, Bud," I bit the mat in the third round with a bloody nose—and literally seeing stars. Something about having someone punch me repeatedly in the face with officially sanctioned intentions of hurting me badly offended my nine-year-old sensibilities.

Back at home, Mom and Dad duked it out that night. She won this round. I fought in the ring no more.

I was much happier contemplating what I should have done when my classmate June Newman, in her parents' recreation room, had suddenly kissed me on the lips one day without provocation.

Meanwhile I was enchanted, progressively, by Sister Mary Jean, my first-grade teacher, whose clean-cut visage garbed in harsh black and white introduced me to a hitherto unexplored realm of imagining; by heart-shaped-faced Sister Mary Rupert, who presided over second grade with radiant enthusiasm; and by the dour but smiling Father Gerst. I can still hear us as we stood up and sang in singsong unison each Friday morning, "Good morning, Father Gerst." In all my years of growing up Catholic, by the way, I never once felt a moment of sexual discomfort from priest or nun. Unless, of course, physical discipline can be considered sexual.

Shortly after the bloodletting in the boxing ring, I tumbled from the jungle gym behind the red brick school building and broke my leg. Aside from safely putting me out of commission as a boxer and lothario, the added benefit of Mom pulling me to and from school in a red wagon was extraordinary because I could insist our route be down College Avenue. Where we would pass the Atterbury house, with the possibility of catching at least a glimpse of flashing-eyed Jeanie Atterbury, my third-grade classmate with the long brown hair. One memorable day Mrs. Atterbury saw us wheeling by and invited us in for cookies and conversation, and I got to bask in Jeanie's sympathies up close and personal while our moms gossiped. I could trust Jeanie not to do anything as baffling as kissing me on the lips.

"I Love to Sleep."

During my midlife crisis move to the west side of LA from my academic sojourn in the Glendale-Pasadena foothills, I signed up for three psychological sessions with a very white-and-shiny, self-created allotherapist, whose name, I kid you not, was "Am." As in the Old Testament Yahweh's, "I am who am."

Am led me to three or four "revelations," each of which ended with a useful takeaway.

The first one was, "If you approach something that disturbs your equanimity in any degree, stop approaching it until you regain composure. Remain in orbit around it until you can either reapproach it while remaining centered or decide to maintain your distance from it."

That's a surprisingly good rule to go by, I've discovered—applying to nearly every kind of relationship and situation, business, personal, or otherwise. It would tell me that I put 1,800 miles between myself and my parents because I found it hard to be closer without losing my cool and getting confused inside.

Especially confused because every approach was somehow associated with *love*.

How could loving something make you confused?

We can all relate to that paradox.

But some people, situations, and things are best loved from a distance. You don't have to own an airplane to appreciate airplanes.

A second thing I remember because it helped me fall asleep and not let dark and confusing thoughts and memories, including memories of nightmares, accelerate to insomnia. Before you try to sleep, Am told me, recite this mantra: "I love to sleep. Sleep is my friend. I feel safe when I sleep." For some reason lots of folks don't feel safe when they sleep. I admit I was one of them, as I imagine are many Roman Catholics who grew up reciting prayers that include, *"Now I lay me down to sleep. I pray the Lord my soul to keep. And if I die before I wake, I pray the Lord my soul to take."*

Here's how the Midwilshire guru told me to deal with recurrent night terrors.

Imagine you're sleeping in the earliest bed you can remember clearly. For me, it was my bed in that upstairs back bedroom on Benton Boulevard from which I'd watched Uncle Wib bid an angry farewell to Mom after Dad kicked him out of the house for being divorced.

Imagine that it's the middle of the night, and you, the hero, are awake, sensing—and fearing—there's a monster in the house.

Instead of freezing with that fear or letting wild thoughts send your mind spinning dark, direct your mind instead to search the house carefully: starting on the bottom floor—the little hallway at the back porch, where the washer and dryer were housed.

Is there a monster on the back porch?

No. You don't see a monster there.

Now check out the kitchen. Any monster you can see? No.

Go through the kitchen door into the dining room, where the family convened for meals. No monster there either.

Behind the little porch, off the dining room, was Dad's home office (though others used it when he wasn't around). No monster there for sure.

No monster in the living room either, the only space left downstairs.

No monster in the little hall between kitchen and living room.

Nor was the cherry wood staircase leading from the living room upstairs concealing a monster.

Now your searching mind is back upstairs, in the hallway around which the bathroom and four bedrooms are grouped. No monster lurks in the hallway.

No monster in the guest bedroom, diagonally across from yours.

No monster in the bedroom on the other side of the wall from yours.

So—Am went on to explain—the monster could only be in *my* room, though looking in the closet and under the bed reveals no monster.

Which meant:

The monster could only be—inside me.

My Self.

The monster that awaits to be confronted and vanquished was born from the "doubling of consciousness" that occurs at the moment in life when the mind first recognizes itself as a separate "self," separate from Dad, even separate from Mom. My "fear" of the monster was a sign of the birth of self-awareness.

I was the monster in the center of my own labyrinth. Against who *I the hero* must battle—as Odysseus did when he escaped the Cyclops by blinding him, or Theseus did when he slew the Minotaur—then found his way out with the golden thread given to him by Ariadne (who, by the way, he later left behind on Naxos).

How can you be afraid of your own consciousness?

Am declared that you cannot.

At the precise moment you become *aware*, you are given the power to defeat the monster, which is the mind trying to control you by introducing fear, dark memories, fantasies—anything it can do to wrest the reins from your ever-calm, ever-present inner awareness, your *very being*—the rock within the whirlpool. You, the real you—what I later termed "the managing editor"—can rise above your maelstrom mind and remain steadfast in the timelessness of being. Later, after meeting director David Lynch when we awarded him the Namaste Award at a Yoga Gives Back banquet, I would learn that Transcendental Meditation offers a similar freeing of the mind. Your thoughts are floating down the river of consciousness—noisy, angry, troubling, fearful—but you are standing on your bridge above the river simply and peacefully *observing* them. Separate from them. Maybe that's why Freddy's favorite song was, *Row, row, row your boat gently down the stream. Merrily, merrily, merrily, merrily...*

Close your eyes, recite the sleep mantra, and sleep deeply and easily. I thought of it as a coming-of-age hero's quest.

The part of me that had just been born, the part of me that is conscious of the doubling and of the power of the relentlessly restless mind (represented in Hindu myth by the mouse squashed by elephantine Ganesh, symbol of pure being), is the splitting (or doubling) of consciousness that marks what we Catholics fondly call reaching "the age of reason." That's when the sacrament of Confirmation can be administered, the sacrament that allows the now-conscious individual to embrace the meaning of the Baptism that was administered in his infancy when consciousness had not yet been achieved.

A comforting theory that didn't *quite* work for me.

Because sleeping is when the monster mind prodded me awake. To analyze the flow of self-delusion in which I led my daily life and to sprinkle fear through my consciousness—until I got out of bed and did something about it all. Like figure out how to keep moving forward, how to keep the whole house of cards that was my creative life from tumbling down around me and those I loved. I always managed, but that didn't keep the monster from biting its nails while "I" slept. As my favorite American poet Wallace Stevens puts it: "It is never satisfied, the mind. Never."

In my recitation of monster-free rooms, I skirted over one room: the one with the closed oak door, my parents' bedroom.

My mind, entering all the other rooms and hallways freely, did not—could not—enter that one.

It was closed for a reason, and I was too young to understand that reason. Why would Mom and Dad want to close their bedroom door on me?

What was going on in there anyway?

Was there a monster in there with them?

Were they doing something monstrous?

Was Mom cheating on me with the very monster she warned me against? Sleeping with the Minotaur! Sleeping with the Cyclops.

Was *sex* the monster that kept me awake?

Suffocating Quilt

In that second-floor solo bedroom on Benton Boulevard, starting shortly after Uncle Wib was banished by Dad, I regularly experienced what I later learned was not just a nightmare, but a "night terror"—a nearly-impossible-to-articulate dream that pressed down on me like a succubus and felt like it was threatening my very existence. I would jolt out of the vision screaming, menaced by the whorl in the half-open oak door to my room, highlighted ominously by the hall lamp.

The terror went something like this, though verbal reconstruction feels pathetically inadequate:

A humongously heavy blanket presses down on me.

I know I can never escape it.

I gasp for air as its moist weight slowly but surely suffocates me beneath it.

My only hope is to unravel it, thread by thread. And I must do it immediately.

But the quilt is enormous—and I possess only a tiny needle with which to do the unraveling. I know it can never be in time—and I scream myself awake.

Sigmund Freud would showcase that little needle.

Something was filling me with fear, something I felt I was unable to overcome in time. It was threatening my life. I imagine Sisyphus felt much the same about the tenth time his rock rolled back down the hill, and he recognized it as his childhood quilt. For the rest of my life I've never stopped reflecting about the connection between dreams and waking life, light and darkness, day and night—between sleep and death. And whether I was unraveling that smothering quilt, or weaving it.

Θ

Dad, not Mom, would hear my scream, which always filled me with greater anxiety. Country mouse Mom was out cold, as usual, by nine. City mouse Dad was, as usual, up half the night working. Her hours were five a.m. to nine p.m., his eight a.m. to two a.m. Even their biorhythms were opposite.

My father marched up the wooden stairs to find out what was wrong, then led me down to the kitchen, opened the fridge, and made me one of his signature "Dagwood sandwiches" (named after the then-famous comic strip character). He began with plain white Tastee (or Holsum or Wonder bread—"Builds strong bodies 8 ways!"), methodically adding mayonnaise, pickles, tomatoes, onion, along with baloney, cheese, and crisp leaves of iceberg lettuce. Yum, that still sounds good, doesn't it?

I would eat at first obediently, then gratefully; my filial alienation, with Mom absent, suspended for this salutary moment. I drank a glass of milk, then went back upstairs, confused by Dad's nurturing intervention, unable to credit him—till decades later—for the recurrent kindness of this nocturnal rescue mission and the vigilant attentiveness that led him up the stairs. For much of my life, I even had mixed feelings about Dagwood sandwiches. They tasted so good, but how could they really be good since Dad loved them?

"Your father just likes company," Mom would say dismissively, when she would find out from me what happened. "He doesn't like to eat alone." She couldn't let me enjoy his good intentions toward me. In my mother's story of her oldest son, the hero wasn't even allowed to accept his paternal ally.

Dad's Last Three Words

Three of my last few conversations with my father cry out for attention:

1) "I'm not disappointed about not going to Las Vegas," he told me, no doubt to relieve my guilt.

2) "You've been a good son."

3) "Don't forget me."

The final one he told me by phone the day before he died.

Θ

I hate Las Vegas. It was my brother's town, not mine. That Freddy believed he was going to win there, and most of the time did—whether as a result of thinking that he'd win, or by skill, or by pure chance—has provided me with a lifetime of uneasy self-reflection.

Las Vegas was my existential antipodes, making me queasy not only when I crossed its city limits, but even when I thought about the confounded place. Its garish enshrinement of mammon was not even symbolic, despite the faux facades it borrowed from the world's cultures. No, it was literal: dollar signs everywhere, amidst the constant ringing of slot machines to remind you, like Skinnerian bells and whistles, that money is flowing freely in this desert where air-conditioning wafts across the outdoor swimming pools like gratuitous manna.

My guilt wounds, and my un-Atchity-like, even un-Aguillard-like, ambivalence toward gambling had been reopened when Mom phoned me a few days earlier. She filled me in on the latest medical details about the cancer devouring my father's lungs. He valiantly decided to stop smoking a year before the final diagnosis made this gesture, like so many life-bargaining gestures we humans make, too little too late.

Medical update duly reported, she was ready to pass the phone over to Dad. But not before adding, "He wants to go to Las Vegas one last time. Please encourage him. Maybe you could join us there."

I couldn't believe my ears, though there was nothing in her statement that should have surprised me in the least.

Spoiler alert: My mother, in her turn, would die at her favorite slot machine at Ameristar Casino in KC. The "boat," as the casino was referred to, had circumvented the state law against organized gambling on Missouri soil by having water from the Mighty Mo slosh in and out of its otherwise purposeless surrounding moat.

"Mom, that sounds absolutely horrible," I said. "In Dad's condition—"

"If he gets tired, you could stay with him in the room." She turned the pressure up, restraining herself from adding, "while I'm playing blackjack."

"What a nightmare: my father dying in a hotel room in Vegas with me at his side while my mother is downstairs gambling."

"There's that imagination of yours," she said. "Don't be so negative."

Why is it that the longer you live, fewer words issuing from family are free from complex insinuations? Who knows your buttons better than the mother who stitched them into your psyche?

My "imagination" was the conversation-stopper. It always had been.

☉

"Is it true you want to go to Las Vegas?" I asked by way of greeting when he got back on the phone.

"That's right, honey," he tried to cover the hesitation in his voice, and I could imagine my mother's eyes making that encouraging squint that had guided my brother Freddy to selling more 3&2 baseball season tickets than his entire team together three years in a row, my oldest sister Mary to straight A's in nursing school, my middle sister Andrea toward taking responsibility for the universe, my youngest sister Laurie toward wanting to run away to clown school, egged on only by Freddy; and me toward my eighth language, thirtieth book, and fortieth film production.

When my mother gave you her "go for it" wink, who could resist?

"I think I'd like that," my father added.

"Dad, let me ask you a question. If you go to Vegas, what will you do different than what you've done there before?"

"What do you mean?"

"I mean, are you willing to take $100,000 from your savings account, pack the cash into a suitcase, and head for Vegas with the full intention of doing something wild like plunking it all down on the first roll at the craps table?"

"No." His voice came out weak and hoarse, but this time expressed *his* mind, not hers. "I guess not," he added, releasing this transient surge of testosterone into capillaries awash with morphine. "Of course not."

"Then I think you should stay in your own bed, and I will visit you there."

"That would be nice," he agreed in a whisper, adding, with what I thought of then as uncharacteristic sensitivity, that I "shouldn't worry about it."

$$\theta$$

A few days before he died, Dad insisted on driving to the bank and asked Mom to drive with him. She told him if *he* drove, she wouldn't go along. So he went alone. When he came back, he told her, "I see why you want to drive, honey."

That day, he asked my mother to move him to the family room, so he wouldn't feel lonely in their upstairs master bedroom.

She refused.

Yet somehow, the day Dad died, he'd made his way downstairs to fall asleep forever in his favorite recliner. Mom later told me that he died rather than giving in to her insistence that he remain upstairs.

I flew in from Montreal just in time to miss his passing. "He was happy knowing you were coming," sister Andrea reported. Was she making that up? Andrea would never make things up. She, of all my siblings, was the dead-serious one, having inherited my father's straight-arrow disposition. But unlike his, hers was laced with the irony only pessimism is capable of—which meant she could communicate with me, whose world view was nothing if not ironic, though mine was optimistic. She was the one I turned to when I needed a direct answer, happily accompanied with pointed commentary and as much deliberation as I had time for. We could have financed an entire phone company between the two of us.

No one would ever accuse Mom of being a straight arrow.

I was relieved that Dad passed away at home, not in a hotel room at the Silver Slipper, the Lucky Horseshoe, or whatever "special discount" hotel he and Mom would have selected for his terminal Las Vegas getaway.

It was thirteen years later that my mother would stroke out at her video poker machine in the Randolph, Missouri casino. Having worked as a nurse most of her adult life, she hated the thought of dying in a hospital.

By that time, she didn't need Vegas anymore; the KC suburbs had found a way around Missouri laws against gambling. Please don't start humming, "everything's up to date in Kansas City." I've hummed that song from *Oklahoma*, involuntarily, all my life. It's an earworm that's dogged me from one side of the country to the other.

Memories of Virginia Avenue

When I was ten, Dad, concerned about falling property values, moved us from our Benton Boulevard homestead because "undesirable elements" were infiltrating that graceful, Dutch-elm-lined neighborhood. Later in my teens, I learned that "undesirable elements" was a polite way of saying "Black folk." I wish I could claim more awareness of the politically questionable situation, more credit for understanding the evils of segregation but Dad's generation succeeded in distancing us from other races—by up and moving every time they got too close. I didn't have a single Black, or Asian, classmate in grade school. Nor did I at Rockhurst High School. It wasn't until my Georgetown college years that I came in touch with an Asian or two and, at a goodly distance, a Black person. In KC we lived in an all-white world and, despite Mom's porcelain skin, were ourselves the darkest-hued kids on the block.

My memories of the quiet Virginia Avenue neighborhood we moved to from Benton Boulevard include my transition from tricycles to bikes, girls, and jobs; making out with the saucy West twins; admiring Mr. Harvey's stamp collection; doing what had to be done to snag Mrs. Letchworth's oatmeal cookies; Dad talking our neighbor Jack Meiner into employing me as his milkman's assistant; and nightmarish four a.m. biking to the Jesuit residence—harried along the way by viciously barking dogs who lay in wait along Forest Avenue for my predawn two-wheeled appearance.

During my rarer and rarer free time, my roaming on Virginia Avenue rarely ranged farther north than Donald Letchworth's house, about six houses down across the street. Donald had a Neanderthal visage, with a wide forehead, single-browed scowl, and coarse black hair on every exposed inch of his body. But I had a very good reason to pose as his pal. His mother, Bea Letchworth, made the best oatmeal-raisin cookies in the known world. They were soft AND crunchy, and best of all, they were shaped more like nuggets than regular cookies. She made so many of them at a time that she didn't mind if I filled my pockets and fists with them when I came over. I'd put in the minimum amount of time required to play with Donald and then split with my oven-fresh trophies to hide them from my siblings under the bed.

Other than the saucy West girls, the only other person I recall between 57th and 58th on Virginia was "Old Mr. Harvey," to whom I was no doubt attracted by my weakness for elder males who might approve of me or at least listen to my babbling. Mr. Harvey was either British or had everyone convinced he was British. He wore tweeds, usually in the shape of a three-piece suit, which in KC humidity gave him a distinctly funky aura. I'd see him caning his way up the street and would head right for him to say hello.

That inevitably led us to his screened-in front porch, where I would sit beside him on a couch-sized glider and sip the lemonade brought out by a nondescript woman who lived there and once might even have been Mrs. Harvey. Our lemonade was normally accompanied by an examination of Mr. Harvey's stamp collection, which he took great pride in explaining to me page by page, country by country, stamp by stamp, breath by bad breath.

Halitosis aside, I was hooked, inspired by an older man who took an interest in me. Even before I had my own album, I started sending away for stamps by mail, further infuriating my father for wasting money in this way. The habit was only compounded when Mr. Harvey gave me my first stamp album, its spine now long ago faded by time and sun, but hardbound front cover still bright red and stamped "Modern Postage Stamp Album," skyscrapers and a biplane embedded on the bottom left. Inside the front cover, I wrote:

> *Kenneth Atchity*
> *5741 Virginia*
> *Kansas City, Mo.*
> *Em-1-1119*
> *Album $2.00*

That last inscription, in pencil instead of blue ballpoint, was there because, at one point, Dad decided I should at least sell any duplicate stamps I'd collected, if not the album itself. At least Mom saved my album. Paging through the old red album today, I see that pencil markings abound—1¢ each, or 10¢ each at the top of German stamps; "complete 25" on the first page of Belgium, and little 3s or 1s on the individual stamps. Maybe the idea was to turn the whole thing into a business and sell off those stamps for a penny fortune.

I put duplicate stamps I encountered along the way in little white slide-open boxes that prescriptions came in in those days, dutifully supplied by Mom from the hospital. When I went off to Georgetown, I left a whole steamer trunk filled with stamp duplicates in the attic of our 75th Street home to protect them from my marauding sisters. But, in absentia at Georgetown, I lost them when Dad, unexpectedly, for the familiar reasons, suddenly sold that house and moved family headquarters way south to 104th Street. On a trip home after that move, I managed to talk my way into the old house on 75th Street and ask the new Black owners if I could check in the attic for something I might have left there. I don't recall what they said, but I know I never saw the trunk of stamps again except as another "loss dream" that dogged me for years, fueled by the fear Dad had sold them out from under me.

After we moved from Virginia Avenue to 75th Street, I heard that Mr. Harvey died.

Fart Fishing

Once in a blue moon, Dad tried to tell a joke, daring to brave the dead silence with which his efforts were generally greeted by our family of stand-up comedians, schooled in timing and delivery by our Cajun storytelling mother. My father's timing was hopelessly off.

But he did take me fishing, mostly at "pay lakes" where you were guaranteed that fish, mostly catfish, would queue up to be hauled in at the end of our lines. Used to fishing in the endless bayous, lakes, farm ponds, and the Gulf in Louisiana, I had a hard time wrapping my brain around "pay" lakes.

How many fathers take their sons fishing? Why did he get no credit from me for that? Maybe because he passed gas loudly as he walked along the shore, stopping when the build-up was serious to shake his leg and grunt. I would stare at him with horror and try to tell myself it wasn't happening. He gave me a look that seemed bewildered by my lack of acceptance. Maybe that's what made him realize he was never going to bond with me no matter how many years went by. Our lack of father-son camaraderie was reinforced by my mother's reaction when I reported his behavior to her, like the disloyal little spy she'd programmed me to be: "Men are animals," she shrugged.

Thanks, Mom.

And what does that make me, exactly?

How awful for a father not to be able to share an honest fart with his son.

How awful for me not to man up for it.

Dad's Optimist Joke

An Optimist falls off the Empire State Building.
"Halfway down," he yells, "So far, so good!"

Defining Event Number Three: Enter Father Z

When we'd moved to Virginia Avenue, the headquarters of our Roman Catholic faith that condemned Uncle Wib to Hell for all eternity had been transferred from Blessed Sacrament to St. Francis Xavier Parish on 52nd and Troost. We thereby made the transition from secular to Jesuit. Situated directly across the street from the Jesuit high school Rockhurst, St. Francis Xavier was a rare Jesuit parish with a stunningly modern fish-shaped church that made me notice architecture for the first time.

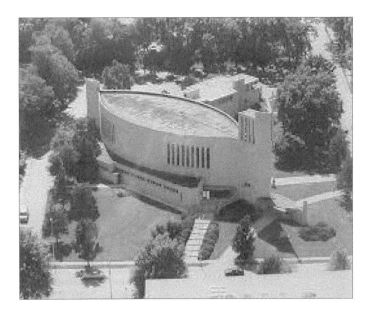

Θ

I have mostly pleasant memories of Blessed Sacrament Grade School where I'd gone through fifth grade, but not so pleasant of St. Francis Grade School due to the tyranny of my seventh-grade teacher Sister Mary Peters, BVM, whose attitude sucked as much as her rotten-egg breath. My fear of her leaning over my desk to berate me for making a mathematical or spelling error shot me to the top of our class and entitled me to skip from seventh grade directly into high school—while half my classmates were herded into the newly invented eighth grade. If it hadn't been for my fixations on porcelain-skinned Cherie Watts and Kathleen Butterfield and my burgeoning friendship with Tom Sullivan ("Sully"), I'd have little good to say about SFX. Seeing the girls in class every day was giving me sensations that were quite different from my pubescent dalliances with cross-dressing.

θ

One extremely hot and humid summer afternoon, still too early for the "locusts" (what we in Missouri called cicadas) to be chanting their twilight litany, I was practicing mounting and dismounting from my new silver bike in front of our elegant Virginia Avenue corner house with the semicircular porch. My objective was to dismount or mount without getting chain-tangled in a tumble to the pavement.

Self-conscious of my physical awkwardness, I spotted a portly man in black, wearing a sporty Italian straw fedora above his Roman collar. He was sweating profusely as he approached our house, watching my determined efforts with the bike. The priest's face was so bright red he looked to be on the verge of heat prostration.

Despite his straw fedora, like the one that had sailed across our living room with my father's "Foghorn" comment, I felt no fear. "Father, would you like a cold beer?" I blurted out, Louisiana hospitality erupting from my mouth.

He stopped in his tracks. "That would be most welcome," he stammered, removing his hat long enough to mop his brow. I was old enough to have learned that a man with a face that red was likely a serious drinker. I was not so sure about what to make of his stammer.

I led him to the front door and called out to Mom, who took it in stride that a strange man—a priest at that—would be dragged into the house on a hot summer day and offered a beer.

He introduced himself as Edmund H. Ziegelmeyer, SJ. A Jesuit, to boot. He would become known as "Ziggy" in my family.

Ziggy explained that he taught "philosophy and linguistics" at Rockhurst College, a few blocks away. He'd even written books! I was all ears. Books I could relate to. I had gone through our entire household library, reading each one we possessed and writing on the inside cover either "Approved Readable," or "Not Approved Readable."

In awe at his refinement and expensive aftershave, I listened to
Ziggy telling jokes and swapping stories with my mother in French
as he sipped his beer. I suppose to keep me quiet he scribbled a
single line in Greek on a legal pad on the table.

"What does that mean, Father?" I kept asking.

He didn't answer me, just went on regaling her with inspiring
eloquence, his stammer dissolving sip by sip. Meanwhile, I kept
interrupting with my questions, and Father Z kept scribbling line
after line on the pad—German, Spanish, Italian, French, Arabic,
Greek again, finally in Latin.

When he was diagnosed with cancer a year earlier, he made a
promise to Our Lady that should she see her way clear to curing
him, he would honor her every day by walking the mile and a half
or so from Rockhurst to the Benedictine Convent of Perpetual
Adoration at 63rd & Myers to recite his daily office. Thanks to
Father Z, I would later serve as an altar boy there, too, for the not-
yet-notorious Bishop John Cody (later, scandal-scarred cardinal of
Chicago who allegedly "kept a woman" on the side and had big
problems with money).

He had, Ziggy told Mom, been cured within thirty days of the
diagnosis. Since then, he had not missed a day, rain or shine or
snow, walking the fifteen long sweaty blocks in each direction.

But the Foghorn could no longer be denied. "What does that
mean, Father?" I repeated, staring stupidly at the written lines.

Father Z stopped to look at me intently. He identified the
languages one by one; then wrote in English:

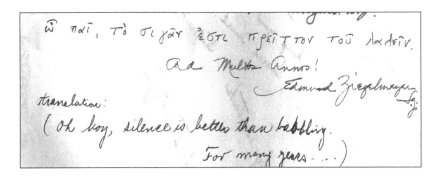

It didn't occur to me until much later that, at least literally, yet again I'd been told to shut up by a male I wanted to admire.

That's the way I recall this Defining Event Number Three in my life, my introduction to Jesuit education—my future lifeline out of Cyclops Island. With Ziggy as missionary landing on the shores of my island of unformed aspirations, the Jesuits took their place as primary Male Authority Figures. They would lead me, through education, self-discipline, and determination, into manhood—first at-home tutorials with Ziggy, then at Rockhurst High School and Georgetown University in Washington, DC.

Meeting this mysterious stranger was tantamount to being inducted into a legion of mentors that would inspire me for the next ten years.

By the way, if anyone was babbling that day, it was he and Mom.

Ꙫ

On that sweltering summer day, I was so awed by Father Z's display of linguistic pyrotechnics that, like St. Paul struck down from his horse, I was accorded a vision of a future potentially filled with accomplishment, self-challenge, and recognition.

"I want to learn all these languages," I told him when he had his frosty beer can to his mouth and could not stop me from talking. Had I been thinking about my precarious position—silenced by the father-male and consequently seeking to bond with a man that folks addressed as "father"—I might have held my breath for his response. But the blessed response came quickly, effortlessly, decisively—virtues I grew to associate with the best of the Jesuits I would meet in years ahead. He nodded, "Let's start with Latin. I'll give you a lesson every weekday," looking at my Mom whose shrug this time was the shrug of complicity and approval—underlined by a wink that implied his thirst would be quenched in return.

So the private Latin tutorial began. In comparison to this blessing, my morning bike rides past multi-headed Cerberus, the unleashed dogs of Forrest Avenue, were, as Father Z would put it, "a mere bag of shells." The stage was being set for me to acquire more languages than I could shake a stick at.

In my brain and spirit, Father Z assumed the place of my biological father.

☉

For the next two years, every weekday on his return from the Benedictine convent, Ziggy stopped in for my mother's brew, a French conversation with her, and a Latin lesson with me straight from Father Henle's *Latin Grammars*, the dark maroon first volume and the gray second. Still on my shelf today, the Henle hardbacks were my first gift from my new *pater*.

By the time I started Rockhurst High School, I could boast two years of Latin in my noggin. I internalized the language even more effectively by serving five o'clock Mass every weekday; in those days, Masses were celebrated in Latin. I can still recite most of the Roman liturgy by heart, from *Introibo ad altare dei* to *Ite, missa est*. Early morning Latin sticks with you like rice and gravy.

That's where my bike rides through the gates of Hell came in—presided over by Cerberus and his cousins. I had to cycle through a Forest Avenue canine kangaroo court of fiercely barking dogs to the Jesuit residence each morning to serve as Ziggy's altar boy. Tears of terror in my eyes, I kicked the hounds of Hell away with one leg, pedaled furiously with the other for the sanctuary of mumbled Latin—where I would hastily throw a black cassock over my miraculously still-intact legs. Going from terror to the cloistered silence of the multi-alcove chapel permeated with incense, where the Jesuit priests, each at his own altar, recited their daily Masses in tandem, was one more great schizoid joy.

I think it "burned Dad up" that I was earning no money by serving all those five a.m. Masses for Father Z. What remained Ziggy's and my little secret was that I was, in fact, being compensated in kind: discarded vestments, slightly outdated liturgical missals, and the bronze crucifix that adorned my basement home altar that Ziggy himself had deigned to consecrate.

My mother might be plying him with liquor, but my personal payback for his private Latin lessons was my faithful bipedal morning service.

It only occurred to me after Mom passed that Father Z, like so many others, was probably as much in love with my irrepressible mother as he was with instructing the over-earnest young man in conjugations and declensions.

She had that effect on everyone she met.

She was a beauty—body, mind, and heart.

My shadow queen.

A Father Z Joke

Jesus is hanging on the cross, attended by his mother, Mary Magdalene, Martha, and a handful of disciples.

They hear a croaking sound coming from Christ's lips. And strain to decipher what words the dying man might be uttering. At first no one can make it out.

"I think he's saying 'John.' His mother cocks her ear to listen, and nods. "Yes…that's it: John…Bring a ladder."

The ever-accommodating John rushes off to borrow a ladder from the Romans and props it against the crossbars.

Jesus is still muttering, so John scrambles up the ladder to make out the words. "Yes, Lord?" he says when he reaches the top. "I'm here."

"John," Jesus says, choking out the words. "I can see your house from up here."

Cellar Sanctuary

Father Z. introduced me to the Latin sonorities of Virgil's *Aeneid*. As I was learning about the mythic underground of Cerberus-guarded Hades, I was associating the cold dank smell of our Virginia Avenue basement with happy merchandising, solemn spirituality, and painful punishment.

In the spirit of our housekeeping venture on Benton Boulevard, Freddy and I built a play grocery store in the basement. It was the year before I was judged old enough to work in my uncles' stores. Familiar with the deployment of cardboard boxes from our garage wars, Freddy and I lined up, cut open, and stacked them in three parallel rows—and then stocked them with Mom's groceries. We'd needed all the cans we could put our hands on to keep the shelves looking well-stocked.

"Where are my peaches?" she would yell from the kitchen. We would exchange guilty looks. But then we heard her coming down the stairs toward us, and the looks between us got more frightened than guilty.

"Excuse me," she said. "Are you open?"

"Uh... Yes, ma'am," Freddy replied.

"What can we do for you?" I asked.

"I need some peaches," Mom said. "I guess I used up the ones I bought last week."

Freddy retrieved her can of peaches from our shelves and handed it over.

Since Dad rarely descended to the basement, the grocery store was immune from his unpredictable diatribes. Mom was the baroness of the basement, that place she marched us when we misbehaved. We had to drop our trousers and hand her one of our belts so she could administer a good whipping on our legs and butts. We screamed from the stinging pain.

But our behavior improved.

For some reason, Dad did not play disciplinarian. Maybe they were both afraid of his temper. The only times I recall him slapping me were enraged moments when I'd answered him back disrespectfully. Like the good Cajun farmer's daughter, Mom administered the beatings without a trace of emotion. As painful as those whippings were, the pain was transitory, but the need to behave within the bounds of reason lingered with me as a lesson that, no matter what, discipline was *necessary* to getting as much out of life as possible. Eventually, you learn to discipline yourself.

The basement held other wonders, some more hidden than others. Although the cardboard grocery store was visible to anyone who walked halfway down the basement stairs, my private chapel was concealed in a cave-like grotto formed by the under-structure of the back porch. As you entered this damp cellar, on the left was my improvised altar, made of a draped ironing board, cast aside when Mom got her automatic ironer. On this makeshift altar, I enshrined the two-foot-high bronze crucifix I'd purloined from the Jesuit residence with the help of Father Z. Next to it, I placed the heavy, bright-red, slightly-outdated, *Missale Romanum*, the Latin liturgy book used by celebrants for the Catholic Mass, from the same source—which I have in my possession to this day.

It wasn't enough for me that I had an original gilded altar book. I had to construct my own version, which I accomplished using crayons and one of Dad's empty hardbound ledgers. For me, until I wrote it down, life didn't seem all that meaningful. What we write, we define.

I enlisted a make-do chalice from a second-hand store and constructed, with scissors, observation, and imagination, the various cloth implements required to array it correctly for the ceremonies I conducted for my sorority congregation, Mary and Andrea. Wearing a Ziggy-sourced cassock and a chasuble Mom sewed for me on her new Singer Electric, I said my daily Mass utilizing white Necco™ Wafers as hosts—after discarding all the licorice ones. I've loved color-coding all my life—from file folders for friends and staff, razor tipped pens so I could use a different color each day, changing my mouse pointer color to match—to my *Shades of Love* movies that form a marketer's dream rainbow when lined up on the shelf: *Lilac Dreams, Indigo Autumn, The Rose Café, The Tangerine Taxi,* etc.

I hated licorice; still do. But I adored the feeling of wearing that black robe.

My shanghaied congregation adored the Neccos™.

About this time, Dad let me confiscate a paperweight he'd received in response to one of his "donations": an actual stone mounted on a wooden base bearing a plaque that read, "The First Stone—Let he who is without sin cast it. John 8:7." I placed it in its own niche in my private chapel.

Father Z, for his part, supported all this because he had hopes that I would someday sign up for the Jesuit order. Besides, it ingratiated him further with Mom, thereby ensuring his supply of cold beer (which, during the cold KC winters, progressed to brandy).

Mom encouraged me because the secrecy of my private chapel was subversive. Or did she really want me to be a priest, and thereby avoid the whole man/woman pileup? As far as I know, Dad never found out about my sanctuary. He was going through his own religious evolution, moving from insisting on us all attending church every Sunday to demanding that *we* go to church while he slept in. I had Mom's back when she swore to him that we'd attended 6:45 Mass.

Bikes & Girls

The advent of my first real bicycle, the silver Schwinn, led to more than early weekday Masses at the Jesuit rectory and early Sunday cooking lessons from Tata on 52nd.

In my sixth and seventh grade classes at St. Francis Xavier grade school, Tom Sullivan was my BFF from the age of ten to thirteen. I lost track of Sully when I enrolled with the Jebbies at Rockhurst High School, and he chose the Christian Brothers' at De La Salle.

My growing stack of 45s included the Big Bopper's "Chantilly Lace," Frank Sinatra's "All the Way," the Poni-Tails' "Born Too Late," Perry Como's "Catch a Falling Star," the Silhouettes' "Get a Job," and Elvis' "Wear My Ring around Your Neck." But Tom and I discovered jazz together—our favorite recording being an excruciatingly cool Louis Armstrong rendition of "Ain't Misbehavin'." We'd sit in his room and play it ten or fifteen times in a row until we were in a bona fide jazz trance. No wonder the vinyl disc finally wore out. Between listening to jazz, the relentless drum rolls of "Topsy Parts I and II," and rock 'n roll, Tom and I became bicycle buddies. His bike—a low-slung 24" (while mine was the more standard 28")—was named "Hildegard." He camouflaged Hildegard with white, red, and black stripes. I named my trusty silver Schwinn "Traveler" after Robert E. Lee's gray steed.

That's one more thing Tom and I shared, in those final prepubescent years before we meandered apart in pursuit of "girls" and high schools. Oblivious, at that age, to all racist implications, we loved the Civil War. He was Robert E. Lee, I, Stonewall Jackson. We studied the codes and ciphers used during the war, and they inspired the one we created for the land we discovered, claimed, and mapped. Between us, we read hundreds of novels and history books about the period.

We biked as far south as 63rd Street and north as Swope Parkway (where it became Blue Parkway and skirted Brush Creek). Brush Creek, as it runs along KC's bedazzling Country Club Plaza, is stolidly contained in concrete. But by the time it snakes its way east to Benton Boulevard, it becomes an almost-river, lined with leafy trees, and punctuated with islands. Tom and I claimed as ours the wilderness "country" between the Benton Boulevard and the Cleveland Avenue bridges. We named our country JKMARAO'RB (which no doubt meant something in code), mapped it, consecrated it, and trekked through it on bikes and on foot.

Eventually would-be usurper Michael Buckley unforgivably cracked the ingenious Civil-War style code by which Tom and I communicated. So we created our own indecipherable language, "Secluniate"—and wrote JKMARAO'RB's declaration of independence on a "scroll" improvised from a ten-inch-wide and sixty-five-inch-long roller window shade, which I discovered on a basement shelf of discarded treasures. Until I ran across the "Grammar of Secluniate," I admit I could no longer read a single word of the code we created—so well-fashioned is our cipher.

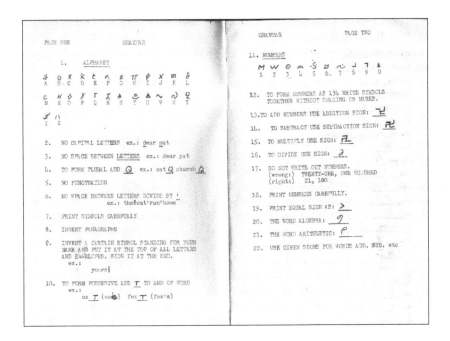

Wild exhilaration would rush through my veins when we dismounted our bikes and marched into the Brush Creek wilderness, a foretaste of the "great escape" to freedom that would later occur when I left KC for DC. We would lose ourselves in our own wild country and talk and plan and dream for hours on end. We were militant in our readiness to defend the land to our last breath, though once Pat Buckley was banished, it harbored no enemy.

Bikes led to expanded horizons: friends, employment, religious service, and my culinary apprenticeship. In short, exploration, discovery, and my first real taste of liberation.

In sixth grade, about the same time as bikes offered the hope of liberation, I discovered that the opposite sex was, well, different. Cherie Watts, a saucy blonde displaying from her navy-blue pinafore an unimaginable creamy-white décolletage when we

63

played Spin-the-Bottle at an after-school birthday party at her house on Forest Avenue, crawled toward me to give me a peck on the mouth.

This time I knew how to respond and kissed her back. But I had no idea what came next, so, out of sheer sexual frustration, I stole her beanie—ran across it recently in a file of all my St. Francis Xavier homework. Filed away, to figure out, like everything else, later. I didn't notice until then that it had been her sister Diane's, Diane's name blued out with ink and "CHERIE" written in front of it. Was it a good sign that Cherie didn't demand her beanie back? I joked with Tom that I was now "going heady" with her.

Kathleen Butterfield had sparkling black eyes and a swan's long white neck. The blood raced between us, but neither of us had any idea what to do with that either. We were both so overcome with longing neither of us could make the first move—or even knew what that move might be.

Tata's Beans

My Lebanese grandmother didn't talk much. They said she was raised in a French convent, where the nuns enforced silence. The silence stuck with her, which no doubt suited Jede. He could speak well enough for both. What I learned from her: **"They also serve who only stand and wait."**

But Tata sure could cook.

Although only nieces and nephews behind their mothers' backs would admit it, my Lebanese beans are the only ones that taste exactly like my grandmother's. There was a good and simple reason for that. On Sunday mornings, I didn't have to serve Mass at the Jesuit residence. But when five-thirty dawned, rain, shine, sleet, and pursuing dogs notwithstanding, I pedaled the twelve blocks from our house at 58th & Virginia to Tata and Jede's house, at the top of the hill at 52nd & Wayne Avenue. What else is a guy gonna do at five a.m. on a Sunday morning?

If I got there by six a.m., when Tata opened her kitchen for business, I would be on hand to witness the start of her cooking process and could be sure to record every single move. The entire Atchity clan would start showing up for Sunday dinner around noon, but my best hours were the ones I shared with Jede and Tata while the food was being prepared and tasted.

Other than her eternally sweet smile and faultless beans, I know all too little about my father's mother. She sold crochet work door to door before she bore her first child. She said *Sa'tanya* to all who appreciated her food—roughly translatable from Lebanese Arabic as, "God bless you. Keep eating!"

I'd learned the hard way that my grandmother's dictated recipes were suspect. If you followed them to the letter of her instructions, the resulting meat pies, beans, cabbage roll, or Lebanese bread would taste a little different from hers. Which, for me, was unacceptable. As a Capricorn, I have the unfortunate handicap of foreseeing how things will turn out—and I didn't care for a possible future without those precisely tangy and palate-satisfying beans. I had to find out whether she was fibbing or just forgetful when she dictated her recipes to my aunts.

Tata cooked her signature tomato sauce navy beans in a large aluminum cauldron that will reprise its pivotal part in this narrative later. It all started with that pot, the same one currently safe on my kitchen shelf covered with a silk scarf to keep dust from crudding up the age-scratched aluminum surface.

Recipe for Tata's Beans

With a ceremonial reverence I've reenacted over the years, my grandmother placed the cauldron into the sink and began to pour the dry white navy beans into it, package by package, until the pot was nearly half full. Kayoko scolds me for never being able to make a recipe smaller than six bags of beans even though there are only the two of us rattling around much of the time. Only late in life did it occur to me that Tata needed six bags because her entire family—five sons, two daughters, and their spouses and spawn—arrived at Jede's for Sunday dinner. That's why she needed Jede's mother's big pot.

I argue to Kayoko that we can freeze the cooked beans if there are any left after our dinner and after the foodies duly request Tupperware containers to take home. I always reserve at least enough for me to make bean sandwiches.

Tata would fill the cauldron with water enough to barely cover the beans and, as the incoming water churned them up, would patiently remove the "bad" beans from the batch one by one. I still do that to this day, though I doubt it changes the final taste one iota—to have an occasional shriveled or brown bean in the mix. It was her convent-instilled manic perfectionism. Once the water reached the right level, Tata would abandon the task long enough to shuffle to the breakfast room, turn on the radio, and say her eight forty-five rosary with Pope Pius XII broadcasting from the Vatican.

That, I didn't do.

Instead, I used her fifteen rosary minutes to chat with Jede. Wearing his white tank top undershirt (called, in those days, a "wife-beater"), my grandfather by now had entered the kitchen with his ever-present unfiltered Lucky Strike cigarettes. His mission was to gulp down, like all his sons and daughters, the first of twenty or more cups of coffee he drank each day—the last one minutes before going to bed. He smoked, slurped, and conversed with me as we waited for Tata's tryst with the pope.

After the last "Glory Be" and sign of the cross, Tata returned to the soaking beans. She transferred the heavy, water-filled pot to the stove. Maybe that's what made her upper arms so hefty? Bringing the beans to a boil, she'd use a perforated round steel spatula—I wonder who inherited that?—to remove the bean-foam that rose to the surface until it masked the beans. She told me it was important to remove the foam before adding seasonings, though I never quite understood why.

The next step was a "dash" of salt; then, she covered the surface of the beans with black pepper. I watched like a hawk to measure the pepper until one Sunday, I concluded it was simply that she covered the entire surface with it.

Once that was done, it was back to letting the beans cook on high flame while she took out one of her wrought iron skillets and filled it with a half-inch of olive oil, into which, when the oil was hot enough to pop, she tossed a large yellow onion chopped fine and about ten cloves of garlic also chopped fine. When the onion and garlic were translucent, she added the sautéed mixture to the beans and let it sit on the surface, drip slowly into, and mingle with the beans. Then she turned the heat to low for the next hour.

The penultimate step was adding Contadina tomato paste—six small cans (or three medium), scooped out with a spoon, and placed on top of the beans. She didn't throw away the emptied cans because you could never get every morsel of paste out of them with a spoon. Instead, she reserved them until the beans needed more water, which she added by filling the cans one by one from the sink with hot water, so the remaining paste would melt and make its way into the pot. Watch the water level carefully: The worst outcome would be to let the beans go dry and burn.

It occurred to me the very first time I got to make the beans using her pot, which had been in my mother's kitchen for twenty years since Tata died, that without Contadina the entire recipe would simply evaporate into history. I've tried using Hunt's or Del Monte, but the beans just don't taste the same. I pray to the kitchen gods that Contadina doesn't disappear during my lifetime.

The exact piquancy required by "Tata's beans" is found only in a Contadina tomato paste can; the acrid under-taste imports the Mediterranean soil directly into the taste buds.

My mother, bless her soul (and I mean it), never got Tata's beans right. For one thing, Mom's beans were slightly too mushy from being over-cooked. Mom, rather than admit her distractibility, claimed my father liked the beans that way because it caused less gas, but, hey, anyone in the Atchity family knows that a little flatulence may be the occasional price you pay for tripping out on those beans. Plus, Uncle Jimmy, the dentist, assured me absolutely no evidence existed that mushy beans produce less gas.

What Mom actually argued, as did all the others who tried and still try to make my grandmother's Lebanese beans, was that "that's the way Tata made them."

Malarkey.

I didn't see anyone else in that kitchen on 52nd Street at six a.m. Sunday mornings to observe how Tata made them. I didn't see Mom there. I learned on those early Sunday mornings that, when it comes to cooking, word of mouth is never a substitute for eyewitness experience. I can't tell you how many times supposedly well-meaning guests have begged for one of my recipes, gumbo, for example.

"If you're really serious, come over next time I make it and watch me," I say.

You can imagine how that goes. They come, they begin to watch, but then they get distracted by conversation, or phone calls, or a knock at the door, or a text message from one of their kids. And they look away. That's when the devil in me could come out and make me add the final pinch of the ingredient they don't write down. I challenge you to find a passionate cook who doesn't!

Speaking of flatulence, another innovation from my mother was the addition of baking soda—two or three spoonsful—to the pre-sauced beans, purportedly to reduce the gas level. Over the years, I'll admit to having experimented with this for various reasons but with identical results. First, it makes no discernible difference in taste. Not a single person, including myself, can tell whether baking soda was added or not. Second, it makes no measurable impact on the level of flatulence—which isn't *that* high anyway. Besides, I learned in Father Young's Greek class at Georgetown that Aristotle supposedly taught that bean emissions are souls of the dead, transmigrating. That's way cool with me.

Tata's final ingredient was also, not surprisingly, the subject of contention in the family. She invariably added a single dash of cinnamon. No measuring spoons in her kitchen, any more than in mine. It was a dash straight from the red and white can.

Folding the tomato paste into the three-quarters-cooked beans, she left them to simmer another hour or so until the smell was heavenly enough to give you visions of cedar trees in faraway mountains. When the beans were very slightly *al dente,* they're ready to be turned off.

While the beans were on simmer, Tata took me with her to the basement where Jede had installed an old-fashioned double oven for her. Starting from scratch from nothing but flour, salt, yeast, and warm water, she kneaded, flipped, flattened, and baked the thinnest, most heavenly tasting, and smelling, bread imaginable. Modern supermarket pita pales in comparison, though Trader Joe's Middle Eastern Bread is a worthy facsimile if you heat it in a hot skillet with a dab of olive oil until blisters start to form on both sides.

We used Tata's Lebanese bread to scoop her beans, each tantalizing bite transporting us to gustatory nirvana.

Uncles Amok

Uncle Victor was the light-hearted flibbertigibbet of the Atchity brothers. Compared to fierce "Eagle" (Uncle Anthony), intense and meticulous Fred (my dad), ebullient Eddy, and polymathically garrulous Jimmy (the only Atchity uncle with an advanced degree), Vick reminded folks of Charlie Chaplin.

Aunt Lorraine "the Beauty" recalls that Victor used to dress up "funny" to make his parents laugh; or distract Tata from her single-minded attention to the *Lawrence Welk Show* and the Pope's rosary. As an adult, Uncle Vick would flit from grocery store to grocery store, his first one at 31st and Brooklyn, then at 34th & Agnes, 36th & Main, and finally way out in Olathe.

Stories of Vick's childhood antics brightened our holiday gatherings like doubloons in a gunnysack of copper pennies. "He was so ornery," Tata liked to say, "he would stand on the kitchen counter, reach into the cabinets and hurl all my plates across the room." She claimed she had to replace her everyday china collection three times before Victor was eight.

Vick and the beautiful Aunt Lorraine made for a dangerous combination. They liked to play cowboys and Indians—she the Indian, he the cowboy. One day, while Tata was at church, my father was quietly counting clothespins on the front porch of the yellow frame house with white columns at 805 Wabash. Uncle Anthony was reputedly babysitting. Vick tied Aunt Lorraine to the bedpost in the girls' bedroom, surrounded her with newspapers, and set the papers on fire.

Which set the room on fire.

Which set the roof on fire.

Miraculously, Lorraine the Beauty survived. As did the house.

I vaguely remember being intimidated by Jede's big yellow house on Wabash. I encountered my toddler cousins on weekends there while our fathers, newly returned from the War, conferred with Jede about reentering American society.

"Buy your store first," Jede ordered, "*then* your house."

Behind the yellow house was a screened-in porch where Tata fed the homeless who stopped in for her Lebanese food.

I liked to hang out in the back yard with its homemade barbecue oven (usually laden with shish kebab being broiled over hickory chips) and its six-car garage, the side of which was mantled

with the thickest grapevines I would ever see. The vines produced
so many grape leaves—harvested for the traditional Lebanese "grape
leaves" stuffed with rice and ground meat—that Jede made a
standing invitation to the Bonahans, Owens, and DeCaros—in
fact, to all the neighbors on the block—to "help themselves" to the
leaves any time.

Frank DeCaro's brood next door was like extended family.
Mrs. DeCaro was a non-stop source of fresh-baked cookies, and her
vivacious daughter Katy, who I would run into at weddings and
funerals for decades, loved to gab—fearlessly rescuing me from my
nemesis Betty Lafferty.

Three American flags flew in front of Jede's Wabash house
because, as beautiful Lorraine reported, Jede was a three-time
"American War Father." He'd sent three sons to World War II:
Dad, Uncle Vick, and Uncle Jimmy. My grandfather didn't take
the flags down until long after the war was over.

Θ

Aunt Lorraine surviving the bedpost burning left its mark in the
triumphant glint of deviltry flashing in dark eyes. Growing up, I
was in awe of her Mediterranean beauty. The fire truck, pulled by
horses in those days, arrived—to startle my father, who was still
playing on the porch. The house was saved, though the bedroom
had to be rebuilt. Victor was no longer allowed to play cowboys
and Indians, but the gleeful deviltry remained in his eyes too—in
sharp contrast with the benign merriment that shaped Uncle
Eddy's aura.

Not that Eddy had no run-ins with excitement.

The milk truck, which doubled as an ice truck, was also pulled by horses. Jede had given his sons strict instructions *not* to ride the red wooden wagon they'd received for Christmas down the driveway into the street. But Jede was gone to the store, and Eddy had no one to play with but Victor.

He loaded Vic into the wagon, pushed off with his leg, and jumped in. They careened down the drive toward what he imagined was an empty Wabash Avenue. Thinking ahead was my father's department, not theirs. Dad, again playing his favorite counting game on the porch quietly, witnessed the scene.

The ice truck was parked in front of the house. By the time the wagon's arc transected the truck, all Victor, who was steering, could do was swerve—right through the horse's rear and front legs.

The horse, rudely startled from an afternoon catnap in his blinders while his driver delivered ice to Tata's icebox, reacted with a kick that trapped my young uncles beneath its abdomen. They tumbled and rocked as the hapless animal bucked down the street, dragging the heavy truck that tipped over and sprayed sparks like a fiery pinwheel.

By the time my young uncles fell free, both boys were black and blue. And laughing hysterically.

Porch-witness Dad was horrified. Before the climax of the scene, he ran inside the house, announcing, "Vic and Eddy were killed by the iceman's horse!"

Tata, still recovering from the last batch of broken dishes, nearly had a mid-day heart attack.

Uncle Eddy's new wagon was shattered. He was not given another one. He would have to "grow up" (Atchity for "Get a job").

Favorite Uncle Eddy Joke

A horse walks into a bar.
The bartender asks, "Why the long face?"

Grape Leaves

Making grape leaves, *warak enab* or *sarma* (the Greeks call them *dolma*), first from the leaves behind the Wabash Avenue homestead, then from the ones on E. 52nd Street behind Jede and Tata's new house there, is an arduous undertaking.

Aunt Carrie's grape leaves were by all votes the best in the family. Not only were they the tightest rolled, which indicated culinary prowess mirroring her tightly rolled personality—but she also counted them. "I made 283 grape leaves," she'd say nonchalantly as she paraded her platter to our living room—as though any of us except Dad had the attention span to count that high. Then she would sit on the floor in casual lotus position—and never stop talking till the visit was over. That, and her ever-present diamond pendant, would cause a lot of eye rolls after she left. Mom didn't know what to make of pretension, or of her faint mustache, or of drama queens, or of women who sat on the floor.

Now that Aunt Carrie is long transferred to that great kitchen in the sky, Aunt Lorraine the Beauty took her place at the top of the grape leaves' ranks. I served as altar boy at her glamorous wedding to sarcastic and dashing Uncle Dave Hake in 1954.

Lorraine looked like a Hollywood star that day, with Jede in white tuxedo escorting her down the aisle.

Aunt Lorraine's Grape Leaves

Though her Lebanese grape leaves could never be as tight as Aunt Carrie's, here is Aunt Lorraine's recipe:

　2 lbs. ground beef (or lamb)

　Uncle Ben's rice

　Salt, pepper, & Lawry's seasoning (or garlic salt, your choice)

　Real Lemon Juice, in the bottle

　5 of the thinnest pork chops you can find

　Grape leaves

Note: If you're not using fresh-picked grape leaves, as we did growing up, Lorraine insists you use the Krinos brand of grape leaves, usually found in the "olive aisle."

Rinse the leaves once and cut off any visible stems that haven't been removed already.

Prepare the stuffing by sautéing two-and-a-half pounds of lean leg of lamb or hamburger meat with Uncle Ben's rice, seasoning to taste with salt and pepper—lots of the latter.

Lorraine adds Lawry's Seasoning, but I sincerely doubt that Tata did that; she might have used garlic salt. Tata may have added a pinch of cumin to the seasoning.

In your saucepan or double broiler, layer the bottom of the pan with the broken leaves as a foundation. Place the pork chops, well-seasoned, tightly wedged together, on top of the broken leaves.

Roll the leaves, with the meat and rice interior, as tightly as you can, tightening them even further by stacking them sardine-like on top of the pork chops, in layers until your whole batch is stacked in the pot.

Cover the grape leaves with a lemon, thinly sliced, and add a saucer on top to hold everything in place during cooking.

Top the packed mixture with water and lemon juice—according to brother Freddy, you can't add enough lemon juice and it's true that the lemonier the grape leaves are, the better.

Cook until they're done. Serve hot, careful not to break the packed cartridges when transferring them to the serving platter.

Lorraine's handwritten recipe ends, "Love you Sweetie."

Catsup Catastrophe

I counted twenty-nine jobs I'd worked from the time, around age eight, when I first got paid to babysit. They included: milkman's assistant; delivering prescriptions and groceries by bike; babysitting; cutting lawns; delivering newspapers; selling popcorn at the Starlight Theater with Melvin Busch, scion of the Busch & Lobby concession fortune; caddying at Blue Hills Country Club; dog-earing books at Reynolds Bindery; working in Uncle Anthony's store, and sometimes in Uncle Eddy's; waiting on cars at Sidney's Drive-in near the Plaza; driving trucks for Minuteman Missile sites; working as an electrician's helper at the GM Plant; inventorying at J. C. Penney's; and counting nuts and bolts at an auto supply store. I filed my first tax return at the age of fifteen: $47.70 refund, applied to my next year's taxes.

One of my very first outside-the-home jobs was delivering prescriptions by bicycle for Spenser's Drugs way across Rockhill Road. Mr. Spenser caught me once, on the hottest day of summer, drinking a purloined Grapette in his backroom—and gave me a tongue-lashing that scared me as much as the ones doled out by the BVMs (nuns of the order of the Blessed Virgin Mary) at St. Francis Xavier grade school. Funny how those tongue-lashings were scarier than our "nuclear drills," where we were ordered to crouch beneath our desks once a week holding our heads in our clasped hands. We took the crouching in stride because it wasn't personal; scoldings were.

My first grocery store job was at Uncle Anthony's grocery store at 43rd and Wayne, working under the protection of Cousin Tony (Anthony, Jr.). Cousin Tony's good humor was as irrepressible as his girth was enormous. When I first encountered Shakespeare's Falstaff in high school English, I was convinced the Bard of Avon had copied my cousin's character. Tony's demeanor grew positive in direct proportion to his stature expanding from his massive love of food, as though it were his fate to epitomize the entire family's exuberance for eating in his single jolly self. Tony's demeanor rarely changed from ebullient. When I, at that same age of fifteen, drove his shiny brown and white '56 Chevy station wagon into a clump of evergreen bushes in the middle of The Paseo one Sunday morning when he was "letting me drive," Tony just laughed. He took the rap for the accident.

Tony's pattern was to swing by our house at four a.m. (if I was lucky, even earlier) to pick me up. He handed me an apron and put me to work lugging cases of cans on my shoulder from the cellar of the store, then trimming and arranging the produce, and "running the shelves"—our term for straightening and restocking the merchandise from the opened cartons tucked beneath the shelves. Then I would dust the restocked and realigned shelves with a feather duster because Eagle (Tony's nickname for his father; Uncle Anthony's dark eyes missed *nothing*) demanded a sparkly clean and orderly store. I knew every inch of that store. For years I could recite the grocery products, label after label, on every shelf of every aisle by heart.

On the few occasions when I was "loaned out" to Uncle Eddy's store at 24th and Linwood, I could barely hide my surprise and disdain. Although my father claimed Eddy's store "did well," I found that hard to believe: It was sheer chaos. The aisles were filled with so many topsy-turvy "specials" that navigating with a grocery cart was impossible; customers abandoned their carts at the end of the aisles, darted in for something they needed—Uncle Eddy, hoping they'd be nabbed by a stacked-up special display, was oblivious to the logjam created at the ends of the aisles.

Eagle's store was the opposite of Eddy's: No special displays of any kind. If a product didn't fit into the orderly grand scheme, Uncle Anthony didn't carry it. He catered to an upscale clientele.

Uncle Eddy focused on thrifty. He had no doubt been imprinted with that demographic when my grandfather arrived in *his* store to discover that a younger Eddy, who'd been sent to City Market at the crack of dawn to pick up fruits and vegetables, had secured a "bargain" on 100 pounds of strawberries and loaded the flatbed truck with them. "Eddy was a sucker for produce," Victor would explain years later. The only problem was that the strawberries were about an hour away from going bad—which my grandfather's nose detected before he even *got* to the red-leaking truck. "*Majdoob*," Jede swore. "You have one hour to sell all those strawberries. Or don't come back," he added and turned on his heel.

Uncle Eddy, who'd just learned to drive, thought hard—and drove away—fast. For the next hour, he motored up and down the side streets of downtown Kansas City, yelling, "Ripe strawberries— fifteen cents a basket. Eat them now!" He managed to dispose of the whole near-rotten bunch before driving back to the store and handing his father a small profit that earned him a small grin. Uncle Eddy was more careful buying strawberries after that and less trusting of the produce vendors at City Market.

Uncle Eddy's grin, like Jede's, was infectious, especially when he was playing the piano—which he did by ear, entertaining the entire family on those rare occasions when Sunday dinner was held at his house on 69th Terrace. You'd ask for any tune you could think of, and he'd begin playing it, dropping into a performance trance that ratified the healthy negative ions in any size room. Being around Eddy Atchity was sharing in an all-pervading good mood, as though he embodied an artistic Boyle's Law. Ed inherited the power Jede exuded when he was playing his oud. Even my grandfather's explosive vitriol rolled off my uncle's back like water off a duck.

Funny how dispositions ricochet around the gene chain. Tony, Jr., the oldest of the Atchity cousins, inherited Uncle Eddy's good humor. Tony's dad, the Eagle, had very little of it, and what he had he reserved for his country club or for the retelling of the one joke he'd bring back from each round of golf. Eagle's store was shipshape because his perfectionist's temper was immediate. Good-natured Tony was impervious to the outbursts that sent others scurrying to the nearest corner to lick their wounds. Others, of course, included hyper-sensitive me, who still hated it when anyone yelled in my direction.

One day as I was dusting the condiments shelf, I knocked a bottle of Delmonico's catsup to the floor in full view of Eagle, who was peering imperiously from his eyrie behind the meat counter. As though it were falling in slow motion, I watched the bottle head for its gravitational denouement—centering my entire observational powers on the cap on which "23¢" was clearly stamped with that purple ink we used in the price marking machine.

I distinctly recall the dreadful pride I felt in knowing with certitude the exact interim that was about to occur between one event and another—the explosion of the bottle and the explosion of Eagle's temper. The Jesuits at Rockhurst High hadn't yet taught me Aristotelian cause and effect, but I knew it in my bones.

I was correct.

This may have been, in fact, the first time I was consciously aware of what I later termed my "Capricorn curse": the ability to foresee the future precisely without any attendant satisfaction therefrom. Cassandra in Homer's *Iliad* was a Capricorn. Like my lifeblood spattered in that boxing ring at Blessed Sacrament Grade School, the catsup and glass splattered on my black trousers, on the floor, on the adjacent shelves, and on the early-morning serenity.

"What the fuck's wrong with you? How can I run a business like this?" Adding a few Lebanese curse words I'd heard around Jede's house, Eagle bellowed his lungs out, removing his cigar to enhance the thunderous resonance of his deep and manly voice. I cringed. Loud manly voices aimed against my frail sensitivities tended to devastate me.

As I bent to retrieve the broken glass and my dignity, I glanced at Tony. He was standing at his second-in-command post behind the counter at the telephone where he sweet-talked the old ladies who phoned their orders in, for me to deliver on the black bicycle with the "Atchity's Finest Foods" sign. Tony was winking at me. The wink that gave me perspective and helped me manage to keep from bursting into tears. "Eagle, calm down, for chrissakes," Tony said to his dad. "Kenny's never dropped anything before. It's no big deal. He'll clean it up." Lightning Rod Tony weathered the next blast and left me in the clear.

A chastened automaton, I headed for the backroom to get a broom and dustpan, ignoring the blood-red spatters on my tennis shoes and white apron. I risked a glance at Eagle, only to find his eyes slit, squinted, and smoldering like twin volcanoes as he followed my every movement. We called that "getting the Lebanese eyes."

Five minutes later, Uncle Anthony was chatting up Mrs. Carraway at the meat counter, upselling her from two lamb chops to a leg of lamb as diplomatically as though he were a pastor greeting parishioners after Sunday mass at Christ the King. The good thing about Eagle was that once the storm subsided, the sun was soon shining brightly. The laughter returned, and his laugh, too, was a high point of my memory, the kind that comes from so deep and penetrates so deep it gives you goosebumps and makes you wonder why anyone does anything but laugh.

Uncle Anthony Joke

A man goes into the confessional. "Bless me father, I have sinned. My last Confession was one week ago. Since then I had adultery four times with a married woman…"

The priest interrupts. "Who was it my son?"

"Father," the young man says, "I can't tell you that. It wouldn't be right."

"But my son, you have the seal of the confessional to protect you. No one will ever know."

"I can't say, father. It would be ungentlemanly."

"Was it Mrs. Ryan?" the priest asked.

"No, father," said the young man.

"Was it Mrs. O'Shannahan?" the priest persisted.

"No, father," said the young man.

"Then it had to be Mrs. Fisher," the priest concluded.

But the young man remained silent.

So the priest gave him his penance, five rosaries, gave him Absolution, and bid him good-bye.

The young man knelt in a pew and recited his rosaries. Then he left the church.

Outside, he was greeted by his two waiting buddies. "Well?" they demanded.

"Yeah," he said, "You guys were right—I got us three new leads."

Tennis Lesson: Errors

Here's the thing: Your score isn't usually determined by the great hits you make. It's determined by your number of "unforced errors." So convinced am I that becoming increasingly *aware* of your errors will automatically improve your game I invented an error-counter to click in my pocket.

I notice that even the best players, measured by the height of their slice or the force of their forehand drive, are sometimes clueless to the fact that they're making 60% unforced errors. The key to defeating them is to hit to their weak spots and *force the error.*

And to know in advance that they'll be hitting to yours.

The great thing about tennis—like life—is that it's *never* too late to improve. You can restart tomorrow or, even better, today, or, best of all, with your next shot. "The game begins every instant," as an Israeli doubles partner liked to put it. And you don't have to be a perfect player to play a good game.

"Be there, and be square," I tell myself, using the one lingo I picked up from Cub Scouts. Meaning: Move your lazy feet, get to the ball, and hit it fully and forcefully. If you do that consistently, you can count on your opponent to do himself in with unforced errors. "Let *them* make the error," I urge my double partners. "Just hit it back and give them that chance."

Morning Pickles

The best hours with Tony were when the two of us were the only ones in the store—usually between four and seven a.m.

After that, the Eagle arrived: *Dun ta dun dun!* Both of us intoned the theme of *Dragnet* as he walked in.

Even before eight, the phone started ringing; by the time we opened the front doors by eight, it already felt like noon from the swirl of activity that crowded the last pre-opening hour.

But from four to seven in the morning, we left most of the lights off—to not attract the stray customer, who'd think nothing of banging on the front door for access to a bottle of aspirin or sanitary napkins or a chicken—and prepared the place for the scheduled invasion.

The goal was simple: The store had to look perfect each morning, as though the previous day's incursions into the bright silver cans of LeSeurs Baby Peas, Libby's Cranberry Sauce, and dark green Delmonico Fruit Cocktail had never occurred. Every shelf had to appear as seamless and undented as a new battleship about to be launched from dry dock.

Early in our solitary hours, Tony would pick up the phone and order a take-out delivery, or a pick-up—usually from Gates Barbecue at 49th and Paseo, or from Sidney's Drive-in (where I sometimes moonlighted on weekends as Carhop #21—still have the button).

The food arrived around five-thirty or six. Sometimes we drove to pick it up. Tony taught me to drive "off the record," to push toward the time he could send me solo. I had to pretend I was just learning to drive at high school, and from Dad—though I'd been driving tractors and pickup trucks during my Louisiana summers since I was nine—a fact left unmentioned since Dad got jealous of anything positive I said about Louisiana.

All work stopped as the two of us sat at the back counter, both in our crisp white aprons that were not yet stained with the day's toil and accidents and joked as we relished the barbecue. I particularly savored the crisp sour contrast between the dill pickle chips and the tangy-sweet barbecue sauce. Nothing after seven a.m. could possibly taste this good. It made the backache from lugging boxes of cans up the steep stairs recede from consciousness as the camaraderie and savory satisfaction of the ribs and pickles washed over me.

Uncle Anthony hand-made the best Italian sausage I've ever known, piquant with fresh dill and fennel seed. I loved how he rolled up his sleeves and started humming as he carefully lined up his seasonings, ground the meat himself in an old-fashioned but heavy-duty hand grinder directly into sausage casings as though he were creating great art. The art of food is the opposite of all other art—except performance art. Where art usually strives for permanence (Horace's *exegi monumentum aere perennius*, I have built my monument longer-lasting than bronze), food is truly, existentially, soulfully *momentary*. The seriousness of chefs is a celebration of the temporary nature of human existence. More than anything else, it's taught me the power of Now.

Tony, the oldest of my cousins, was also the first to pass away—from a perforated intestine, no doubt caused by a lifetime of exuberance. Like Dom DeLuise's character in my favorite movie *Fatso*, Tony was equally "heavy"—Falstaffian from head to heart—leaving me to marvel at his prowess among the young women who frequented the store. I sometimes got to meet them when Tony let me tag along on his romantic dinners at Jimmy & Mary's Steakhouse on Main Street. How romantic could those dinners have been for the ladies, with me in tow? But that never stopped Tony from inviting me. I think he liked me as a buffer, and maybe for the sake of educating me in *carpe diem:* **Eat, drink, and be merry!** Another Male Authority Figure shows the way!

Tony's jokes were unending, his humor irrepressible, his charm with women of all ages working its magic from morning to night. None of his ladies seemed to mind his formidable heft.

Cousin Tony Joke

Two single girlfriends are buying their weekly two sausages from the neighborhood butcher. When the butcher tells them the price, they hand over several bills but say they're sorry they don't have exact change. The butcher bundles up the sausages and pushes them across the counter. "Since you don't have change," he said, "I gave you a third sausage."

Exiting the store, the two of them look at each other.

"What do we do with the extra sausage?" one of them asks.

The other one says: "Eat it?"

Double Entry

It was the combination of being Tony's apprentice at the grocery store and being my father's son that led me to keep a double set of books from the time I was ten.

Dad had long ago given me my first ledger and showed me how to keep track of income and expenditures. My father expected me to account for every single cent. It didn't take long to realize this was a monitoring operation as well as a lesson in life accountability. I remember him telling me, "You don't round out numbers. Numbers are numbers." They're simply what they are, neither more nor less, which explains why my father felt more comfortable with them than with human beings who would not accept anything for what it was. And who were always asking to be rounded off.

The problem announced itself at our first weekly meeting when Dad reviewed my ledger and raised holy hell if I spent too much on candy, gum, or school supplies.

On top of that, Tony, with a wink, had taken to slipping me five or ten dollars "on the side," usually on the same day I received my printed check as payment from Broadmour Market.

What to do? If I recorded the extra income I received from Tony, it would end up in that savings account Dad opened for me with the silver dollars I'd received as birth presents. That had the opposite effect on me than the one Dad intended, since it instilled in my heart an aversion to savings it took years to overcome. His depositing those silver dollars, which I saw as symbolic of my idyllic Cajun roots, made me view him as the all-controlling Cyclops. Given my ongoing resentment and distrust of Dad, that was a fate I could not suffer for my "on the side" funds.

So, I bought myself another ledger like the one Dad gave me and kept it as well: the original, to present to Dad weekly; the duplicate, concealed beneath my mattress, to keep track of the actual expenditures and income.

Two different stories, both told with numbers.

Date	Description	Dr.	Cr.	Balance
3/4	lunch	.35		60
3/4	Reynolds G: 7.50		7 28	7 88
3/4	gum	.05		7 83
3/4	Broadmoor	.	2 00	9 83
3/4	gas	2.00		7 83
3/5	Church	.25		7 58
3/6	Southeast game	1.00		6 58
3/6	coke	.15		6 43
3/7	milk+role	.20		6 23
3/8	milk	.10		6 13
3/9	milk & gum	.15		5 98
3/10	milk	.10		5 88
3/10	bus	.25		5 63
3/11	pop	.10		5 53
3/11	Reynolds G: 8.00		7 76	13 29
3/11	party (Band + cokes)	.50		12 79
3/12	Broadmoor		4 00	16 79
3/12	Church	.25		16 54
3/12	gas T: 2.00	1.50		15 04
3/12	tux	1.00		14 04
3/13	milk + roll	.20		13 84
3/14	milk	.10		13 74
3/14	phone	.10		13 64
3/14	apple	.10		13 54
3/15	typing paper	.25		13 29
3/15	milk	.10		13 19
3/15	bus	.25		12 94
3/15	razor blades	.36		12 58
3/16	shoes	10.67		1 91
3/16	milk	.10		1 81

At the time, in the ingenuous duplicity of youth, I thought I was getting away with something. Only later, I think it was in my Georgetown years, did I realize Dad had the better of me after all: An accountant's son, I couldn't be content to *not* record my cash economy. I needed that second set of books to validate a separate reality base, one that was entirely mine. I was in training to deal with the Hollywood studios.

The Chicken Game

Uncle Eddy told us the legendary story of Jede closing his grocery store for the weekend at half past eight one Saturday night.

As my grandfather was turning out the lights, he heard someone banging on the front door. Glancing up, he saw that it was his most lucrative customer, Mrs. McGilley of Melody McGilley Funeral Homes (the final way station of so many KC Atchitys). She looked desperate, so what could he do? He let her in.

"Thank God, Mr. Atchity," she said. "I don't know what I would do if you hadn't still been here." She told him she had unexpected guests drop in and needed another chicken for tomorrow's dinner. In those days, grocery stores in Missouri and Kansas had to close on Sundays.

He led her back to the meat counter, donned his apron again, and discovered, looking in the compartment beneath the counter, that he had only one chicken left. He looked up and asked her, "How big a chicken do you want?"

She answered: "I think five pounds should be fine."

Jede stuffed ice into the chicken's cavity just in case, then pulled it out and dropped it on the scale where it weighed in, ice and all, at precisely five pounds.

Mrs. McGilley could see the chicken, and her face fell. "I'm not sure, Mr. Atchity. Maybe I should just get a four-pounder."

"No problem," Jede replied, removing the chicken and taking it with him below the counter, where he deftly removed some of the ice; then returned it to the scales.

"This one is four pounds, five ounces. What do you think?"

Mrs. McGilley nodded at first, but then the troubled look came over her again. "You know what?" she said. "I'm being silly. I'd rather have too much than too little. I'll take both," she said.

Family history does not record how Jede got out of that one.

Making Out

Aided and abetted by seventh-gradeclassmate Mark Carney, I finally figured out what comes after the bottle-kiss. We made our move on the enticing West twins down Virginia Avenue. Their mother was recently divorced from their father, whose last name was Ruppert, and now they lived with their stepfather Lew West. Jan was the foxier, Ann the more serious—and my favorite. They had a younger sister named Jo, who was also quite pretty. Their father was either alcoholic or angry (for good reason!) or both. Though we all dreaded him, we managed workarounds.

Carney and I invited Ann and Jan over one night when my folks were out. Mark and Jan on one bed, Ann and I on the other, we steamed up the windows of my front bedroom, doing everything that could be done within the strict laws of Roman Catholic celibacy—clothes on, of course. Ann and Jan, not Catholic, had a hard time understanding the lines we wouldn't cross.

It was called "making out." Lots of moaning and cooing—ending in good Catholic frustration. The sweetness of these first erotic kisses lingered long after we'd moved away from the neighborhood and headed farther south to 75th Street and even more daring liaisons.

Keeping Track

Dad kept track of things. That's what he did. He was an accountant.

I've done it too, all my life. Not only kept track but retain the records. Not only retained the records, but report them to you, dear reader.

At first, I didn't know for sure who in the heck I was keeping track for, but it felt somehow imperative. I eventually concluded that I was collecting evidence in case I could ever figure out who I was and what my life was all about. I was collecting for future me to use in defining myself. I was collecting so I, that future me, could tell you this story.

I even kept a log of every letter I wrote and each one I received. To this day, I've kept running lists of every movie I've seen (at least since 1963); every play and every book I read, including the total and accumulated page count; and every airline flight, starting with the TWA Constellation I flew from DC to KC for my grandfather's funeral.

Even though I had no idea at the time what the usefulness of all this record-keeping was, it reaches a certain critical mass where you hate to consider stopping because you've done it for so long.

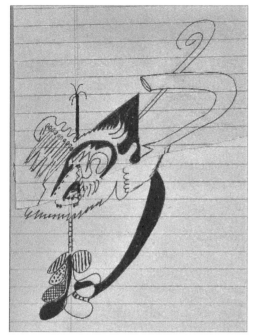

I even kept a file of my doodles.

For years I recorded my dreams long before I started studying how dreams influence life and literature, then went on to co-found *DreamWorks* with my like-minded Occidental College colleague, the brilliant Marsha Kinder, who was studying how dreams impact film. *DreamWorks* was a journal devoted to the relationship between art and dreams and was published by Human Sciences Press in New York for nearly ten years. Our advisory board included Ursula LeGuin, Joyce Carol Oates, Denise Levertov, and John Fowles. Contributors included novelists William Burroughs, Stephen King, Anais Nin, Carlos Fuentes, Alain Robbe-Grillet, Diane Johnson, A. E. Van and Carlos Fuentes; filmmaker Federico Fellini, and musician/philosopher John Cage. When Jeffrey Katzenberg and Steven Spielberg founded their Hollywood studio and gave it the same name, we wrote them a polite letter asking if they'd be interested in pursuing synergies with our magazine.

Apparently, they weren't. We received a rude letter from their legal department warning us away. LOL.

Θ

One curious list I kept reveals all the letters I sent to my high school sweetheart Carrie Catherine Curran. I would meet Carrie Catherine Curran in 1960 when I was a junior at Rockhurst, and she at St. Theresa's Academy. I interviewed her by phone for a school assignment, asking her a hundred questions about her favorite things (her favorite priests were Jesuits; favorite instrumental, the theme from *Picnic*; favorite means of transportation, "feet"; favorite snack, "shoestring potatoes"; and favorite Bible quotation, "Suffer the little children to come unto Me." She had twelve siblings!).

That we both attended unisex schools sparked a fire in our progressively more intense relationship. I lived for interminable weekend phone calls with her and our once-a-week evening out, ending in front of her family's big brick house on 74th & Wyoming. Driving, which meant I could borrow the family car, opened the gate to amorous exploration, though our testing the envelope of chastity never even got close to "doing it"—as it was rumored that manly classmate Tom DeCoursey and a few more macho others had done. I recorded a total of 341 letters to Carrie Catherine between September 9, 1961 and April 6, 1963.

Go figure.

Tom DeCoursey Joke

It was a family legend that Paddy O'Reilly's great-grandfather, grandfather, and father all walked on water on their eighteenth birthdays.

In August when Paddy's eighteenth birthday came around, he and his pal Danny took a boat to the middle of the lake. Paddy stepped out of the boat—and nearly drowned.

Danny managed to pull him to safety.

Furious and confused, Paddy went to confront his grandmother.

"Grandma," he asked. "It's me eighteenth birthday, so why can't I walk across the lake like me father, his father, and his father before him?!"

Grandma looked deeply into Paddy's troubled eyes, and said, "Because, ya fekin idiot, ye father, ye grandfather, and ye great-grandfather were all born in December when the lake is frozen."

Cold Turkey

Dad was about thirty-five when he stopped drinking. Cold. No family intervention. No drug assists. No AA meetings. Only the sheer power of will—and prayer.

What inspired him?

We were driving home from a party—maybe at Bill Reynolds' house near Independence. Heading back to 58th and Virginia, up the divided-lane Paseo Boulevard, with the wide grassy meridian where I had crashed Tony, Jr.'s Belair station wagon into the evergreen bushes.

It felt like the middle of the night. My brother and I were half asleep in the back seat of the family Plymouth, Mom riding shotgun, Dad driving. As I was being stacked into the car, I recall her grumbling about something or other.

We had just passed 55th Street when a huge jolt shook us awake, and we were suddenly in the center meridian staring at a tree that had crumpled the front end of our car. Dad had driven off the road. Was it an icy night? Was it the thick snow that clogged the wheels and stopped the car?

Baby Mary and brother Freddy were crying, Mom was whiter than her natural porcelain, and Dad was hunched over the wheel, stunned at what he'd done. I was filled with fear and anger—two familiar patches of my suffocating quilt of negative feelings toward Dad woven from my mother's unhappiness.

A few beers too many for a Semitic-alcohol-processing-gene-deficient man who for too many years valiantly tried to compete in the drinking game with his hollow-legged Irish employers and who was now no doubt worried by something at work that he knew was going to happen.

Θ

According to Dad's own account, from that day forward he formed a pact with St. Jude (the "patron saint of lost causes"): that if the good saint would help him, he'd never have another drink so long as he lived.

And he never did—not even a sip of champagne on a festive occasion, or a single bite of Christmas fruitcake if it even faintly smelled of rum.

That's the kind of will my father had.

If only he could have applied it as well to the smoking that led to his lung cancer that led to his death.

But when all is said and done, something *has* to kill us all, doesn't it? I guess Dad figured it might as well be something he enjoyed.

Ο

During our last year on Virginia Avenue, I desperately applied myself to the Latin language. I was bonding with Father Edmund Ziegelmeyer, SJ—and, by extension, with the entire Jesuit order. By way of Father Z's mentorship, the Jesuits became not only my gateway to escape but also my intellectual and spiritual role models.

One day, Ziggy could see from my countenance, never good at masking feelings, that something was amiss. I shared with him my latest crisis with Dad. His response was to scribble a Greek phrase on my homework paper. Raising my linguistic ambitions even further, he translated it into Latin, German, and French. The English translation: "Even this will pass away."

When Ziggy departed for the day, I proceeded to translate the phrase into Secluniate, the secret code grade-school pal Sully and I invented for the "nation" he and I had created. If you don't *know* a language, make one up.

That afternoon Father Z had proceeded to recite, from memory, a poem by Theodore Tilton I would repeat to myself until the day I left home:

Once in Persia reigned a king,
Who, upon his signet ring,
Graved a maxim true and wise,
Which if held before the eyes
Gave him counsel at a glance
Fit for every change and chance.
Solemn words, and these were they:
"Even this will pass away" ...

The poem, which I've recorded here from memory, goes on, stanza after stanza, through travails experienced by the ancient Persian king. I compared them with my own litany of woes:

- Tears streaming down my face night after night as I sat at the top of the stairs, listening to Mom and Dad fighting in the kitchen.
- Watching my father walk out the door with a suitcase and praying that he'd never come back.
- Listening to Dad go through the grocery store cash register tape, comparing each price against each item, screaming at Mom for "buying two pairs of nylons again."
- Being asked by Mom to get something in her pocketbook and feeling paralyzed by the conglomerated odors of chewing gum and lipstick that I associated with forbidden femininity so much that to this day I freeze when a woman asks me to hold her purse. It makes me feel as though my masculinity is being challenged. I felt queasy, even as an adult, when Mom took my hand or my arm. What does that tell you? I was never quite sure what it told me.

"Even this will pass away," I kept chanting to myself.

Kibbeh Nayeh

The first step in making this signature Lebanese dish begins at the grocery store, whichever store has the most trustworthy butcher in your town. In Los Angeles, we prefer Gelson's though Whole Foods is also possible on a friendly, not-too-busy day. In New York, Grace's Marketplace on 3rd Avenue. In KC, the only choice for serious foodies in the Atchity family, after our own stores were no more, was for a long time McGonigle's Market near Waldo, on 79th Street. A tribute to the growth of diversity is that Pak Halal in Lenexa now not only sells excellent lamb but will make the *kibbeh nayeh* for you.

To end up with two pounds of ground lamb, you may have to buy a whole leg of lamb since the bone, fat, and gristle must be trimmed away. Besides, purchasing a leg that you've eyeballed and asked about ensures that the lamb is fresh, which it must be to eat raw. A trustworthy butcher will advise you. Nowadays, due to hygienic obsession, he will also almost surely advise you that it's never safe to eat meat raw. I roll my eyes and thank him for the warning. He will roll his eyes back, and you'll get what you need.

Then I ask him to grind the lamb three times and to make sure to clean the grinder's blade before he begins to ensure no shreds of beef or pork stray into the mix.

Buy a pound of bulgur wheat, as fine as you can find it.

The proportions are two pounds of lamb to one full cup of wheat.

Soak the wheat in a large bowl with filtered water for about half an hour.

Next, in a big enough mixing bowl, put the ground lamb along with the drained wheat and a fourth of a cup of water. Add plenty of black pepper, several pinches of salt, and, yes, a generous dash of cinnamon. Cousin Bruce Prince-Joseph's mother Adele mixed in chopped fresh mint as well.

Finely chop a large white onion—or a bunch of scallions (Tata used white onion, Freddy preferred scallions)—and add them to the bowl.

The traditional way of mixing kibbeh is kneading it by hand, which I always do, following Tata's example. Wash your hands and dry them, making sure to eliminate all traces of soap, and reach into the big bowl to knead the mixture. Knead until the consistency is perfectly blended—a light pink color. The better the grade of lamb, the faster the kneading produces desired results. Some people, and I won't name names, use a food processor to mix the ingredients, which gives the resulting dish the texture of baby pablum.

When the *kibbeh nayeh* is mixed, shape it into a tight ball, leave it in the bowl, and add a few ice cubes around the sides. Place it in the refrigerator to congeal until just before serving—at least an hour, but as long as three or four hours.

When it's time to serve it, remove it from the bowl, and dry it off with a paper towel if necessary.

Preferably on a long oval serving plate, spread the ball of kibbeh out to cover the entire surface of the plate. I use a fork to tamp it down and create grooves to catch and hold the olive oil. If you like, you can surround the plate with wedges of white onions or red radishes cut in half as garnish.

Once that's done, use your wrought-iron skillet to brown in butter as many pine nuts as you like. When the nuts are dark brown (but not black), they're done. It's time to pour them evenly across the surface of the *kibbeh nayeh.* If some of the butter flows with them, that is *not* a problem.

Bill Reynolds loved the pine nuts so much he would scoop as many as he could into his every helping of *kibbeh.* After a while, to avoid accusations of ungenerous greed, he'd deftly turn his *kibbeh* upside down, so the pine nuts weren't showing! Mom would always catch him and wink. He, whose whole life was one big wink, winked back. That's what I learned from Bill: **No matter what life brings you you can always wink.** Mom liked Bill, another of her "real characters." He comforted her when his wartime buddy, Dad, was on the warpath; and when he died.

Finally, drizzle your best olive oil across the surface—and serve a cruet of it on the table for those who like even more oil. With your piece of Lebanese bread, you scoop up onion or radish with the *kibbeh nayeh* and pine nuts. The bread should always be warm (though careful not to warm it so much it becomes stiff; it must be malleable to do its scooping job).

Nothing brings me back to the warmth of Tata's kitchen like a scoop of *kibbeh* with a sliver of onion and plenty of pine nuts. Preferably served with Lebanese beans. If I had my way, I'd put pine nuts in everything—and usually do.

By the way, cooked *kibbeh* is what most folks are familiar with. It's made by baking or frying *kibbeh nayeh*.

Uncle Jimmy

If Cousin Tony, Jr. was my favorite cousin and psychological role model, Uncle Jimmy the Dentist was my intellectual role-model.

Doc Atchity moved "far away from the family," all the way to Overland Park, Kansas, on the other side of State Line, to a wonderful white-frame house that was reportedly "too big for him." I got to hang out there with sloe-eyed cousin Pam in her upstairs bedroom before we got called down to dinner. If I were lucky, I'd get to spend the night longing to do God knows what with her.

Rumored to be "in debt up to his ears," Uncle Jimmy was my hero—an Atchity that went for it and never looked back! Eventually, he moved from Overland Park to an old-fashioned small-town, white-framed house in Cameron, Missouri, "to start over again" (according to the family rumor mill, which quietly reported that life in the fast lane had gotten to him). Doc Atchity proceeded to become not only the most beloved dentist in this small town, but also its preeminent bass fisherman—and mayor. A citizen would report: "Here we have a lot of little farm ponds—some aren't any bigger than this room—but there might be a six- or eight-pound bass in it. If there is, Doc'll get it."

That's what I love most about America, what my grandfather loved: It offers you as many chances to start over as you have the will and energy to take. I witnessed a yoga master once at a Satsang in India when a supplicant, who'd traveled 8,000 miles for the purpose, asked him, her voice faltering, "But, Master, how many times can I pick myself up?" answer simply, "Sister, how many times can you fall?"

"There's no penalty for failure here," Jede repeated to me frequently, reminding me of the Arab saying he'd learned as a kid: "There's nothing to fear! Kick the road—and go!"

I would discover that principle also holds in the Hollywood jungle, where I've battled to get stories produced for more than a quarter century. The alleged show business truism, "You only get one shot," is blatant nonsense. Nobody's counting! You get exactly as many shots as you have the hunger and stamina for. Show business, founded by immigrants, after all, is another microcosm of the American dream that continues, I hope, to attract immigrants from every opportunity-impoverished or dream-challenged part of the world.

I will never forget the mix of pain and pleasure I experienced when I visited Uncle Jimmy's office during my growing up years to have my cavities filled. He was always happy to see me because I brought him *kibbeh nayeh* which the Germanic Aunt Bobbie, his wife, and sister of Uncle Vick's wife, Aunt Leona, wouldn't *think* of eating, much less making. Doc Atchity's waiting room displayed a sign that read,

Service
Speed

Economy
Choose Two.

But it wasn't only the sign on his office wall that appealed to me. It was the opportunity to hang with a male member of the Atchity clan who talked about anything other than money and business.

Of course, it was primarily *his* talking—since my mouth was otherwise occupied by his fingers and tools. My responding would have been painful for us both. I listened to my uncle discourse on Aristotle and Plato, philosophers I'd reported I was reading in the original Greek at Rockhurst—as though they were still his nighttime reading. His learning and intellectual curiosity were equaled only by his wisdom about life, his perspective on family ("Distance is necessary," was the gist), and above all by his sense of humor.

He was my *only* Atchity uncle who never ran out of jokes.

Uncle Jimmy, from his newly created position as "the only offspring who moved out of KC" (Cameron was an unimaginable sixty miles north), encouraged me, as Jede did, to explore the world beyond "the Heart of America."

His passion for literature and philosophy—chatting about Homer as his instruments probed my mouth—was both inspiring and deeply troubling. Inspiring, because it taught me the stirring in my blood when I read a language as foreign to KC as ancient Attic Greek, was shared by another human from the same gene puddle. Troubling, because that imitable person had still not escaped completely from the sphere of the family monitoring every single action of his life.

Maybe complete escape was impossible?

For the rest of my life, by far the most dismal moments of my existence were those spent in a dentist's chair other than my uncle's. Without the classical Greek repartee and the family Male Authority Figure bond, all that's left me to think about in this prone and passive position is The Meaning of Life. No matter how hard you strive to figure it all out and be happy, life inevitably leads back to this electric chair in which mortality is paused, confronted, and calibrated tooth by skeletal tooth. After all, it will be your dentist that the police will enlist to identify your remains in the event of a catastrophic demise. Thank God audible.com now makes it possible to listen to books during dentation. The spoken word pushes the pain, like the thinking, safely aside.

The summer following my freshman year at Georgetown, in the silent intensity of Uncle Jimmy's electric chair, I vowed that not only would I follow the humanities to the max, but also that I would escape from and would never return to live in KC.

Uncle Jimmy Joke

Moses, brow furrowed, climbs down the mountain lugging the commandments under his arm. He turns around, looks up, and says, "Wait a minute, have I got this right? The Arabs get all the oil and we have to cut off the end of our dicks?"

Nervous Breakdown

The year before I was to enter Rockhurst High School, two things happened. Dad announced we were moving away from Virginia Avenue. But not before having what folks called in those days a "nervous breakdown."

The six-month-long event would haunt me many years later as I struggled through the pressures of my own career transition from professor to producer—wondering whether the next setback might be the one that brought my tightrope of a brain crashing to the mat.

Dad's mind was rudely brought down, to the point of incoherence, to the point of electric shock treatments that must have rattled his captain's dignity to the core.

What he believed was lifetime security at Lafferty & O'Gara Company had been ripped away from him when the Lafferty boys lost the business—rumor was, from over-consumption of their own product.

I remember a painting hanging in our dining room, of a group of distinguished-looking colonial white wigs sitting and standing around a table laden with serious looking documents. Out the one window in the room could be seen a discreet "Pabst" sign hanging from the wall of the next-door pub. The painting was so classily rendered I blushed with embarrassment the day it finally dawned on me that the painting was an ad for the beer company. Duh!

Dad hadn't needed to go for a college degree after the army because he'd met Joe and Bill Lafferty, as he'd also met Bill Reynolds, in Europe. By the time they all returned after V-E Day, the four young Kansas Citians were fully bonded. For about fifteen years my father worked as the presiding accountant at the Lafferty distributorship, bringing home the bacon—and lots of beer and neon Pabst signs for the family room. And for decades, he also moonlighted on Saturdays at Bill Reynolds' bindery. Between poker parties, VFW and American Legion gatherings, picnics at Swope Park, and the work itself, job security was never a consideration for him.

Until the Lafferty brothers were forced to take early retirement. Leaving Dad high and dry, with his four children (youngest sister Laurie would come later, on 75th Street).

To my father, whose guiding value in life was security, counterbalancing *his* father's madly joyful but manic and daring entrepreneurial drive, the shock must have been devastating. Yet, optimist that he was, he had to press on.

At first, Dad thought he could rely on his accounting and made the brave decision to open his own accounting service, its office on the second floor of a shotgun-style building. "Atchity Bookkeeping & Tax Service," at 1101-A E. 47th Street. His service made it through June, but then, after tax season, business became too sporadic to support the family. Dad had to close his heroic little office. He didn't have the college degree or even the "CPA" after his name to give him the edge he needed in a tightening job market. My father was in despair.

And finally lost it. Optimism did not suffice. Dad couldn't sleep, began hallucinating, and was judged "clinically paranoid." Did he believe Mom was having an affair with Father Z.? He told Uncle Jimmy, the closest thing we had to a medical doctor in the family, that Mom was trying to poison his coffee. Though she may well have fantasized about doing that from time to time, I'm quite sure that accusation was groundless. Uncle Jim came to the same conclusion. Jimmy talked to the family doctor, who referred Dad to a neurologist. Who prescribed Thorazine, which only made things worse. Thorazine is an anti-psychotic, according to my sister Mary, totally wrong to prescribe for someone who's depressed.

No doubt at Mom's prompting, I wrote Dad a letter when he was away from us, at the hospital:

Dear Dad,

How are you? We are all fine... I have been working at Junior's store for two weeks now. The first week I made $8.10 and yesterday I got paid $12.80. I put $5 in the bank and gave Freddy $1 for helping Mom. $3 I used to pay for some groceries. The rest I saved for bus money. Today is Victor Michael's birthday and Freddy is going bowling with him at 11:00 at 12:30 we are going to Aunt Catherine's for dinner. After dinner we are going to the show at the Brookside. Mother is going to see you today at 2:00. I play my record once in a while but I don't have very much time to do anything. Every day at 3:15 I take the bus to the store. On Saturday I work all day. So I don't have time to do anything. Junior closes at 7:00. Sunday is my only day off. Thanks a lot for that candy you sent us. We miss you a lot and we can't wait to see you. Well I have to say good-bye for now.

Love Kenny

I can feel my mother's presence hovering over this pious epistle, one more daily paradox I had to deal with: "You really should write to your Dad. You really should talk to your Dad. You really *should*"—even though most of the time she was making me despise him with reports of her own Dad-induced anguish.

I never got to be a graphologist, but there are too many lumps in my name. The "I" is slurred into a "we" where I wrote, "can't wait to see you." Most notably, the handwriting at the end changes from pencil to pen, in a cursive suspiciously resembling Mom's.

Θ

What's the difference between being depressed and having a nervous breakdown? The question haunted me for years until I figured it out: "Depressed" means you're not thrilled, but you're still handling it; "nervous breakdown" means you're no longer coping. Nothing is adding up. For an accountant like Dad, what could be worse?

Mom came home from one shock treatment and reported that Dad had begged, "Get me out of here." One of his letters to Mom read:

> I enjoy your letters more than I can say, but I wish you could come visit me too. The days are so long without visitors. Please do everything possible to get me home soon. Honey, I think our 30 days of Blue Cross is about up and this hospital charges $16.00 per day. Honey, if that is the case and your mother is coming, I can finish the treatments in the doctor's office—there will be some I have to finish there anyway, we can't afford $16.00 day after me being out of work 5 months....
>
> You are right, Keny, that wasn't the record I had in mind namely, "April Showers." It was "Come Rain or Come Shine"
>
> Honey please, get me out of here as soon as possible—they moved Earl downstairs today, and the minister. I'm well enough to come home now.
>
> I think of you always and love you very much.
>
> Here's a kiss for all of you.
> Fred
>
> P.S. Please get me released. I'm O.K. now. Do you know right now just Jimmie is authorized to visit me? I don't understand why he didn't authorize you.

My father spelled my name wrong. Did he drop an "n" because I was adding one? Because Mom added one too? Was it another subtle sign of our estrangement? Or was it nothing at all? As Freud would say, not every single slip of the hand is meaningful. Homer had already made the point: "*Many are the birds that fly across Zeus' heavens. Not all of them mean anything.*"

Working for the beer boys kept us all alive for years. When Dad lost that, he nearly killed us with his drinking that night on Paseo. Then, to live again, he gave up drinking entirely—an algorithm enough to challenge anyone's mental equilibrium.

The only thing that would cheer him up during this dark night of the soul was Bill Reynolds taking him on long rides. Rides with Bill would cheer anyone up.

Eventually, some sort of intervention on the part of friends and family helped Dad find employment. His medical condition didn't help his employability. But he *was* a World War II veteran, a captain on Eisenhower's staff. Somehow, he got a break and began working as an in-house bookkeeper again, a job that lasted him until the International Brotherhood of Electrical Workers discovered him and made him their health & welfare administrator for the rest of his working life.

Work restored, mental issues went away—never to recur. Work was the rock upon which my father's sanity was founded.

It's been mine as well. When in doubt, chop wood, carry water.

Work is our waiting strategy. We don't wait around for life to become perfect or to reveal its plan. While we're waiting, we work. It was Dad who taught me this secret: if you love the work you do, the waiting is pleasurable—and a working life is a perfect step along the way to happiness. That's why St. Catherine of Siena said, "All the way to Heaven is Heaven."

I do the work I love while waiting for life to interrupt me. My children or grandchildren walk in from their outing. I abandon the work gladly to be with them. Kayoko comes back from yoga, a shoot, or shopping. I welcome her home and relish her presence. A guest is joining us for dinner, and I whistle my way into the kitchen to make a seafood pasta. I don't regret turning away from the work because the work will be dependably waiting for me, just as I am using it to wait.

"I wish I could catch up," I mumbled one day long ago within earshot of my son Vincent, who was staring at my heaped-up desk.

"Dad, you'll never catch up."

I'm happy to admit he was right. Work, unlike time, is infinite because work generates more work (as I describe in detail in *A Writer's Time*). What could be better than a perpetual motion machine—as long as it's moving in a worthy direction and the machine's mechanism is one you designed? When my boat comes in, you will find me happily scrubbing the dock, whistling while I wait. Or, as my favorite Zen koan puts it,

> *Before enlightenment,*
> *Chop wood, carry water.*
>
> *After enlightenment,*
> *Chop wood, carry water.*

Uncle Anthony Prince

One of my favorite family guests was Uncle Anthony Prince from Portland, Oregon. We always called him Uncle Anthony Prince to distinguish him from plain Uncle Anthony (aka Eagle).

I did consider Uncle Anthony Prince princely. Mom called him "a real character," usually when she was inventorying gifts he brought us from his automobile trunk: expensive and odd-shaped jars and cans—of sardines, caviar, salmon roe, smoked oysters—and little bottles of capers, green peppercorns—all items a Cajun farm girl had no idea what to do with. He was a traveling salesman, a merchant of exotic foods. Mom either re-gifted them to the omnivorous Bill Reynolds or sent them with me to Eagle's store "on consignment."

Uncle Anthony Prince is the one who'd been victimized by the goose Jede shot when my princely uncle attended Christmas dinner on that fateful day on Benton Boulevard when we ended up chowing down on hot dogs in a house blackened with smoking goose fat. Mom, shrugging, admitted she'd never cooked goose before.

When Uncle Anthony P. visited us on 75th Street, his sleek green, immaculately clean Oldsmobile made an exotic fashion statement parked in front of the house. He dressed in a designer three-piece suit and kept his jacket on during dinner—unheard of in our house. It made me want to dress up too.

I noticed his gorgeous cuff links, gold crescent moons, each with a sapphire nestled inside its crescent. I'd never seen anything like them before. "Your cuff links are beautiful, Uncle Anthony," I piped up.

Before anyone could protest, he deftly detached first one then the other and handed them across the table to me. "They're yours," he said. "Enjoy them, honey."

Staring at the glittering objects now in my hand, I couldn't believe my good fortune. I didn't own a shirt that needed cuff links, but I damned sure would go out and buy one. "Thank you," I managed to stammer.

"Don't ever do that again," my mother told me after he left that night.

"What did I do?"

"Don't ever admire something out loud that a Lebanese person is wearing," she explained. "Their culture requires that they give it to you."

I wasn't quite sure what was wrong with spontaneous generosity, but I nodded in pretend understanding. For years after, before those cufflinks disappeared into the twilight zone where all small valuable gewgaws seem to prefer to spend eternity, I honored those cuff links—more for what they stood for than for any utility they enjoyed in my rarely sartorial life.

I was careful not to admire out loud anything a Lebanese person was wearing, especially that gorgeous blue satin tie the Lebanese ambassador was wearing at Bruce Prince-Joseph's house the day I showed off my scant Arabic.

Hit the Road

It wasn't long after one of those long nights sitting at the top of the stairs on 75th Street, where I was sometimes joined by Freddy, sometimes by our sister Mary, that I decided my only way out of my own private lion's den was to run away from home.

During a particularly fierce fight between Mom and Dad, I slipped unheeded into the kitchen, loaded my pockets with cooked kibbeh sandwiches (Tastee bread slathered with mayonnaise plus a slice of white onion—*red* onions I'd only sighted at Eagle's store but *never* in our home), stuffed a change of clothes into a make-do backpack, and headed out the back door. Between Mom's farm-raised nostalgia and Dad's Depression-spawned frugality, we ate only plain white bread despite distant rumors of rye and baguettes.

I had no idea where I was going, except away. Away from the constant bickering, the violent arguments, the hollow feeling caused by the eternal, chemically palpable atmosphere of oppression that hung in the air the moment Dad came home from work. I swear the actual ions that filled the rooms seemed to whimper with unhappiness.

I turned left at the bottom of the driveway and headed west on 75th Street. In ten blocks, I'd reached Katz Pharmacy at Waldo, as the area where 75th Street met Wornall Road was dubbed; then decided I would head south along the railroad track that skirted the Katz parking lot.

After all, railroad tracks meant escape. I walked down the middle of the rails, eating kibbeh sandwiches through my tears.

By 80th Street, I'd stopped crying. And started being confused about what in the world I thought I was doing. Could I really walk all the way to Louisiana? Did I really want to abandon Rockhurst and the Jesuits?

By 85th Street, three things happened: I finished my last kibbeh sandwich. I saw Christ the King Church ahead on my right, telling me that not only was I out of food, but I hadn't even made that much progress. And Dad picked me up as I crossed toward the church. All this before cell phones. Neither of us spoke a word all the way home.

Flying Fisticuffs

My years at Rockhurst High were filled with all the intensities of adolescence, built on my rapidly expanding foundation of Latin, Greek, French, and English studies—with just enough algebra, geometry, and trigonometry thrown in to keep me humble.

The solid study habits I'd learned from the BVM nuns at Blessed Sacrament and St. Francis Xavier Grade School came in handy. And so did, it turns out, that brief stint in the Blessed Sacrament boxing ring.

At our high school newspaper, *The Prep News*, I started as an assistant to the News Editor, progressed to News Editor, then to Editor in Chief. I and the other editors congregated in the multi-neon-painted *Prep News* office deep in the school's basement before our eight a.m. first class. Here we would work on our journalistic assignments, finish homework, plan investigative scoops, analyze girls, and shoot the shit.

One morning our privileged enclave was interrupted by Dan Matula, an irate classmate always enraged about something or other that no one could recall a week later. No one recalled how it started, either, but the next thing I knew, he and I were tumbling around on the floor of the newsroom in a combination wrestling match and fistfight—from which, to my surprise, as well as the other editors', I emerged victorious. Matula limped away with a bloody nose and avoided me for the rest of the semester.

☉

That was my year for getting slugged. Shortly after the fistfight on the floor, I stood my ground to face Jesuit scholastic Mr. Herson in his "Speech & Drama" class. "Herson in Person," as we called him, assigned me to memorize a speech from Budd Schulberg's brilliant screenplay, *On the Waterfront*: "I came down here to keep a promise. I gave Kayo my word that if he stood up to the mob, I'd stand up with him. All the way. And now Kayo Dugan is dead. He was one of those fellas who had the gift of standin' up..."

Herson listened to me reciting the lines from memory, then leaped to his feet, shouting me down. "No emotion?" he yelled. "Unacceptable!" He moved toward me, Black Irish eyes flashing with disappointment and anger. "Do I have your permission?" he demanded. Without waiting for answer, he hauled back his fist and socked me on the cheek so hard my head was ringing, and I could literally see those damned stars again. "Now!" he screamed. "Now do the goddam lines."

My enraged recitation merited his applause. The class started to join in the clapping but thought better of it. No one wanted a face as red as mine. It was still red the next day when I woke up. I'll never forget that feeling of speaking with my face on fire.

The Jesuits loved to hit us—on the back of the head with a yardstick if you missed a word in a recitation from the *Aeneid* in Latin class; by grabbing your ears in each hand and banging your forehead on the surface of our wooden desks if you got a B- instead of an A on a history paper; by an outright slap, if you happened to be an over-sized football player like poor Nick Ventola; and on the outstretched hand, with the yardstick, on general principle, because we needed to be on our toes. Once, because I erased the black stripe on a cartoon skunk's tail in my Sophomore English book, I even got kicked in the back of the knee by a passing scholastic as I stood facing the corridor wall in punishment.

I can't say I regretted the Jesuits' martial arts treatment. It inspired me to excel at both Latin and Greek. Anything to avoid a yardstick to the back of the head.

Besides, it was way better than being at home.

Danny Thomas Glasses

Dad came home one Halloween day with a new pair of black-frame glasses. I didn't notice anything particularly new or striking and kept my nose in my Greek grammar at the kitchen table until brother Freddy rushed in from baseball practice. And started laughing hysterically. "I love it!" Freddy said. "Where did you get the Danny Thomas glasses?!"

"What are you talking about?" my father asked.

"Can I wear them to my Halloween party tonight?" Freddy asked, serious.

I realized what he was talking about only a few beats before it dawned on my father. The harsh frames so accentuated my father's "Roman nose" that my brother thought they were a pair of those big-nose party glasses you buy in novelty stores and associated with Lebanese American entertainer Danny Thomas.

"These are *not* Danny Thomas glasses," Dad finally said.

"They are, too," Freddy insisted. "Take them off."

It was more than surreal when my father reached to take off the glasses. Looking up from my book, I halfway expected to see his nose come off with the frames. But it didn't. There it was, still larger than life on his face.

I wish I could have recorded my brother's expression when he saw the nose was still there and not with the glasses. Not sure whether Freddy had been joking or serious, Dad looked bewildered.

Vocation Revoked

The Jesuits must have been getting to me because sometime in my sophomore year at Rockhurst, before I discovered girls up close and personal, I found myself seriously considering the priesthood.

In those days, it took eight years beyond high school before a Jesuit could be ordained. But it took only four years to become a Maryknoll father. As a Maryknoller, I could undertake a mission to my mythic homeland, the South, where their work was focused—and be free at last of the Cyclops' lair. Besides, Maryknoll fathers sported cool white cassocks with dashing dark cinctures—"pope with a black belt," I thought.

Hiding his increasing alarm, Dad invited one of the order's recruiters to visit me on 75th Street. I sat on the dark blue living room couch with the good father while Dad and Mom made themselves scarce until the interview was over. I have no recollection of what the MAF in white skirts said or what I asked him but only that I lost interest in the priesthood that day. I guess it's all how you tell the story.

I remember only that at the end of the session, I watched from the door of my dad's den as Dad wrote out a hefty check—no doubt recorded in his little black book as a "donation." Maryknollers never troubled us again. With the stroke of a pen, Dad had ended my flirtation with permanent drag—although every time I find myself sitting across from aspiring writers at a writers' conference pitch session, listening to their stories, I still feel like a priest in a confessional.

The vocational loss was made bearable because my interest was shifting to females. It began with an uneventful date with pretty family friend Pam "Pug" Calegari, but quickly accelerated to a double-dared kiss in the dark living room of Allison Seidlitz's mansion with the highly-perfumed, pinkly cashmered, and adorably giggly Porky Karnes. Finally, my attraction to the female moved to heated front-seat entanglements with Catherine Callahan.

God help me, puberty had struck.

Mortal Sins

When I discovered "sex," I lost all interest in organized religion, not necessarily in that order—all because of a petite red-headed and freckled sweetheart named Catherine Callahan.

I can't recall how or when we met, nor what we did on the first half of our six-hour dates. All I remember was the second three hours, parked in front of the Callahans' home on a side street near 70th and Troost, fogging up Dad's Pontiac windows and exploring the width and depth of each other's mouths. Hard to believe, in retrospect, that our hands never strayed below our waists. Trust me, they didn't need to.

The problem was that our oral explorations usually occurred so late Saturday night it invariably became Sunday. Which presented, to me, the dilemma faced by every Catholic teenager in those days when sin was still, adamantly, sin.

Venial sin might have been a kiss on pursed lips.

Mortal sin was defined with textbook precision in Father Kalamaja's Honor Program Religion class, where we were forced to memorize a thin Jesuit-authored manual called *Modern Youth and Chastity*. Within its well-worn pages was inscribed the "F.E.A.R. Rule" that governed when a kiss was venial (meaning, that should you die after committing the kiss, your soul would be consigned to Purgatory for an additional thousand years or so) or mortal (meaning you'd be dispatched directly to Hell forever—"Do not pass Go! Do not collect $1 million dollars").

Here is the F-E-A-R rule: If kisses were

Frequent

Enduring

Ardent, or

Repeated

they were mortal sins. What could be clearer?

Well, as I was learning, a number of things.

I wasn't an expert logician (confirmed a few years later when I received a "D" in Logic at Georgetown) but, fortunately, my Honors Class included the irrepressible Robert J. Riley. Bob, generally first in the class or at worst tied with Rusty Lusk for first, went on to become an Augustinian monk and ended up on the cover of *Newsweek* as a self-defrocked leader of the National Gay Liberation Front and finally became a broker at J. P. Morgan. All this, to avoid his doting mother, the bane of Rockhurst High social events she insisted on attending with her son. I ran across an article by Bob on Google, "The Importance of a Gay, Lesbian, Bisexual, and Transgender Student Group at a Catholic University." Go, Bob!

To me, on post-Callahan Sunday mornings, the F.E.A.R. rule was, pun intended, the kiss of death for any hope of partaking of the privileges of the Communion of Saints—at least until I could route myself to the next available Confession.

Bob raised his hand in class or rather twirled it in the air like a crazed dervish. When Robert J. Riley raised his hand, it was with the blushing eagerness of a zealot on steroids. Never mind the probability that calling on him might lead to trouble, no zealot can long be resisted by the argument-addicted Jesuit mind.

So, Father Kalamaja called on Bob. "What is it, Mr. Riley?"

"Father," Bob began all in one breath: "I don't consider these four categories truly logically exclusive, and I, therefore, question their overall validity." He gulped and smiled with pride. This, from our classmate least likely to have ever kissed, to be kissing, or even to someday kiss, a member of the opposite sex for whose osculatory frontiers we hopeless heteros benightedly figured the F.E.A.R. rule was designed.

"What do you mean, Mr. Riley?" Kalamaja ventured, with a trace of warning and a sliver of dare in his voice.

"I can understand," Bob said, provoking a susurrus of guffaws—no one wanted to laugh too loudly and risk derailing a line of questioning that could have a direct impact on our Friday and Saturday nights and Sunday mornings, "how a kiss that is Enduring can be distinguished from a kiss that is Frequent or Repeated. But I don't understand how a kiss can be Ardent without being either Enduring, Frequent, or Repeated; not to mention, how are we to know when venial Enduring is approaching mortal Enduring?"

I wonder how the F.E.A.R. rule applied to actors kissing on a stage.

But Riley was flashing his wild Irish eyes at his classmates and still smiling widely.

Oh my God, I thought, is this a case of self-immolation? A request for crucifixion? It wasn't entirely out of the question. Masochism was being ingrained in us by our Jesuit taskmasters. For anyone starved for male attention, sacrificial violence might be preferable to being ignored.

Before I report Father Kalamaja's reaction to Riley's Kiss Challenge, dear reader, let me roll back the calendar about a week to this same class's discussion of the seventh commandment. Without that for context, Father Kalamaja's response and the complete and utter undermining of my until-then obsessive adherence to Catholicism hook, line, and detail, could not have occurred.

That previous week, Father K had explained to us the difference between venial and mortal when it came to the sin of stealing. Stealing under five dollars (around thirty-two dollars today) was a venial sin, ushering the unshriven sinner into prolonged incarceration—no doubt complete with holy water-boarding—in Purgatory.

Stealing *over* five dollars was mortal. Eternal fire. Forever and ever. Amen.

As simple as that: Five dollars and one cent—and it's off to the eternal crematorium.

It wasn't Father Kalamaja's job to paint the "Hell picture" for us boys. That had been covered at St. Ann's Retreat House by the "Other Father K," our feared and revered principal Father Carl

Kloster, SJ. We called Father Kloster "Peaches" because his cheeks had that pink/yellow sweet fuzziness found elsewhere only in the expensive fruit bin of Uncle Anthony's Broadmour Market, the outrageously expensive food court of Takashimaya department store in Tokyo, or my mother's beloved side-of-the-road Louisiana farm stands during high peach season.

Peaches' hair-raising portrayal of Hell went something like this, and it was hard to judge whether James Joyce's *Portrait of the Artist as a Young Man* stole it from Peaches or Peaches stole it from Joyce:

> *Imagine a globe the size of the earth, made entirely of solid stainless steel. Once every million years a white dove touches that globe with the tip of its wing (the dove no doubt being the Holy Ghost, the only dove we knew of who could withstand the rigors of airless space, much less fly through it). By the time the dove's wing-brushes have worn that steel globe down to nothing, eternity is just beginning.*

Yikes.

But Riley's hand was dancing the whirligig that day, too, and the rest of us were on the edge of our seats, hoping our class logician might offer us some kind of reprieve from Purgatory.

"Yes, Mr. Riley," Father K finally said. Didn't he realize his track record for these Riley inquiries wasn't conducive to his blood pressure? Riley, I suppose he figured, was his own private Purgatory, so he might as well get it over with in this life to shorten his afterlife consignment to Mount Torture.

"Father," Riley began, "suppose I were stealing frozen peas, using my butter knife, moving them one pea at a time off my mother's plate onto mine. There would come a time when all that would divide $4.99999 and $5.00 was a single pea."

Father K may not have been sure where Riley was going with this; but the rest of us certainly were. "Yes, Mr. Riley, that is precisely correct."

"So, what you're saying is that God would condemn me to Hell for all eternity for stealing a single pea!?" Bob's face was positively cherubic, blood rushing to his cheeks with the surging self-confidence he had, no doubt, not even once experienced in his mother's house. He glanced sideways at the class for support but was met with the pitiless stares of a coliseum crowd watching a gladiator poke a tiger in the eye.

Father Kalamaja's reaction was a slap in the face: "That's *exactly* what I'm saying, Mr. Riley," he stated.

We all thought hard as Kalamaja expounded his lesson that day. He was indeed honestly saying that we were worshipping a God who would condemn a human being to eternal punishment for stealing a single pea. Because that single pea was a sin of willful disobedience.

So much for our fuzzy, incense-induced, feelings of holiness and sanctity and being warm and cozy with a loving Jesus.

With this incident as context, you can better understand what occurred after Riley's foray into the logic of F.E.A.R., his challenge to the kissing rule.

Instead of responding with affirmation to Riley's logic gambit, Father K hurled his Religion book to the classroom floor. "I'm through with you boys," he said, unjustly indicting the entire class as though we'd willfully chosen the least socially-mainstream of us as a spokesman.

Then he turned and, very un-Jesuit-like, stomped from our homeroom. Were those tears in his eyes?

The momentary silence was broken by simultaneous applause and cheering which, Bob later told me—when he visited me at Yale to explain the sudden change of heart that led him from the Augustinian monastery to Wall Street—was the high point of his adolescent life. He had cracked a Jesuit's composure—to a full and appreciative jury, at that.

Remembering those glass-fogged nights in the family station wagon parked in front of Catherine Callahan's house, my heart went out to my friend Bob.

The elation of our Honors Class that day didn't last long. Minutes later, a ruddier-cheeks-than-usual Peaches stormed into Room 202. The principal didn't mince words. "Do you know what you boys have done to Father Kalamaja?" he demanded. No one answered because none of us, even Riley, were quite sure how to put it. "Take out your textbooks. For the rest of the semester, you will copy the entire book by hand, starting with chapter one, during Religion period. I will come to collect the papers at the end of the hour. He has refused to teach you because you're not worthy of being taught."

He waited impatiently until all writing arms were moving across the page. For twenty minutes, we copied. When the bell rang, he walked up and down the aisles scowling and collecting our penmanship. Then he walked out the door, nonchalantly tossing our work in the Army-green trash basket.

With that by way of further background, we return to that fateful weekend that began, for all practical purposes, in the fogged-up station wagon outside the Callahan domicile where

Catherine and I were eagerly committing mortal sin after mortal sin, running variations on F.E.A.R.:

We kissed Frequently.

We kissed Enduringly to see how long we could do it without coming up for air.

And we kissed Repeatedly.

We tried our best to distinguish between Repeated kisses and Frequent ones until we giggled ourselves into increasingly passionate Enduring kisses that expressed Ardent in the thickening of window fog.

Body heat was intense, venial sin left behind in the dim memory of our first contact on a party couch when the lights went out at Allison Seidlitz's house. Or was that with Porky Karnes of the violet cashmere sweater and intoxicating perfume?

We somehow disentangled ourselves enough to release a disheveled Catherine into her house and send me home in time to pretend all was well as I awakened at six after two hours sleep.

I'd been an early riser since birth, but this Sunday morning, I had a religious reason for getting up early. My only hope for escaping my family's judgment was attending six forty-five Mass instead of nine-fifteen with them. I walked the five long blocks to St. Elizabeth's at 75th & Main, snuck into a pew safely halfway back, where sinners could sit without being too obtrusive. I had come to this Mass for those of you who've never experienced the moral dodges of being raised Roman Catholic because my family would never drag themselves to a Mass this early. My folks went to the nine-fifteen, or sometimes even the eleven. Funny, as my father aged, he who insisted on Sunday church regardless of his abusive behavior during the week, and ragged on my mother's recalcitrance (her Louisiana family took church of all kinds with a grain of salt) about doing her weekly duty, Dad became less and less insistent on attending himself—while she started going to Mass. But that was long after I'd flown from the nest.

Uncle Eddy and Aunt Catherine lived in St. Elizabeth's parish, as did Uncle Vic and Aunt Leona, which meant cousins galore within a stone's throw. The reason it was necessary to go to a Mass unattended by family was to avoid witnesses to my failure to walk up to the Communion rail and receive Holy Communion.

The sacrament of the Eucharist was reserved for those who had no mortal sins on their souls. Venial sins were okay and could be taken care of by a "good Act of Contrition":

> *O my God,*
> *I am heartily sorry for*
> *having offended Thee,*
> *and I detest all my sins,*
> *because of thy just punishments;*
> *but most of all because*
> *they offend Thee, my God,*
> *Who are all good and*
> *deserving of all my love.*
> *I firmly resolve*
> *with the help of Thy grace,*
> *to confess my sins,*
> *to do penance,*
> *and to amend my life.*
> *Amen.*

That Act could even be recited en route to the Communion rail if necessary.

Unfortunately, mortal sins associated with the ecstatic heights of F.E.A.R. required the full official shriving available only in the darkened wooden retreat of the confessional. But confessionals in those days were closed on Sundays, the sacrament of Penance available only on Saturday afternoons between three and six.

Intricate discussions were conducted with the Jesuits about the validity of this whole Confession drill. Suppose you did go to Confession on Saturday afternoon, just to start the evening with a level playing field. Was it morally valid to receive Absolution from your confessor when you knew beyond a shadow of a doubt exactly what you intended to be doing, God willing, in front of the Callahans' home a few hours later?

The surprising answer the Jesuits gave us was Yes! The sacraments were "effective rituals" dependent solely upon their correct performance and not upon intention. That didn't seem cosmically fair, since sins of intention, we were told, were purportedly as deadly as sins of action. If you daydreamed of murdering Father Puricelli, our exuberantly belligerent Latin teacher, you were guilty of mortal sin as surely as if you'd driven his yardstick through his black heart (the yardstick he used to smack the back of the head of anyone who stumbled on a single word while reciting the *Aeneid* in front of his Latin class). Dreams themselves, by the way, were immune from this "sins of intention" rule. You could murder anyone you liked in your dreams.

Happily for this teenager having the intention to sin again, ill intention didn't keep you from receiving Absolution. Think how much this has done for *la cosa nostra*, for example—murder on

Saturday morning, Absolution Saturday afternoon, and public Communion on Sunday.

So, just in case I might be killed in an out-of-control skid en route to the party on that cold Saturday evening, I'd gone to Confession Saturday afternoon. By three a.m. I was blissfully back in the state of mortal sin.

Hence dispatching myself to six forty-five Mass the next morning.

Imagine my surprise when, from my back-of-the-church viewpoint, I saw the entire Callahan family—Mr. Callahan, Mrs. Callahan, and my fellow F.E.A.R. Felon Catherine—walk in and march to a pew close enough to the front of the church to give me distinct trepidations about Catherine's intentions—not to mention distinct relief that she hadn't spotted me.

As Communion approached, my dread only increased.

A few months earlier, we'd been assigned to read Graham Greene's *The Heart of the Matter,* and my mind now flashed to the protagonist Henry Scobie's approach to the Communion rail in a state of mortal sin. Scobie knew he was condemning himself to Hell for all eternity by receiving the sacrament of the Eucharist without the benefit of shriving his soul of his adulterous acts—but needed to preserve the lie or risk shattering his marriage and the routine life that enslaved him.

With a soul besmirched by F.E.A.R., I knew I could not approach that rail.

Θ

Row by row, communicants rose and filed toward the Communion rail.

When it was time for the Callahans' row, I watched Catherine stand with her mom and dad and move toward the altar. I could see her lovely Botticelli face clearly and detected nothing reflecting the mad osculation that she'd been party to a few hours earlier. The serenity on her sharply-etched features mesmerized me.

I surmised her plan. It could be no other: She would approach the rail, kneel with her parents and the others, to await the host-dispensing priest, but as he approached her, she would discreetly put one finger to her lips the way we'd been taught by the Jebs to signal the celebrant to skip her and not try to dispense the Body of Christ to her. Supposedly, the priest would handle this signal so deftly that people in the church wouldn't notice. One's public reputation could be preserved without risking the eternal jeopardy of sacrilegiously receiving the consecrated host into a Temple of the Holy Ghost (as we were taught to call our bodies), that had been fouled with F.E.A.R.

Like an owl watching his oblivious prey, I knelt and observed with maximum concentration.

Catherine's face displayed no emotion, no vestige of either passion or uncertainty. The priest with the ciborium full of hosts approached her. The moment arrived: her soul at the crossing point. Her white palms were joined in the ritual position of pious prayer.

Her blue eyes gazed up at the priest as he proffered the consecrated host. No warning from her eyes. No flicker of finger. Catherine opened her mouth, the same mouth that a few hours ago had been completely open to mine—and received into it the Body and Blood of Our Lord Jesus Christ.

I couldn't believe my eyes. I was flabbergasted.

As Catherine rose from the Communion rail and turned back toward the family pew, her eyes were properly downcast. She chewed the sacred bread with jaw motions as subtle as some of her most Repeatedly teasing kisses.

Having read enough catechism and James Joyce, heard enough sermons, and bristled through enough lectures to be certain of what should come next, all I could do was stare in horror. I awaited a lightning bolt from above, as God the Father, Zeus-like, smote Catherine's sacrilege with the punishment it merited.

Absolutely nothing of the kind occurred.

She took her place back in the pew, her family none the wiser. She did what she had to do, the Scobie Sacrifice. Who knows whether the parental units insisted on this God-awful early Mass for the precise reason of putting her to this test? If that were the case, would they share in the responsibility of her eternal damnation?

But the Callahans walked out of the church as calmly as they'd walked in.

$$\theta$$

Something inside me snapped that morning.

Despite the Kalamaja Peas' Pronouncement, until that moment, I had been an unquestioning, staunch believer—nay, more than staunch: fanatic. This religion had given me the strength to suffer the Cyclops. I obeyed the letter of its law because

133

I'd been taught that the devil was in the details—"idle hands are the devil's workshop"—and *all* the details were equally important.

My eyes now opening, I could no longer believe without question. Instead, I was awash with questions. Not the logical questions that delighted Riley, but emotional and spiritual ones that slowly but surely led me to renounce organized religion entirely and all self-righteous sects that declare they alone held the keys to some eternal reward. It was simply easier to believe that no sane God would condemn a man to Hell for eating a single bite of hotdog on Friday, a single pea, or a single Ardent kiss.

Years later, when the church decided it was okay to eat meat on Friday, I wanted to call Riley to find out what happens to all those souls in Hell condemned eternally for eating hotdogs. They'd get a pass to Heaven? Unh-uh. Church doctrine insists being condemned to Hell means you'll *never* get to Heaven, *never* see the face of God.

I never called Catherine for a date again. I had too much reconsidering to do on the moral-spiritual front and was embarrassed that she was obviously way ahead of me. I recognized that morality and spirituality were separate from religion; for the first time that moral strength must come from within, not from an outside God. Don't get me wrong. I was still a masochist. By then I'd studied Plato's *Apology*, wherein he describes his master Socrates' execution by the Athenians for worshipping an unseen "god inside." But I preferred Socrates' suicidal execution over the Roman Catholic version. At least more was at stake than a hot dog or a single pea.

I'm glad I was raised Catholic, though my faith was subtly undermined by Mom, from her south Louisiana countryside where the line between Baptists and Catholics was blurred from sheer inattention and the struggle of getting to church even once a week. It was my father, from an adamantly Catholic family that saw religion as a social binding force but didn't take the rituals and beliefs that seriously (despite Tata and her weekly rosary with the pope), who set the pace for me by his choice of grade schools and Jesuit high school. I was glad to have been exposed to it all, though in retrospect, it was an unintended over-exposure that led to my almost complete rejection of the institution of religion while continuing to embrace its spiritual principles.

Can you build character from the outside in? I dunno. After that fateful morning witnessing Catherine's casual blasphemy, I didn't feel I had it from the inside out anymore—or maybe never had. Determination and follow-through aren't the same thing; them I have, in spades. The nasty irony about extreme Catholicism is that it eats away the very moral code it's intended to establish, riddles it with holes that it may take a lifetime to figure out how to fill—if you bother to keep working on it. The history I was devouring at Rockhurst and Georgetown included all the bad actions taken in the name of the Roman Catholic Church, and of most all organized religions. If the golden rule's morality persisted, it was despite the faithful professing it on Sundays while betraying it much of the rest of the week.

Fortunately, the Jesuits, those most skeptical of Catholic operatives, had given me the tools to figure all this out. As I studied atheism at Georgetown in Father Edmund Ryan, SJ's class, I wondered whether he was an atheist at heart. I suspected Father Joseph Sebes, who taught me Asian religions, preferred Buddhism to Christianity.

So it was that much of my adventure has led me through the colorful areas that form the ever-widening border between black and white. Only in that space are you on your own. Vulnerable. You are never going to be secure there, but you *are* free. I used to hear the phrase "conflict of interest" as a challenge, as a judgment, until finally I began hearing it as a battle cry. Don't avoid conflicts of interest. *Seek* them because in their space, more than anywhere else, achievement and progress are born. Of course, there may be castigations, accusations, lawsuits in that great borderland. By my third lawsuit, I *welcomed* the trip to court. The situation in question had become so goddam complicated *I* had no idea who was right and who was wrong. When the jury told me, each time, that my side had done nothing wrong, I was relieved to hear it because, amid the fray, and in the midst of decisions made by my overly-sensitive conscience, I'd honestly lost track. The most provocative thing about this life we all live, this game we are born to play, is that there's nothing cut and dried about it.

One day I had an enormous epiphany regarding respect. Self-respect is the only respect you need in life because it's the hardest to earn. Only *you* know your own potential, and only you know whether you are doing your best and living up to it. The flash came as I was sitting in an otherwise empty conference room at a big agency at a meeting where the agency head didn't show, so it was only the author of *The Big Nasty* and me. We worked out our deal and I didn't have a moment of thinking, "she's showing me no respect." Why? Because (a) I don't think she thinks that way; and (b) I don't need her to show me respect. I know that, in general, she respects me, and I also know that, in general, it doesn't matter at all whether she respects me or not.

The only thing that matters is that I respect myself.

I can do a better job of that, of course. But the great thing about it is that it's something I can feel good about moment by moment, hour by hour, day by day—without needing the outside world to reflect anything. I just try to undertake every single action cheerfully and do the best I can with it because that's how to maintain self-respect. Maintaining self-respect is just another word for integrity. He does things the way he thinks they ought to be done.

My self-respect has nothing to do with how much money I currently have; it has to do with what I can do with what I have or don't have.

It wasn't until my forties that I became capable of Catherine's audacity: In church for a cousin's funeral with Mom, at the nudge of her elbow and wink, I, a divorced and therefore excommunicated man, followed my mother to the front of the church, the memory of sweet Catherine tugging like a ghost at my elbow.

By that time, the Communion rail had gone the way of all flesh.

And I'm still here to report, no lightning struck.

Tom DeCoursey Joke

An Irish daughter had not been home for over five years. When she finally arrived at her parents' cottage door, her father cussed her roundly. "Where the fook have ye been all these yars? Why did ye not write to us, not even a fookin' line? Why didn't ye call? You terned your grand back on ye poor parents, did ye? Can ye not understand what ye put yer old mum thru?"

The girl, crying, replied, "Sniff, sniff.... Dad....An' it's even worse—I have to confess to ye. I can't bear hiding it any longer. I took meself down to Dooblin Town and became a prostitute!"

"Ye what!!?" The old man's face turned as red as a ripe tomato. "Git ye out of this house, ye shameless harlot! Sinner! Ye're a bloody disgrace to this family."

"Okay, Da—as ye wish. I thought ye would say that. But I wanted to give Mum this pure white sable coat, title deed to a ten-bedroom mansion plus a two million punta savings certificate. For me little brother, this gold Rolex and for ye, Daddy, to show me sincere gratitude, the sparkling new red Mercedes limited edition convertible parked outside—plus a lifetime membership in the Dublin City country club...." (takes a breath) "....and an invitation for ye all to spend New Year's Eve on board me new yacht in the Italian Riviera after a private audience with His Holiness..."

Her da' took a deep breath and stared fiercely at her. "For the love of God, girlie, that's different. You know how much we love ye. Now what was it ye said ye had become?" he asks at last.

The lass, crying again: "Sniff, sniff.... a prostitute dad! Sniff, sniff."

"Oh! Jesus Christus begab, there's Daddy's sweetest girl! Ye scared me half ta death! I thought ye said 'Protestant.' Come here and give ye old da a grand hoog!"

Bill Reynolds

If Uncle Wib was my substitute Louisiana father, portly, diminutive, pipe-smoking Bill Reynolds, Dad's best friend forever, played that role up north in KC. Bill and Dad met in the war, and remained buddies until Dad's funeral when Bill, tears in his eyes, put his hand on my shoulder and said, "Your Dad loved you, Kenny."

Though Dad never once said that to me, Bill told me that a lot.

Bill was my trusted ally and confidant, another Male Authority Figure I could confide in, who, like Cousin Tony, winked at me behind my Dad's back. Reynolds Bindery, at 1703 Lister Avenue, a few blocks south of Truman Road, is today an abandoned shell of urban decay, a mournful gash to the eye. To adolescent me, it was my thrilling Saturday job. I would drive there with Dad, so he could update Bill's accounts in Bill's office while I worked back "in the plant" dog-earing books—unbending all those little bent-over flaps created by readers marking where they'd left off reading. So good was I at dog-earing that Bill decided to hire me full-time for the summers when the bindery handled thousands of text and library books to prepare them for the next school year.

What could be more fun for a scholarly introvert than working in a bindery where books flowed to me from all directions? Except that those infernal dog-ears dimmed my literary enjoyment. They had to be taken out because a book trimmed for binding with dog-ears still in place ended up with freakish flaps sticking out from the newly trimmed pages when the binding was done.

So, I, and a few other child laborers, were enlisted to flip through the books and make sure the flaps were undone *before* the book went to trimming. The trimming machine was run by the dour bindery foreman E. J., whose hollow dark stares reminded me of Shakespeare's Hamlet, without the existential panache. E.J.'s disapproving scowls were no doubt caused by my father's close relationship with Bill—which, in his mind, had nepotized yours truly.

One day I had a bright idea. Watching E. J. slouching over the industrial vacuum to rid his work area of the paper-trim dust that accumulated in piles every day, I determined to wait until E. J. timed out, which he did at noon on Saturdays. After he and his metal lunchbox were safely gone, I rolled the industrial vac over to my workstation where I'd spent the morning dog-earing. I held the vacuum mouth in one hand, book in another, and, as I ruffled through the pages, flipped on the switch. And watched the powerful vacuum pop up the dog-ears as though it was born for the task.

I showed Bill. He was delighted, not only at the discovery but at me for making it.

Bill got a kick out of me. He delighted in printing little scraps of leather with puns on my name, like "Hatch with Atch." They made him howl with laughter, and the little cardboard chits he left around for me to find with pathetic limericks based on my name:

> There once was a young man
> Named Achity
> Who turned out bad
> Jokes by the batchity.
> Ever since just by luck
> He received a big yuk
> His head has become
> Very fatchity.

There once was a young man
named Achitly
Who turned out bad
jokes by the batchity
Ever since just by luck
He received a big yuk
His head has become
very fatchity

Bill made a few adjustments in the vac's intake hose, patented the "dog-earing machine," and we used it at the bindery regularly from that day on. E. J. had to buy a new industrial vac for his book dust, which only made him scowl the more.

Saturday lunchtime, I was dragooned into accompanying Dad and Bill to Dixon's, a few blocks away, a chili parlor they attended with reverence for reasons I never quite figured out. Like zealots, they raved about Dixon's chili, which was served on an oval white platter and was completely bean-less and, to my taste, so dry as to be nearly tasteless. No doubt that's why both Dad and Bill doused their portions with Tabasco. I followed suit and, not to be a killjoy, dug into it with pretend gusto.

I suppose compared to the army rations they'd both shared in Europe, it was scrumptious.

Contrasted with our Aunt Najeba's chili, it was downright pathetic.

Θ

Because Dad's temper was so frightening, whenever I could get away with it, I chose to stay at the bindery and read a book, while munching on a peanut butter and tomato sandwich from home.

Dad worked at Reynolds only on Saturdays, so to work at the bindery for the whole summer I had to find my own ride to work every weekday. My bike became the obvious choice, though it was a good seven miles from the house on Virginia. I had to leave at five-thirty to get to work by six-thirty. It was worth it.

One day Bill asked me to load his shiny new candy-apple-red 1962 Invicta Buick station wagon with books that had just been bound sans dog-ears for William Jewell College. I told Bill "*invicta*" meant "unconquerable" in Latin. He grinned at me and winked. "Why don't you come with me?" he asked.

I was thrilled. "Really?"

"I'll tell E.J. I need you to help me load and unload."

That was the first of a dozen gleeful trips I took with Bill through the hilly highways of Missouri and the flat highways of Kansas on his deliveries to the bindery's far-flung customers: libraries, elementary and high schools, and colleges where he'd deliver bound books and pick up boxes of beaten-up books headed for the bindery.

We stopped for burgers on the road and talked about everything under the sun once Bill had pumped me dry of my latest supply of jokes. Both of us prided ourselves on being able to come up with a joke on *any* subject, each trusting that as we listened to the other person's current joke our minds would unfailingly come up with the perfect response joke. My storytelling talent came from both sides of my family—Atchitys and Aguillards alike—in a nonstop onslaught that seemed to have evolved to force laughter into every available nook and cranny of life, probably because humorless silence was too painful. I learned from Bill the value of cultivating your sense of humor and keeping your perspective—the first I had no problem with mastering, the second was long a work in progress.

Sometimes Bill would let me drive a country road even though I was only fifteen—both of us delighted to be pulling something on the all-controlling Cyclops behind his back. "Our little secret," Bill called it.

It was Bill who encouraged me to show him my thick collection of retyped songs, quotes, favorite passages from Shakespeare, and every other major author I'd run across. Dad must have told him about it, lamenting the time I "wasted" typing. A Jesuit told me early on that physically copying great thoughts or great writing would eventually make it impossible for your unconscious to produce mediocre stuff. Maybe that was my excuse, or maybe it was because I was obsessive-compulsive and a good typist; maybe, also, it was because Dad had trained me to type his clients' tax returns, and I would rather be typing anything else! Bill, when he learned from my father that I was wasting my time doing that told him, "Tell Kenny to bring it to me and I'll bind it into a book."

Bill, whose typing was the painfully slow "hunt and peck" method, was astonished at my digital proficiency. He paged, wide-eyed, through all 696 pages, marveled at the lack of typos, praised me roundly, bound it all in bright blue leather, and stamped it "Blue Book" in gold letters; then, a year later, he bound Blue Book

II. A Male Authority Figure had given me his literal stamp of approval. When he asked me why I called it my "Blue Book," I told him I typed into it when I felt blue. He hefted it from the countertop and stared at me.

The title page of Blue Book proclaimed, from the song "Bali Hai" in *South Pacific*:

> *Most people live on a lonely island,*
> *Lost in the middle of a foggy sea.*
> *Most people long for another island,*
> *One where they know they would like to be.*

That was how I felt in KC growing up, and later for much of the first half of my life: longing to be on another island, distant from where I happen physically to be.

Bill's endorsement made me feel I'd created a real book. I still have it on the shelf that displays my published books today, along with its second volume. Next to them are two others Bill sent me with my name on the spine: *What I Know about Basketball* when, in 1971, he learned I'd broken my femur playing faculty basketball at Occidental College; and *What I Know about Women*, when news of my second divorce reached him in KC. Both books were comprised of blank paper. Humor! Perspective! I asked Bill once what his secret was for a happy marriage—he and Connie were married till the day he died. His answer: "Yes, dear!"

Since college applications required a personal reference, I called on Bill. He made a copy of the letter he'd sent to Princeton:

> *Since I have been a friend of his since his childhood, I have*
> *observed that he has always been an honor student...For several*
> *years now he has mentioned to me that he has a strong desire to*

*teach and wants to make that his occupation in life. Know him
to be steady and determined in his pursuits, I feel that he is certain
about his desire and will do everything in his power to attain that
end...He has the power of concentration and the necessary
ambition...His character is of the highest and I consider him a
good Christian gentleman, a good boy, who has never been in
trouble with the police.*

Years later, when Dad and Bill were in their late seventies, Bill
came to the lake cottage one day to give Dad a matching baseball
cap stamped with the inscription, "Old Fart." He howled with glee
at the bewildered look on Dad's face as my father reluctantly took
it from his hand.

I frowned.

Like Dad, I hated that particular F word.

Hated the O word too. "Old" was "out of it."

One evening about the same era, Bill came by the family house
on 104th Street to pick up Dad for one of their rare "boys' night
out." Wearing his OF cap. He insisted that Dad wear his too. As
they marched out the front door toward Bill's Cadillac, Mom bade
them good-bye from the same little porch from which she greeted
us for holidays.

"You sure you don't want to come with us, Myrz?" Bill asked
my Mom.

"No, thanks," she said. "That's the last thing I want—to hang
with two old farts who can't even hear what I'm saying."

"Hunh?" Bill and Dad said simultaneously.

A Bill Reynolds' Joke

What's the Mormon punishment for bigamy?
Two wives.

Unwelcome Gifts

The Christmas before I escaped to Georgetown, my insensitive sarcasm at its height, I bought my father two gifts he did not appreciate.

One was Tiny Tim's new album, "Tiptoe through the Tulips." Although Dad was the first to claim distant kinship with Danny Thomas as a fellow Lebanese American, Tiny Tim was quite another matter. Even the mention of this long-curly-haired falsetto-lilting singer was enough to reduce my father to apoplexy.

In the smartest-aleck moment of my smart-aleck adolescence, giving Dad that album was an indication of how far from filial propriety my sense of humor had strayed.

The second gift was a bottle of cologne I saw advertised in *Mad Magazine.* The cologne was called "Money," with a label that counterfeited a paper dollar and that boasted it contained the "intoxicating odor of old bills." When it arrived, I showed it to Mom before I wrapped it. She thought it was funny.

When he opened it on Christmas morning, Dad did not laugh.

I understand why only in retrospect. I had broken the code of never articulating the elephant in the room that stood between Dad and Mom. I only realized later that it stood between Mom and me as well. He knew all too well my views of what I saw as his worship of money, the religion my mother accused him of when she was with me; and which I realized much later was, in fact, as much if not more hers than his.

A harsh word to me, a harsh argument between him and Mom later in the day, and I withdrawn to my room with my usual feeling of loss wondering what was going on, what was wrong with what I did and why I'd done it. My father thought I was guilty of disrespect. His feelings might even have been hurt.

He was right.

Dad, that really sucked. I'm sorry.

Months later I went to the downstairs bathroom one day to borrow Mom's eyeliner to draw lines under my eyes so my Rockhurst classmates would think I was exhausted from studying all night.

I saw the Money bottle was sitting on the medicine cabinet shelf. I opened it. It *did* smell like money. It was only half full.

A Tony Joke

A man walks into a store and asks the clerk what aisle the Polish sausage is in.

"Are you Polish?" the clerk asks.

"Yes, I am," the man replies huffily. "But let me ask *you* a question. If I asked for Italian sausage, would you ask me if I was Italian? If I asked for tortillas, would you ask me if I was Mexican? If I asked for French wine, would you ask me if I was French? So why are you asking me if I'm Polish?"

"This is a hardware store," the clerk replied.

Act 2

Purgatorio

---

*In which the Odysseus-like narrator plants his flag in the academic groves
of Georgetown, Cambridge, Yale, Occidental College, UCLA, and the
venerable University of Bologna and, like a rolling stone gathering no moss,
continues editing and writing in his quest to spin tales of his own and get
his story straight.*

"I think the only immoral thing is for a being not to live every instant of its life with the utmost intensity."

—José Ortega y Gasset

The Great Escape

I was taught by the Jesuits that the worst thing about Hell, aside from never getting to see the face of God, is that no one leaves it. In Dante Alighieri's *The Divine Comedy,* no one leaves the inferno except the pilgrim Dante, led by poet-guide Virgil. My Virgil was Father Kalamaja, Father Z's stand-in, who talked Dad into letting me accept the Ignatian Scholarship to Georgetown. Any way you slice it, getting out of Hell and into Purgatory is cause to celebrate. Even though you may suffer thousands of days of pain there, you're no longer in the Big Burn.

Odysseus escaped the Cyclops clinging to the belly of a sheep, I reflected with grateful elation, as I departed home for college in Washington, DC, whizzing past the KC limits in the much more comfortable 1960 Oldsmobile I'd contracted to deliver for its owner. My joy that day surpassed even what I experienced as the Southern Belle backed out of Union Station en route to Louisiana. That car was my sweet chariot swinging low to take me across the river to the promised land—my chariot of the gods, wafting me from KC bondage to the French-designed city where a statue of freedom presided above the Capitol building.

Prometheus was now unbound. Turning my back on Cyclops' island and the fearful, hurt, angry Foghorn persona, I would lay claim to a hallowed grove of academe, where I would speak fearlessly in my Honors classes; debate eloquently either side of an issue in the Philodemic Society against Bob Shrum, Ted Kennedy's future speech writer; write on any and every subject for the campus newspaper, *The Hoya*; and create my own program of Broadway musicals at WGBT radio. I hoped I was shedding my role as designated loser overshadowed by Freddy's birth and all-trumping tantrums, as well as my gnawing feeling of existential hopelessness, expressed in night terrors of suffocating quilts.

What I packed along with me was my insatiable hungering for approval by Male Authority Figures, my embracing of the Jesuits' love of learning and aspiration—and a heart beating with mythic heroism.

Years later, after a Roman cab driver had outlined the dismal plight of the Italian economy during a long taxi ride to a party at the American embassy on Via Vittorio Veneto, I told him as I climbed out: "*Coraggio!*" He grunted his response: "*Sì. E sangue di pecora.*" *Yes, but have the blood of a sheep.* That's why I love the Romans. Always be prepared to run away.

That late summer day in 1961, I was positively and absolutely running away. Evidence of the urgency of my escape trajectory was my being stopped for speeding—and having to beg the Ohio Highway Patrol to telephone the Cyclops, so he could confirm that I had the right to be in that car. That I had packed my rod and reel with me was an indication of how unprepared for East Coast city life I was. What did I think—that I would be fishing in the Potomac? LOL, as folks say today.

I know now, and maybe even knew then, that this whole entangled ball of twine wasn't the least bit fair to KC. Now with Mom and Dad passed away, I feel increasingly comfortable visiting family there. Parental pressures removed, I love seeing Rockhurst

154

High School pals and playing poker among the non-stop wisecracks of Aunt Lorraine and her rascally progeny, my dear Atchity cousins.

But as I drove off in the Olds I relished the first unwinding of that suffocating quilt. I hoped that I was moving too fast for it ever to catch up with me again.

I was seventeen, and outward bound.

Cobblestoned Awe

Father Z didn't just teach me Latin. He taught me not only to *respect* learning but also to be awed by it—as I am to this day. I probably hit Google more often than anyone I know. Did the Empress Theodora really dance with bears? How is "octodecillion" defined in Great Britain vs the US and France? Am I right about *further* vs *farther*? Which is more closely related to Latvian—Estonian or Lithuanian?

Georgetown University is indeed my alma mater. Each time I revisit the bastion of Jesuit learning, I approach the campus reverently down cobblestoned "P" Street, heading toward monolithic Healy Tower, positioned for maximum photogenic effect behind the "O" Street Gate. I'm overwhelmed with nostalgia for the feeling I'm entering a brick-and-stone time warp into the first days of the Republic. I, who'd never left the Missouri-Louisiana corridor, was in awe of the history embedded in these very streets. The university was founded by John Carroll, Jesuit Archbishop of Baltimore, the province to which Georgetown belonged long before a District of Columbia was born. The smell of the leafy trees—white and English and pin oaks interspersed with magnolias—and stolid beige cobblestones—wafted my imagination back to the times when literary and military heroes walked or rode on horseback or carriages down these very streets. I felt academically fulfilled already, and I hadn't even signed in. The place was so heavenly alien from Cyclops' Island, I knew I'd achieved escape to a different world—a world for me to conquer.

Here I would leave behind Peaches, Father Kalamaja, Father Puricelli, and Ziggy and meet goggle-eyed Father Young in Attic Greek, the universally detested Father Durkin in American Studies ("the most evil person I've ever met"), Father Edmund Ryan who made me wonder if Jesuits really believed in God, Father Joseph Sebes who seemed to know more about Hinduism, Buddhism, and Taoism than about Christianity, and the handsome, dapper courtly and eloquently intimidating Father Joseph Sellinger, Dean of the College. By my junior year, after I was elected editor-in-chief of *The Hoya*, which became the university-wide newspaper under my management, I was even dining on Sunday evenings with Father Edward Bunn, Georgetown's 40th president, at the brand-new 1789 Club. We would order roast beef and Yorkshire pudding and a bottle of fine Bordeaux so expensive it created aspirations I'd never dared to imagine, much less entertain.

I would soon discover that some of my best mentors at GU weren't Jesuits at all, but laymen like Rudy Schork in Latin, Greek, and Old Testament studies, Raymond Reno in Renaissance drama ("Scholarship is not a game of shuttlecock!"), the austere Thomas Walsh in Modern American Poetry, and Wilfrid Desan, whose *Planetary Man* was a major influence on my thinking about humanity's place in the grand scheme of things.

156

Probably the most important thing I learned from Jesuit institutions was not to rest until I could say I'd explored my full potential, honoring the motto inscribed above the stage in Gaston Hall: *Ad astra per aspera*, to the stars through obstacles. On that very stage, years later, I would introduce Clint Hill, Jackie Kennedy's Secret Service agent, to premier our film for Discovery, *The Kennedy Detail*, based on Jerry Blaine's and Lisa McCubbins' New York Times bestseller *The Kennedy Detail*.

Career Decision

In the euphoric oblivion of my senior year at Rockhurst, half-focused on maintaining my grade point average so I could graduate with honors, and half-focused on my passionate but never-consummated affair with Catherine Callahan's successor in my affections, Carrie Catherine Curran, my father convinced me that if I were being permitted to go to Georgetown, it would be to enroll in pre-med.

Willing to sign any bargain with the Cyclops that would enable me to leave his island, I agreed. I'd have agreed to anything, except changing my name to Freddy. I must have figured Dad was entitled to his pound of flesh (my future) for letting Father Kalamaja persuade him that I should travel 1,200 miles away for college.

In high school, I excelled at all things literary—including Latin, Greek, English, and history; spending uncounted hours at my high school and parish newspaper—and became averse to all things that had to do with numbers. I was hopelessly stymied by algebra teacher Mr. Petersen's seemingly disarming and properly didactic ending to every baffling session: "Any questions?" When Mr. Petersen cornered me, "I don't understand why you don't ask questions in class," I looked at him and said, "Sir, if I could *ask* a question, I wouldn't need to." That would mean I had at least a clue to whatever the hell he'd outlined in his blackboard-filling hour. I didn't. We looked at each other impassively, mutually baffled.

Years later, sailing across Houston's Clear Lake with GU college buddy Michael J. Rees, I realized that I'd have had a shot at understanding geometry if someone had simply named those abstract vectors "wind," "current," "angle of keel," "angle of prow." Or if they'd referred to the angle of the ball in tennis, that would later make me instantly aware the incoming ball was heading out of bounds. If algebra and geometry could be tied in with something practical, this grocer's nephew and grandson might have comprehended their usefulness.

Michael Rees, by the way, was one of the weirdest and funniest friends I would encounter at the Hilltop. He wrote me this random letter from Marine Corps training camp:

> *Dear Ken...*
> *I'm ashamed of myself...forgive me.*
> *Now that I've got that off my chest (I had it tattooed on at Camp LeJeune), I can get down to some real letter writing:*
> *Afjska; fjdksla; fjdksla; f djska; a ffjdksla; fjdl...*

Copy editor for *The Hoya*, Mike was the pal I chose to have breakfast with at Britt's on Wisconsin when we put the paper to bed at four a.m. It was Mike I chose to accompany me to New York for Vice President Lyndon Johnson's Waldorf-Astoria address to the Georgetown alumni—partly for Mike's humor, partly for his sonorous glee-club voice and knowledge of and ability to parody Broadway lyrics equal only to mine:

> My name is Jesus, the Son of God,
> Hello, hello, hello, hello, hello.
> I've come to save you, to heal your bod!
> Hello, hello, hello, hello!

But I admit what really nailed Mike's shotgun position was his promise to hook us up with two Manhattanville girls in matching black cocktail dresses. For a long time after I could no longer recall my date's last name, I still remembered that her first name was Barbara, and she had six fingers on one hand.

After a massively hung-over Sunday Mass at St. Patrick's, Michael exited the cathedral, white-faced, after the Collection. At my fingerful date's prodding, I rushed back to check on him. "What happened, man?" I said.

"I put $50 into the collection by mistake," he said. "It's all the money I have left."

Ө

In retrospect, it could not have been surprising to anyone except my father that on the day I arrived at the Georgetown Hilltop, I took a dramatic, self-propelled change of course from the McDonough Gymnasium pre-med registration line. The line for pre-med was the longest in the gym, I noted, from my position fifty places back from the moment of destiny when you picked up the packet and inscribed your name among the cadre of future Hoya medics. During the time it took to move from #50 to #42, my mind wandered in earnest. I was about to decide my *curriculum vitae*, the "course of my life," and I just wasn't feeling it in this line. I mourned to think my beloved Latin, whose resonant onomatopoeia rode daily through my mind, *Quadrupedante putrem sonitu quatit ungula campum, (their) hooves with four-footed beat pounded the dusty plain,* would end up trivialized into the curt phrases I heard from my mother the Nurse: NPO, "*nil per os,* nothing by mouth"; q1h, "*quaque hora,* every hour"; c̄, "*cum,* with"; s̄, "*sine,* without," and the more familiar "Rx, *recipe,*" prescription. My eyes darted desperately, around the gym.

They came to rest on a dapper man in a suit, hair slicked down, with a Cheshire Cat grin of contentment on his face. Rudolph J. Schork, "Rudy," as I would soon learn he was known to his loyal students, stood with no line at all confronting him, at a position at a sign-up table that displayed a gorgeous white-figure vase from the classical period of Athens. The lines from a favorite poem by Wallace Stevens sprang to mind:

> *I placed a jar in Tennessee*
> *And round it stood upon the hill.*
> *It made the slovenly wilderness*
> *Surround that hill.*

I instantly became Rudy's slovenly wilderness. Body and mind and soul ("*Mens sana, in corpore sano,*" a mantra of the Jesuit order), I surrounded Professor Schork's hill. I moved, almost in a trance, from my forty-second bumper-to-bumper position heading for medical registration (with another fifty behind me) to the wide-open road not taken leading to Schork's vase.

Without even flashing back to my vow made in Uncle Jimmy's dentist chair, I signed up on the spot to be a classics major.

After all, I couldn't stand even the sight or smell of blood.

Two weeks or so later, lines of Horace and Catullus love lyrics floating happily through my mind, I finally let reality penetrate my state of liberated bliss. I marched myself through the drizzling overcast evening into a corner payphone on leaf-laden Reservoir Road to confess my transgression to the Cyclops.

Characteristically, my mother answered the phone.

Uncharacteristically, I decided to take the manly path: "Hi, Mom. Can I talk to Dad?"

"Hello. What's wrong?"

"Dad, I have to tell you something. I didn't register pre-med."

Dead silence.

"I registered for classics."

Deader silence. I could hear my Dad thinking, *Damn that Father Z.* "What are you going to do for a living?" he finally asked.

"I don't know right now. I'll figure something out. But it's what feels right to me."

"I'll let you talk to your mom."

Mom, of course, approved, though I'm sure she couldn't say that directly to me. I'm sure she was shrugging at him when she got off the phone.

My Alpha MAF, grandfather Jede, later gave me the clearest family blessing. "I'm proud of you, Kenneth," he told me one early Sunday morning when I returned for the Christmas holiday by Greyhound bus.

Uncle Jimmy echoed his father's words when I went in for my cleaning the summer after my freshman year before we launched into my new studies of Aesop and Herodotus and Galen (read for Greek, not for medicine): "I'm proud of you, honey. Stick to your guns."

"But my Dad—"

"Don't worry about your dad," he interrupted. "He doesn't understand. Do you what makes you happy, and you'll be okay."

He saw the look on my face—the look that asked if he could possibly understand the price I and my mother were paying with my father for this most un-Atchity-like career aberration. "I know, I know," he read my mind. "She can deal with it. You can deal with it. *He* can deal with it."

I was liberated from Dad.

I thought I had grown up.

Laham b'Ajeens

My reward from Mom arrived a few days after the drizzly phone call, a brown-paper-wrapped cardboard box, the oily spots on its wrapping a dead giveaway. The box contained meat pies, my most comforting of Lebanese comfort foods.

Everyone in our family would also have a slightly different take on preparing the meat pies. They've provided lifelong sustenance, from the times in Tata's kitchen when I dipped them in the bean juice on my plate, to Mom packing them along with fried chicken for my train rides south—to lugging them along with me to Sedalia when I left at the crack of dawn Monday mornings to put in another week driving trucks to and from Minutemen silos.

For me, the perfect Lebanese meal consists of *laham b'ajeens*, preferably made by Son Vincent, who took the time to learn them from Mom; *kibbeh nayeh;* and Tata's beans served with tiny wedges of white onion.

Here's all you need to make the "little meat pies":

3 lbs. ground lamb (or beef, depending on your dietary attitude. I prefer the lamb as it's more traditional, but I'm sure Tata used beef when lamb was too pricey).

1 large white onion chopped (we like a lot of onions!)

salt

pepper, lots

(pine nuts, Vincent's ingenious addition)

1 cup lemon juice

Fry the ground meat and onion and season to taste. Add the lemon juice, and simmer for a while till the lemon permeates the meat—the more juice, the better. Add the browned-in-butter pine nuts at any time.

Chill the meat mixture overnight. Or not, if you're in a hurry.

For the dough, you need:

3 cups flour

5 tablespoons of shortening. Mom used Crisco.

Salt

1 packet of dry yeast, dissolved in 1¼ cups of lukewarm water

Mix the flour, shortening, and salt with a pastry blender or by hand. Then slowly add the yeast/water mixture until the dough "can be shaped into a smooth, round ball" (Mom's words).

Leave the dough to rise, undivided, in a dark warm place for at least thirty minutes.

When it's risen, flour the surface of a table liberally and roll the floured dough out lightly to make it as thin as possible without being transparent.

Cut the dough sheet into roughly two-inch squares and place a teaspoon of meat mixture in the middle of each square. Then roll each square up as neat as humanly possible and place it on a lightly buttered cookie sheet. Some family members shape the pies into the tri-cornered-hat pattern that may have been their traditional shape—no doubt inspired by the French occupation of Lebanon during the crusades. As Tata did, I just pinch them together.

Put a small dab of butter on top of each formed pie.

The more diligent the chef, the smaller the meat pie.

Bake at 375° for 20–25 minutes on the buttered cookie sheet.

When they're dark but still golden brown, they're ready. You'll know it by the heavenly aroma.

Keeping Tracking on Track

At Georgetown, where coats and ties in class were mandatory, I even recorded "clothes combinations"—a list of all the clothes I had on hand and a day-by-day account of how I combined them. Good grief.

7

Clothes Combinations #5 (p. 9).

1	new suit jacket (green)
2	new suit pants (green)
3	new sport jacket
4	old sport jacket
5	new black trousers
6	old black trousers
7	new brown trousers
8	green vest
9	blue tie
10	brown tie
11	bright red tie
12	dull red tie
13	gray tie
14	yellow tie
15	gold-green tie
16	striped tie
17	black tie
18	old suit jacket
19	old suit pants
20	old gray pants

9-15	1-2-15
9-16	4-2-16
9-17	18-19-14
9-18	4-6-16
9-19	3-6-12
9-20	4-7-9

Another list was rooted in my college years' affectation of the pipe-smoking habit, in emulation of Uncle Wib, and as an attempt to give up cigarettes. I kept track of tobacco combinations, though not for long enough to become certifiable. I wish I could remember what I did with my pipe collection, which had become extensive by the time I finished Yale and left the habit behind.

And, of course, I didn't stop typing into my Blue Book. Blue Book II reflected my gleanings while at Georgetown, 1961-1965. It includes enormous chunks typed out from E. V. Rieu's translation of the *Iliad*, from a dozen Shakespeare plays and Thomas Hardy novels, and from the works of Salinger, Steinbeck, Dostoevsky, Carson McCullers, Fitzgerald, Herodotus, and John Donne. I typed in dozens and dozens of songs from all the great American musicals along with sections of Tennessee Williams' plays, John Henry Cardinal Newman's *The Idea of a University*, and Walt Kelly's "Many Happy Returns," which I read to one female victim after another through the years. About a fourth of the thick blue volume is in Latin—favorite poems of Horace, Catullus, Martial, Virgil; and at least that percentage of its 618 pages I'd committed to memory.

I also kept scrapbook after scrapbook detailing the highs and comic lows of my grade school, high school, and college years. I kept things so fervently because I was seeing everything at a distance, not *being there*, but observing my own life flowing by, with me on the periphery instead of in the center. My confused and confusing feelings for Dad *and* Mom had turned me into a sleepwalker walking through someone else's dream. I kept things because I didn't understand at the time what they signified, what pattern they were forming, and because I must have hoped, unconsciously, that if I kept them, I could relive the life I was missing out on and make sense of it.

Without all the "keepings," I couldn't have written this book.

Jede Passes Away

My beloved Lebanese grandfather, Jede, died on March 16, 1963. He was born on December 4, 1891, in Tripoli, then "Turkish Syria," now Lebanon.

"Your grandfather was a real character," I'd hear Mom say to one of *my* siblings not old enough to know him as well as I did. No one was quite sure what she meant by it. When pressed for more details, she just shrugged. My mother's shrugs were notorious for their expressiveness.

When the news reached me in DC, I was at first numb, then progressively angrier. How could he go and die like that and leave the rest of us behind to figure things out without him? That was pretty much my response to the death of anyone I loved from that day until a few years ago when I finally acknowledged the notion that death was, probably, inevitable. "No one of intelligence," Arthur C. Clarke wrote, "resents the inevitable."

Dad duly authorized the unbudgeted expense of my returning to his father's funeral, allowing me to withdraw money for my ticket from my Boatman Bank's account because he knew how much Jede meant to me. Besides, I'm sure he rationalized, this funeral was a family command performance, a ritual gathering of the clan. My first airplane flight was in a white and red TWA

Constellation from DC's then National Airport that lumbered bravely westward into a blizzard.

I wasn't afraid to fly in a blizzard because I happened to be reading, in my sophomore Existential Philosophy class taught by Father Ryan, SJ, Albert Camus' *The Stranger,* and digging the Frenchman's cool approach to an absurd existence. What could be more perfectly absurd than going down in a snowstorm en route to a funeral while reading about absurdity? Years later, producing my first movies between Montreal and Toronto, taking off in an even heavier blizzard, I wasn't worried even when the airline offered to substitute a later flight if I had any hesitation. I figured if I were going to die in that blizzard, I'd be dying in the middle of my dream.

I already understood that it's not life's job to offer the symmetries so laboriously constructed by art.

Mom told me that Uncle Jim had arrived at Jede's house in twenty minutes from his rambling white house at 4900 Oakdale Court, in Overland Park—after Tata called him to announce, "Your father keeled over at the breakfast table."

The funeral itself was a jumble of memories. I served as my grandfather's pallbearer along with my cousins Eddy, Jr. (Uncle Eddy's son); Tony, Jr.; Aunt Selma's son Robert; Uncle Victor's son Victor Michael ("Mike"), and brother Freddy, Jr. How name-bearer Freddy managed to upset first-son balance by serving as the sixth wheel in this honorable procession I can only imagine. I tried to focus on what I'd learned from Jede: "There's no penalty for failure here," express your gratitude for the freedom this great country offers by kicking the road fearlessly, and joyfully move forward toward your dreams.

That was the only time I saw Tata break down. Kneeling before the coffin, she burst out crying. "You went and left me, didn't you, Jim?"

When we got back to my grandparents' house on 52nd Street, someone brought out Tata's stash of family photos. They included my favorite of him: Chieftain Jede seated on his living room couch on Wabash with Uncle Bob Martin (Selma's husband) perched behind him, saucy Mom, meat pie in hand, giving Jede her "he's such a character" eye, and Dad leaning forward tentatively. Aunt Catherine and Uncle Anthony, on the left, stare solemnly at the camera. Jede is the only one smiling. Which indicates his appreciation of the respect and deference accorded him.

I loved Aunt Selma's husband, Uncle Bob, a ruddy and rugged railroad man with a ready smile and honest red face who refused to hide his feelings. He and Dad ended a family picnic in Loose Park one day in a fist fight over whether Baptists, of which Uncle Bob was one before he converted to Roman Catholicism to marry Aunt Selma, can get into Heaven. I'm sure I knew Dad's position on that. Those who disagreed with my father earned the epithet "hot-head."

Until Freddy reminded me, I'd completely forgotten the story of Jede and the Easter Eggs. The whole family had adopted my grandfather's passion for egg-cracking—where you pitted your favorite dyed Easter egg against your siblings' eggs to see which one cracked which. Each family's champion came to Jede's clan conclave for Easter dinner, triumphantly bearing his or her uncracked egg. Then all the winners among the cousins, aunts, and uncles went at it until only ONE egg was left uncracked. Only at that point did Jede bring out *his* egg—and invariably cracked the winner's—to dismay on the erstwhile winner's part, uproarious glee on his. Later we all learned that he, the grocer with know-how and resources, was deploying a *goose* egg against our mere chicken eggs!

It was that day in 1963 at St. Mary's Cemetery on 22nd and Cleveland that I noticed one gravestone simply inscribed "Atchity Baby" that marked the grave of my unborn baby brother. And also spotted the grave of Jede's father, Antoine (Anthony) Atchidi, the shoemaker from Tripoli by way of the mountain village of Hadchit (aka Habchite), who died in 1918 after only a dozen years in the New World. Jede's generation called America the "New World" and referred to their origins in the "Old World."

We were "Syrian" for a while, by the way, before we started calling ourselves Lebanese. The fact was that when Jede and his family arrived on the SS Pennsylvania from Boulogne-sur-Mer at Ellis Island on April 13, 1906, they were logged in as citizens of the Syrian province of the Ottoman empire, the territory which was later carved out as modern-day Lebanon.

My grandfather sailed across the Atlantic at fifteen, with his forty-three-year-old father, Antoine, and his mother Sulimé, twenty-eight, along with three siblings, and a total fortune among them of $120. Disembarking in the United States of America, my great grandfather, former shoemaker and future grocer, real estate investor, inventor, and candy and ice cream cone manufacturer, was welcomed to America by being required to take this oath:

> ...I am not a disbeliever in or opposed to organized government or a member of or affiliated with any organization or body of person teaching disbelief in or opposed to organized government. I am not a polygamist nor a believer in the practice of polygamy. I am attached to the principles of the Constitution of the United States, and it is my intention to become a citizen of the United States and to renounce absolutely and forever all allegiance and fidelity to any foreign prince, potentate, state, or sovereignty, and particularly to "Mehemmed VI [sic] Emperor of the Ottomans" of whom at this time I am a subject, and it is my intention to reside permanently in the United States.

Nine years later, in November 1915, Jede became a US citizen. Later we would learn that our Atchity name may not be our original name at all (which, according to Dad was "Helou") but a typical Ellis Island miscommunication. The family was associated with the village of Hadchit, northeast of Tripoli, founded by the Phoenicians. When they asked my great grandfather what his name was, he thought they'd asked, "Where are you from?"

"H'adchit'i," he replied—"from Hadchit."

Not comfortable with what linguists call "aspirates," the authorities wrote down "Atchity"—and so our New World family was born. If you run into an Atchity anywhere, he must be my relative. Variations in transcription from Arabic include Habchiti, Aschidi, Atchidi, Atichity, Achity, Hatchety, and, so many times, it became a pet peeve, "Atchison-Topeka-Santa Fe."

Jede explained all this to me at that Formica-topped kitchen table over the years of Sunday mornings during the cigarette and coffee portion of the bean vigil, the only time he could get my attention away from Tata's aluminum cauldron. He never thought of himself as a Turk once he set foot on American soil. He hated the Turks. They were the reason he left the Old Country. As far as he was concerned, he was Lebanese, and that was that. No one in this brave new world dared say different.

Θ

We still called them "Syrian beans," even though technically they were now "Lebanese beans," and originally may even have been called "Turkish beans." Friends and my brother visiting Istanbul reported from time to time that a similar bean is served at restaurants there.

When we arrived back in the long black limos from St. Mary's Cemetery that day at my grandparents' house on 52nd for photo-browsing, the smell of Tata's beans—along with *kibbeh nayeh* and *kusa*—welcomed us. My grandmother, true to character, had risen early to prepare the traditional dishes even on—especially on—the day of her husband's burial.

While we waited for her to heat everything up, I roamed around the house, feeling how suddenly empty it felt without Jede. I opened the door leading to the staircase to the attic. There on the lowest step, I spotted my grandfather's oud. For a wild moment, musically untrained as I was, I wished it mine. But it was not mine to take, and I left it on the stairs. Uncle Jimmy, Jede's namesake, ended up with it. For the rest of his life, he displayed it with pride on his dining room wall.

Jede's smile still shines in my memory, a smile that flashed the depths of experience—suffering and joy, toil and relaxation, laughter and tears.

And his quiet pride. Pride in the family he'd rescued from the Old World, proud of the modest wealth he'd amassed—far more than anything he could have achieved in Tripoli as the son of a shoemaker. Pride in himself, for figuring it all out and enjoying it. Jede, always thrilled by fireworks on the 4th of July, was our own Zorba the Greek, whose dancing and singing lit up this new world for us.

Θ

At the Formica-topped table those early Sunday mornings, Jede made it clear he was proud of me, too, beginning with the promising speed of my ingestion—the acquired habit of eating too fast, as he did, that I later found very difficult to break.

My grandfather was in love with speed. He smoked Lucky Strikes quickly, spoke in lightning bursts on the phone, gulped his coffee from dawn to midnight, and drove too fast. No wonder he conked out from a heart attack. His racing brain finally hit a brick wall. He lived all-out and died with the same intensity.

I'm certain he died with a smile on his face. According to Tata, he'd just downed a cup of coffee and eaten a plate of her beans (Uncle Jimmy confirmed that the dish he slumped into was clean).

He'd led a life filled with entrepreneurial zeal that ended up well off enough; in his late years, he consolidated his various efforts into a variety of real estate holdings that would be managed later by his progeny. To this day, I have—all my siblings have—framed on our walls, labels marked "Atchity's Shurgood." That was Jede's brand: bottled barbecue sauce, canned cabbage rolls, and chili con carne.  Cardboard cases full of Shurgood products disappeared bottle by bottle and can by can from the basement on 52nd as the last of his

unsold stock was distributed to the extended family, who dutifully consumed them well after posted expiration dates.

Decades later, Aunt Lorraine, nibbling her double pastrami sandwich at Longboards at the age of eighty-four, told me that when Jede first went into business, he went down to the bank to establish "a business relationship." The banker welcomed him and set him up with his first checking account. "Now, Mr. Atchity, you can write checks anytime," he informed my grandfather, who was unfamiliar with the banking system.

So Jede did. He wrote a number of checks.

One day the banker called him and said, "Mr. Atchity, you need to deposit money to cover these checks you've written."

My grandfather, who'd never suspected this "catch," rushed down to the bank and made things right.

Jede's Royal Mercantile Company manufactured and patented the waffle cone's predecessor—the first ice cream cones made in KC. RMC also manufactured candy until the company was wiped out when a trainload of sugar arrived at KC's Union Station COD—on the very day the price of sugar doubled to five dollars a sack because war had been declared on Japan.

Eventually, Jede also learned from his banker that his accountant was stealing money from him but refused to prosecute her. Atchitys don't believe in suing. They believe in karma. Either something good would come from forgiving the accountant, or at least he'd never have to deal with her again.

Once he recovered from that little setback, Jede moved into the grocery business with dreams of having a store for each of his five sons. Jede opened stores on 9th Street, 24th & Denver, 40th & Holmes—and at the height of his grocery empire he was operating, with his sons Anthony, Eddy, and Victor, four stores at the same time (one run by grandson Tony, Jr.).

When they were kids, Jede left Vick and Eddy in charge of the grocery store while he made a delivery. As I heard the story, it was Uncle Eddy who started the bean fight. They were loading packages of dried lima beans onto the shelves Jede liked to fill to bursting.

One of the packages did.

The beans that spilled out transformed into projectiles, and Eddy lost no time pelting Vic.

Vic, in turn, opened a bag of his own, and the bean battle began. Losing their minds to childish glee, they ran from aisle to aisle, firing at each other until the floor was carpeted with beans that would never make it to Tata's big pot on Sunday.

If only Freddy and I had thrown beans instead of rocks!

Before my warring uncles regained their senses, the front door slammed, and Jede was back.

"You won't believe what happened!" Eddy shouted.

When Jede stopped laughing, it was Vic who paid hell for it. He couldn't quip fast enough.

On the side, in 1928, Jede patented the replaceable mop head.

As family legend has it, he also invented a sanitary napkin that he dubbed "Motex" (because we lived in Kansas City, MO). Johnson & Johnson imitated his idea, came out with Kotex across the river in Kansas, and released theirs at such a low price they drove Jede out of that business. More likely it was Jede who copied them with his brand.

June 24, 1930.

J. A. ATCHITY

1,765,364

MOP

Filed June 25, 1928

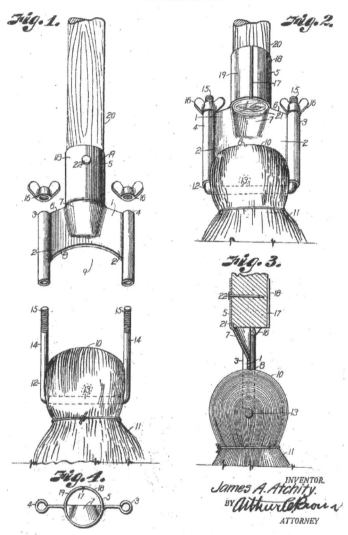

Fig.1. *Fig.2.*

Fig.3.

Fig.4.

INVENTOR.
James A. Atchity.
BY *Arthur LeBrou*
ATTORNEY

No wonder my uncles owned retail stores! The family needed outlets for the patriarch's inventions. Later in life, when I was simultaneously managing a poetry quarterly, a Pasadena arts journal, and another journal called *DreamWorks*, Occidental College's president asked me, "Atchity, what other entrepreneurial projects are you involved in?" I smiled fondly, thinking of my grandfather.

There were rumors that Jede even made bootleg liquor during Prohibition. The only corroborating story I recall was one Uncle Victor told of supplying "Holy Water" to the cantankerous Father O'Malley, pastor of St. Aloysius Parish on 11th Street—where all the siblings walked to grade school and where my parents were married. "Holy water" was the Prohibition euphemism for anisette, which Victor delivered to the rectory a gallon jug at a time.

Jede liked to smoke his Luckies in a cigarette holder, which indeed gave him the appearance of the tribal chieftain. He was a proud one at that, proud of his own accomplishments, proud of his sons—though he never stopped giving them hell to his dying day—and especially proud of his grandchildren. Though my father never quite admitted to me his own acceptance of my Georgetown career decision, Jede said the words I couldn't hear too often from a Male Authority Figure, "I'm proud of you, honey." What his own sons didn't understand, Jede celebrated.

Jede confided in me that all his children were too careful. They didn't take enough chances—they who had been nursed in the laboratory of his risk and had seen his fortunes—and theirs—rise and fall with the price of sugar. For Jede, it was not about keeping what you have. It was about tapping into the abundance of America, pulling its flow in the direction of your will. "In this country, there's no risk to failing, honey," he told me more than once. Which translated, "Go for it!"—my mother's favorite exhortation.

On one visit home from Georgetown, I was driving Jede's car, chauffeuring him on a business errand. As we headed north on The Paseo, he saw a stoplight turn orange—and urged me to "step on it." "I hate stoplights," he added.

My grandfather did not go gentle into that good night. I'm grateful he didn't live long enough to suffer through the mushroom-like proliferation of speed bumps in the modern world. He gave me the paternal recognition my father was unable to because my rebellious mother blocked him.

Another Cousin Tony Joke

A priest, a minister, and a rabbi bumped into each other in their adjoining parking lot, each bearing a collection basket in his hand. They looked at one another sheepishly, embarrassed by the coincidence.

"Well," said the priest. "What's your method of dividing the collection between God's needs and your own?"

"You go first," said the minister.

"Okay," the priest replied. "I draw a line in the parking lot and stand right on it. I toss the cash into the air. Everything that falls on the right side of the line goes to God's purposes. Whatever falls on the left side, I use for my expenses."

"Ah, I see," said the minister. "My method is remarkably similar. I draw a CIRCLE and stand in the middle of it. Then I toss the basket into the air. Whatever falls INSIDE the circle goes to God, outside goes to me."

The rabbi shook his head and smiled. "I see we all have very similar methods," he says, "though I believe mine is based on a faith even stronger than yours. Because of this faith, I don't draw lines at all. I toss the money into the air. I figure whatever God needs he'll help Himself."

Tata's *Kusa*

Tata's squash recipe is made either with *kusa* (yellow squash), my favorite, or long, green zucchini. The process begins with owning a squash-cleaning implement that Jede manufactured by the bunch and provided to his daughters and most of his daughters-in-law. I inherited Mom's—or rather purloined it from Mary, whose kitchen drawers were formerly Mom's since she inherited the house on East 104th on Mom's passing. It's a long, thin, aluminum implement used to hollow out the squash, careful not to push it too far and rupture the base you want to keep intact to contain the flavor.

Once the squash is hollowed out, you insert the same mixture used for grape leaves—rice and ground meat (lamb or beef), heavily peppered and lightly-salted, packing the mixture tightly into the squash.

Pack the bottom of your pot with thin pork chops. It's the pork that gives the best flavor to the dish. Layer the stuffed squash on top of the pork chops and, between layers, add green string beans, ends removed (Trader Joe's has deliciously fresh ones frozen). Also, intersperse in the packing a can of Contadina chopped tomatoes for the best flavor of all.

Fill the pot with water to the top of the squash and simmer until the stuffed squash are easily cut with a fork.

Sedalia Summers

From the day I first walked the bricks of Georgetown, my Hoya years were a lightning blur of activity: the intensity of the Honors Program; jousting with our George-Clooney-handsome Jesuit dean and his drop-dead gorgeous and fiercely loyal assistant Mary Joy over disciplinary issues; taking advanced courses on Chaucer and Elizabethan Drama at the Hall of Graduate Studies with Professors John McCall and Bernie Wagner, a font of Elizabethan trivia; being inducted into Eta Sigma Phi (national honors society); winning the Vergilian Academy silver medal before an international panel of Latinists; my Broadway musical show on WGTB-FM, where I met my first wife; a brief stint with the Philodemic Society, which I abandoned to the more eloquent voices of Bob Shrum and Phil Mause; and working my butt off for *The Hoya*.

Through Dad's machinations, and no real willingness of my own, I landed a summer job for "good money" in Sedalia, Missouri. I was to drive trucks for the IBEW's (International Brotherhood of Electrical Workers) installation of Minuteman missiles in the Missouri countryside. Who would have thunk that literally dozens of nuclear missiles were being drilled into the

Midwestern soil in readiness for retaliation against the Soviets? When I worked there for two summers during my Georgetown years, Sedalia, ninety miles southeast of KC, was famous for being the alleged birthplace of actor Andrew Vabre Devine, better known as "Andy." Andy Devine had achieved nationwide fame by playing Jingles, Guy Madison's wheezy-voiced sidekick in *The Adventures of Wild Bill Hickock*, one of the first shows we watched on television. Long before the days of Wikipedia.org, it became known that Andy was actually born in Flagstaff, Arizona. But Sedalia, desperate for attention, insisted that *it* was his birthplace.

For me, "good money" brought with it enforced exile from my new girlfriend, Kathy Desser, better known to herself and her world as "Dess." But it at least was a lot more interesting than my previous Dad-arranged summer job, counting and greasing nuts and bolts at the Western Auto Parts company. I could use my rural lunch breaks memorizing more of Martial's deliciously salacious lyrics:

> *I have sworn ten thousand times*
> *To write no more epigrams.*
> *But when I see your face, Vacerra,*
> *The old sickness comes upon me.*

I moved into Mrs. Reynolds' Boarding House in Sedalia, 319 W. 6th, a few blocks from the railroad tracks and spent my evenings writing letters to Dess and poring over hers—at least one a day in both directions.

What did I know about driving big trucks, hauling electrical conduit across the rolling farmland of north-central Missouri? Absolutely nothing on my first day on the job but more than I ever dreamed of knowing by the time I moved on with my life. Today my filing still contains maps to all the Minuteman sites, in eight "flights," named after the letters of the alphabet starting with "A."

My first day on the job was explosively unpropitious. I had parked my long-bed truck at a gas station to grab a bite of lunch. When I came back to the truck, I checked the side mirrors and backed up.

Smack into a fuel pump. Which blew up, setting the gasoline on fire but, fortunately, not the truck.

When, a few minutes later, the union chief's helicopter landed in the extended parking lot next to the station, I figured my job had set a record for brevity and that I would be sent back to the big city in disgrace. Imagine my surprise when instead of rage what I saw written on John Simms' face was laughter. He alighted from the helicopter and approached me. "What did you learn from this, Kenny?" he asked.

"Not to trust mirrors," I said.

"It's called a blind spot," he nodded. "Always check your blind spot."

A few years later, March 4, 1965, John Simms' personal blind spot, it turns out, was tucked beneath the chassis of his T-Bird convertible. He was blown to kingdom come from his front seat by an unidentified anti-union activist inside my Dad's office building parking garage on Washington Street. Dad speculated, very quietly, that John's death had been arranged by the KC mob—in those days still called "the Prendergast machine," though Jim and Tom Prendergast were long gone. Something to do with Teamsters and Las Vegas. The same political machine had rewarded the Pabst distributorship to "Big Bill" Lafferty because he'd voted in the legislature to end Prohibition.

Θ

That began the first of two surreal summers driving up and down Missouri farm roads, delivering coded cardboard duct-taped boxes from one supply base to another, or from Base to one of the sites. One of the boxes I packed with a live baby raccoon, a practical joke that could have startled its recipient right into a ninety-foot-deep silo.

I got to stare into those dark deep silos and greet the electricians who were the first ones to crawl the sides of the newly-dried concrete cylinder to lay the conduit I brought them that would carry the wiring that would make it possible to blow the evil Soviets to smithereens.

Driving was mentally relaxing work, providing plenty of time for memorization and contemplation, mostly about why I was working for money instead of writing—a condition humans often find ourselves in.

The tedium could be exhausting. I pulled an eighteen-hour shift one day and found myself driving a twenty-foot trailer truck up and down the rollercoaster hills between two far-separated sites. It was after midnight, and I had to pinch my cheeks to keep myself from falling asleep. We didn't have iPod then, not even Walkman, and the trucks were not equipped with commercial radio. The next thing I was conscious of was the squawking of the two-way, begging me, "Atchity, come in, please. Over!" I opened my eyes to see the sun rising over the eastern hills. My truck was in a ditch, the engine off. Before conking out, I had pulled over and turned it off. I reached for the radio, grateful to be alive.

That would be one more story to report to Dess.

The rest of that summer I amused myself by stopping to retrieve turtles from the middle of the road, those that were not yet squashed by heavy vehicles such as mine. I set them in the back of my pickup and, on the weekends, drove them home to our garage on 75th Street to entertain my sisters. Before summer's end, our 75th Street garage was filled with turtles. Recalling Betty Lafferty's digs about sleeping with turtles under the bed, I made sure none of them got into the house.

When Dad started muttering about "turtle soup," I opened the garage door before the crack of dawn one Monday morning before leaving for Sedalia and let them all escape—no doubt forever altering the zoological balance of St. Elizabeth Parish.

Corporate Waiting Room

The blur that was my Rockhurst high school years gave way to the blur of my Georgetown college years gave way to the blur of Yale graduate school years that gave way to the blur of my teaching years at Occidental College where I was professor of comparative literature. When you live as intensely as I always have, packing every instant with work I either love or need to do to survive, I suppose it's not that surprising that life itself can blur a bit. I recorded it, I collected evidence from it along the way so that I could slow it down here for you, maybe also so that I could someday understand it better than I did at the time.

My predecessor as *Hoya* Editor-in-Chief at Georgetown recruited me for Yale. At Tom Scheye's invitation, I drove up from DC to visit Yale's New Haven campus during my senior year (I was married by then, with son Vincent born in December 1964). I was pleasantly surprised to see Tom had a fireplace in his private room in the Yale Hall of Graduate Studies on York Street. He urged me to apply to the Theater History department, because it was much smaller than my first choice, Comparative Literature, and might therefore be easier to get into.

Ignoring Tom, I wasn't accepted in comparative literature, even though I won an NDEA Title IV fellowship that would have supported me and my new family for three years of graduate school. I saw the wisdom of Tom's advice too late.

But another door immediately opened. I'd been interviewed on campus by AT&T a few months before graduating from Georgetown. They were visiting campuses, looking for management recruits. AT&T offered me a position in their Long Lines' Immediate Management Development Program. That would lead to assignment as a manager in one of Long Lines' many offices in DC. After conferring with NDEA to make sure their fellowship could be postponed by a year, I immediately made two decisions:

1) I would accept AT&T's funds-producing offer.
2) I would reapply to Yale, this time in Theater History.

In a majorly intense week at the Bear Mountain Inn in upstate New York, I learned how to combine my highly-advanced time-management skills with the skills required to *manage* corporate people and situations. I was taught that a good manager doesn't *do* anything; he gets someone else to do it. The week passed like an hour (another blur), and I was given an amazing job assignment:

I was to report, as a "Communications Engineer," to the AT&T Long Lines NASA Headquarters Account, where I would report to the account's general manager.

Suddenly I needed to buy a second and third suit—and learn what the word "commute" meant (since we lived in Falls Church, Virginia, a twenty-five-minute drive to the Long Lines' office on K Street, NW. I was put in charge of three seasoned execs in the DC office and one in Houston, all four of them vying for the position I had just lucked into out of the blue.

I got to be in a control room when Ranger impacted on the moon—thanks to Long Lines' communication lines that reached from Cape Kennedy (as Cape Canaveral would soon be called) to the Manned Spaceflight Center in Houston. Why would a spaceflight that originated on the Florida coast be controlled from a thousand miles away? I wondered. But it became clear to me very quickly. Lyndon Johnson, who had regaled Mike Rees and me and our Manhattanville dates at the Waldorf, was now the president. Which came to mean that NASA headquarters was relocated to Texas no matter how impractical that might seem.

By the way, the White House Account was the desk next to mine. The conversations I overheard were sometimes hilarious. Each morning a technician was dispatched to the White House to replace the carbon filter in one of the President's phones. Normally, these filters lasted months. But President Johnson insisted on having phone conversations in the shower, so his had to be replaced daily.

Our job at Long Lines was to reduplicate every voice and wideband data line between Florida and Houston. Some we buried underground, some ran on old-fashioned poles, some were transmitted via microwave. But no matter how ingenious our communications engineering might be, we still couldn't engineer enough communications clarity to enable Houston to control the first few seconds of a space flight. That required visual contact with the rocket; so had to be done in real time, at the Cape. Once the rocket was inserted into orbit, control could be passed to Houston.

My analytical skills, honed through years of Jesuit education and polished at Bear Mountain, served me well at Long Lines. I designed and implemented "The Green Network," a green telephone on the desk of the director of each of NASA's twenty-six installations throughout the US and the world. He could reach any other center by dialing only two digits.

I got to travel—*had* to travel—from Florida to Huntsville, Alabama, where Werner Von Braun built the big Saturn rockets; to Houston; to Ames Research Center in Silicon Valley; to Lewis Research Center in Cleveland; to Grumman Aircraft in Downey, California, and JPL (Jet Propulsion Laboratory) in Pasadena.

The California trip was my first experience of the Golden State. I *adored* being awakened by my hotel's alarm radio with the Southern California weather report: "Early morning low clouds in the LA Basin but clearing before noon; ten degrees cooler in Santa Monica, Venice, Redondo; unseasonably hot and clear in the San Fernando Valley, ten degrees cooler in Topanga and Thousand Oaks; a bit cooler in the San Gabriel Valley, both topping in the low nineties; ninety to one hundred in the low deserts; over one hundred in the high deserts; foothills in the eighties." My God, I thought, is this a city or a country of its own? I learned that there are ninety-three urban centers in Greater Los Angeles. I vowed to visit them all someday.

But it was the California roses (along with camellias and azaleas) blooming in December that eventually, four years later, led me to choose California as the place to commit to my first academic job offer from Occidental College. I couldn't imagine a better place to raise my young family than a state where roses bloomed in December.

Even with such glamorous and exciting activities and surroundings, corporate life was not my cup of hemlock. Earlier, I had decided not to pursue a career in either politics or journalism, because I was convinced they'd bring out the worst in me. Now I couldn't see myself thriving in a corporate environment where everyone was either fearful of losing his or her current position or viciously competing—often surreptitiously—to take someone else's. The stress and lifestyle were already taking a toll on me. Within the twelve months of my assignment to the NASA Headquarters account, I gained thirty-five pounds—many of which I would never lose. I longed to be back in the academic world's security where I could apply my brain to ancient thoughts and languages that might isolate me from the unruly real world.

In this winter of my corporate discontent, the light at the end of the tunnel started shining when I heard, in January, from LSU (Louisiana State University) that I was accepted into the Comparative Literature department. The Woodrow Wilson Foundation granted me a year's full tuition at the graduate school of my choice, and finally, from Yale, I learned I'd been accepted into the Department of Theater History.

Escape, again, loomed on the horizon, although it would soon present itself as yet another crossroads.

I flew to Baton Rouge, Louisiana, to meet with LSU's Comparative Literature department. Uncle Wib drove me to inspect the married student housing, neat brick apartments adjacent to the sprawling lake-centered and willowed LSU campus. We celebrated with pork roast, rice, and gravy my imminent return to my native state—a dream come true for both of us.

Then came a phone call from the Woodrow Wilson Foundation (recently renamed The Institute of Citizens & Scholars). In lieu of the stately letterhead of a prestigious ivory-tower foundation, here was a real live person at the end of the line. To congratulate me on winning the prestigious award, and to reassure me the NDEA Title IV could still kick in at the end of the one-year Wilson fellowship. Then, to my surprise, the talk turned to my choice of graduate schools. The Wilson exec told me they were aware of LSU's comparative literature department's distinction but wanted me to consider Yale instead. "Yale is Yale," was their bottom-line argument. "The mere name will open doors for you for the rest of your life."

Once again, I was torn, facing a choice between the idyllic dreamland of my birth and my mother's family, and the equally mythic nirvana of rarefied academic distinction.

The Jesuit, the urbane, the Dad in me won out. I chose Yale. The dye was cast, and I turned my back on fried chicken, pork roast, and crawfish étouffée in favor of spartan New Haven apizza. Yale was my ultimate dream of serious education, one step above even Georgetown.

Yale

Perhaps because I was by then a married man, my most memorable relationships at Yale weren't with my fellow graduate students, but with my professors. Because libraries where I might hang with my classmates always spooked me, I immediately began my routine of checking out twenty plus books at a time from the Sterling Library. That was the limit for graduate students. That way I could devour them at the ruckus of the family kitchen table. My Yale mentors who made an enormous impact on my life. My first night on campus, I stood outside the Drama School waiting to see Megan Terry's *MacBird!* Kingman Brewster, then president of Yale, stood behind me. I recognized him from the brochures. He greeted me cordially and welcomed me to Yale.

Alois Nagler, Prussian ramrod straight, presided over the Theater History department. His demeanor was so intimidating that when he assigned me to make an oral presentation in German about *Die Meiningen* theater company, I accepted it without question though my German was nearly non-existent. You needed Latin, French, and German to qualify for your Yale degree, but could master one of the three before graduation. I'd qualified with Latin and French and wasn't allowed to substitute my eight years of Homeric and six years of Attic Greek for German. I'd have to learn that before completing my degree.

But I never thought I'd have to cram-learn the language in sixty days—until I could read and cite, summarize, and analyze the research—mostly from contemporary nineteenth-century German newspapers—and stumble through it, just passably, in the class. Afterwards, in Nagler's office—atop a winding staircase that had the effect of intimidating anyone who managed to negotiate it to face the stern professor—the good professor congratulated me on my German. I admitted I was baffled that he'd assigned me to German, which I hardly knew, and my classmate Andrew Bose to French, when *he* spoke German fluently. Nagler's face went red. Is he blushing? I thought. "That was my mistake," he said. "Why didn't you tell me?" "I thought this was what being at Yale demanded," I said. We both had to laugh out loud, for quite different reasons.

True to Scheye's prediction, I was able to switch to comparative literature by the end of my first year. My first comp lit class was with Lowry Nelson, Jr., a friend until he died in 1994 in Talinn, Estonia, where he was tracking down that language's relationship to Lithuanian and Latvian. Lowry was the primary MAF who guided me through Yale, a place where I felt I didn't belong. He serenely, sincerely, urged me to follow my instincts, and to do what I was doing.

That came after my first mid-term exam for Lowry's class. Instead of answering the questions he posed, I composed a Platonic dialogue, "The Logolos." Lowry awarded it an "Honors" (Yale's grading consisted of Honors, High Pass, and Pass), leaving astute comments in my margins and not once referring to my answer having nothing to do with the question. He invited me to the Elizabethan Club for tea. I fell in love with this man's voracious thirst for knowledge, his mastery of a dozen languages, his emotional involvement in questions that the rest of the world would simply dismiss as ludicrously pedantic. He was the epitome of what the Italians call *pignolo*, a word derived from the pine nut, which means someone obsessed—in Lowry's case joyfully—with the tiniest details. Once he pointed out to me that the word octodecillion was a "cardinal number represented in the US and France by a one followed by 57 zeros, but in Great Britain and Germany by a one followed by 108 zeros." Lowry was determined to find out why if it took him the rest of his life.

One night, a few years after I'd moved on from Yale to Occidental College, I returned to New Haven for a visit. Lowry had arranged Nathan Hale's room for me, now an alumni guest room in the oldest building on campus. But the room was available only for three days, and he insisted on my staying at his townhouse south of the main campus for my last night. Around two-thirty a.m., I heard a knock on my door. My heart was in my throat. I'd always wondered about Lowry's sexual proclivities. Was this the moment of truth? I shuffled to the door and opened it groggily.

"Do you feel like a cigar and a Cinzano?" he asked.

"Do you know what time it is?" I responded.

Minutes later, we were downstairs in his living room/den where I found a half dozen thick books opened and spread out on the floor. "What are you doing?" I asked him.

That afternoon we'd taken high tea with linguist Roman Jakobson, again at the Elizabethan Club, to which he and Lowry belonged. I recalled the barely crispy cucumber sandwiches. The two of them were deep into an argument about whether Estonian was closer to Latvian than Lithuanian.

"Roman..." Lowry said that night, puffing on his cheroot and gesturing to the books spread out on the floor. "...is wrong!" He insisted on "walking" me through it. I listened and sipped my Cinzano. "Well?" he said finally.

"Well what?"

"What should I do? Lithuanian is closer to Latvian than it is to Estonian. Which is what I always thought."

God help me, the Midwesterner in me came out. "Lowry, it's three a.m. You should go to bed."

Lowry's face went white. "I think if he's like me he would want to know right away," he said. "Shall I call him or not?"

"Not in the middle of the fucking night," I said. "No one is like you."

"I would want to know immediately if I were wrong," he mumbled to himself. The expression on his face was priceless.

"Call him in the morning," I said solemnly, and headed back to bed, leaving Lowry surrounded by his dilemma.

Lowry died in Estonia, still pursuing his truth, the death of a true polymath.

On another memorable night at Yale, I sat on a curb near campus commiserating with my mentor in Greek tragedy and comedy, Erich Segal (I was his TA [teaching assistant] in Greek Tragedy and Greek Comedy), who'd just received word that he was denied tenure. Not because he hadn't published enough—his book on Roman laughter and his anthology of criticism on Euripides were well received; but because he'd also published the bestselling novel *Love Story* and written "The Yellow Submarine" for the Beatles. The faculty weren't sure he was "focused enough" to be granted tenure at Yale. Another brilliant dilettante bites the dust due to academic insecurity!

At Georgetown, I'd studied Shakespeare under Raymond Reno and Elizabethan drama with Bernard Wagner, so I was well-prepared to expand my studies at Yale with Bart Giamatti on the Renaissance epic. One of my favorite courses of Bart's acquainted me with Castiglione's *The Courtier* and led me to fall in love with the concept of "the Renaissance man." Bart defined that as a person who wasn't afraid to explore every talent he was gifted with at the risk of being labeled a dilettante. Painter/sculptor/scientist Leonardo da Vinci, sculptor/painter/architect Michelangelo Buonarroti, poet/composer/King Henry VIII, and sculptor/architect Gian Lorenzo Bernini are just a few Renaissance men who defied "specialization." A dilettante to the world of the Medici was not only *not* a bad word, it was also laudable *aspiration*. Versatile in many things, the Renaissance man prided himself in doing all of them with enthusiastic and casual *nonchalance*–the Italian word *sprezzatura*. Somehow that struck a deep-down chord. I didn't have to be just a writer, just an editor, just a professor, just an *any one thing*. After taking Bart's course, I began to feel more and more at home at Yale–as I felt in the rice fields of South Louisiana and would feel in a lecture hall in Innsbruck, Austria, in a hut with Randy Borman near an iron-tinted stream in the Ecuadorian Amazon, at a podium at Villanova or at the University of Bologna, lecturing in Italian and science fiction in Trieste, or at Rome's Lord Byron Hotel marketing Bob Wald's *Freshhh!* orange juice.

Much later in life I would ask myself if I might have been more successful if I had focused on just one thing, like my upstairs neighbor on 49th Street, Dominick Dunne. But Dunne was drummed out of Hollywood by Bob Evans, and really had no choice *but* to concentrate on writing true crime. I've *always* had choices, and my divided mind was better and better at making them. When the Little Prince is asked if he wants to take a boat or a train, his answer is my lifelong answer: "Yes! I would like to take a boat and a train."

My most memorable moment with Giamatti during my Yale years was when I consulted him, a fellow Wilson scholar, about the subject of my doctoral dissertation. I proposed that my PhD thesis would compare the world views of Homer, Dante, and Joyce. He listened to me go on and on about it. "Atchity," he concluded, "do us all a favor and focus on just one of them. So you can get out of here and go on with your life."

Bart went on to become, first, Master of Ezra Stiles College, where visiting him for advice was like entering a contemporary Stonehenge; then the nineteenth and youngest President of Yale University, taking Kingman Brewster's place; while at the same time being a star of the New Haven Dance Company. Ultimately, he became Commissioner of Baseball and, heavy-heartedly, fired Pete Rose. I would later meet Pete when I produced one of my first inspirational entertainment programs, *Pete Rose: Reach for the Skies*. Ironically, my Yale mentor's disciplinary action against Rose destroyed my video's future.

Sitting in Bart's classroom in the Hall of Graduate Studies, I felt I was in the living presence of Castiglione. I invited him and his wife Toni and their rambunctious sons Paul and Marcus for dinner. The boys spent the evening jumping up and down on our living room couch while we, after my smothered chicken and maque choux, chatted at the table about literature, politics, and everything under the sun until midnight. Bart served as my mentor and friend for years after I left Yale, until his ridiculously premature death at fifty-one (a few days after kicking Rose out of baseball).

A few years after I switched careers from teaching to making movies and living in Montreal on leave from Occidental College, I bumped into Bart in the elevator of our beloved Yale Club in Manhattan. "Atchity, what's this I read about a professor of comparative literature producing romance movies?" he asked. *The New York Times* had done a spread on my *Shades of Love* film series.

"What's this *I* hear about the President of Yale becoming the Baseball Commissioner?"

"Touché," he laughed.

We proceeded to a most jovial breakfast, where I learned that his single complaint about the Yale Club was that it didn't serve fresh orange juice. Within a month, that had been remedied. I persuaded my then financing partner Bob Wald—I served as VP of marketing for Bob's new company *Freshhh!* Orange Juice in exchange for Bob's financing my romance film company—to install a fresh-orange-squeezing machine in the club's kitchen. Bart sent me a gracious thank-you note, now safely treasured in the Kenneth Aguillard Atchity Collection at Georgetown University Library.

Sterling Professor Thomas G. Bergin, Master of Timothy Dwight College, was known equally for his history of the Harvard-Yale Game, his scholarship on Dante, and his first translation of Petrarch's epic *Africa* from Latin into English. He and I bonded when I answered his question in our graduate class, "What is the most important thing to note about Dante's *Purgatorio?*" with the answer, "It's beautiful." It wasn't quite fair, because I was last in his semicircle to respond, and all my fellow students had said something profound or abstruse. In Tom's class on Provençal poetry, instead of following directions to parse the poems cited in the final exam, I translated one of them into English—the *Enueg,* "Complaints," by the Monk of Montaudon. It begins:

> *I hate to hear, if I dare say,*
> *a bungling butler chat all day;*
> *& he who would too gaily slay*
> *another galls me—& a headstrong bay.*
> *And they annoy me (as God knows):*
> *young men who hold their shields too close*
> *& will not risk receiving blows;*
> *monks whose beards conceal their toes;*
> *the jealous man's disjointed nose...*

Sharing evening martinis with Tom, whose 80+ published books included nearly two dozen published *after* he retired, were high points of my Yale days. He smoked Camels incessantly and for years after wrote to me faithfully, missives always posted with an Episcopalian saint's date. "Don't worry about money," he wrote to a financially-stressed younger me. "Money always comes." The sentiment baffled me at the time, and still does, though it's unaccountably proved true.

Another piece of advice from Tom Scheye turned out to be true: "Follow the man, not the course." The Male Authority Figures of this Yale island of the Lotus-Eaters made lasting impressions on me, and many of them remained friends and intellectual confidants for as long as they lived. As I contemplated my next book, I wish Lowry were around to discuss it with. He *always* encouraged me to pursue my wildest ideas, then made sure they made precise sense.

My last few months in Connecticut were another kind of blur. I was just getting used to Yale when the experience was coming to an end. Before I even turned in my dissertation, job offers poured in—from Cornell, Rutgers, Herbert Lehman College in New York, University of Delaware, California State University/Los Angeles, Occidental College, Trinity College Hartford. These offers I could discuss only with my faculty friends—my classmates that year received not a single offer among them. By my last year at Yale, I'd amassed a page-long resume of publications, including the book reviews I started writing at sixteen.

John Freccero, my "Modern Italian" prof, called me "an idiot" for not taking Cornell's offer. But after a freak blizzard that hit New Haven during a barbecue on May 6, I'd had my fill of snow and ice, and Ithaca seemed to me to be the North Pole. Besides, by then, I'd already taken the airport bus from Los Angeles International to the Huntington Sheraton in Pasadena, where Occidental professor and Chaucerian specialist Lewis Owen met me for an interview amid beds and beds of roses—and it was December in California. Though I've always been an ascetic in my work habits, I was always a hedonist at heart. The Golden State won that heart. California was like Louisiana, but without the oppressive humidity and proud provincialism.

California Bound

California, also known as the "Dream State," became my earthly Ithaka, my ultimate home on this zany planet, from which I would remain content to leave and return for more than half of my life.

I laid claim to being the first one of Jede's clan to go to college, to major in classics, to receive a PhD, the first to be divorced, and the first to be divorced twice, I would have loved to lay claim to being the first Atchity in California. Alas, that wasn't true. Cousin Bruce Prince-Joseph took his shot at Hollywood, living in an apartment in the Baldwin Hills despite the oil wells that populated

it like giant drinking birds. He found Hollywood too tough for him, which led him later to declare it "too superficial" when he cut down my client John Scott Shepherd to size at a luncheon he threw for us after the KC premiere of our *Joe Somebody* film.

Beautiful Aunt Lorraine and her husband moved to Orange Country to expand Uncle Dave Hake's "Victorian marble" empire, and later sloe-eyed cousin Pam and her jovial husband Mike Daugherty moved here too until they, too, threw in the towel and returned to KC.

My father's first cousin, Phil Koury, not only lived in Los Angeles but also worked for Cecil DeMille as his attorney for years; and even published a book about it, *Yes, Mr. DeMille* (which my Story Merchant Books re-published). Phil's son, Bill Koury, later a respected K.C. radiologist, was my classmate at Rockhurst High School. His signature validated the constitution of my pretend

Brush Creek country JKMARAO'RB. From what I gathered from Dad and Mom, Phil, like Bruce, got fed up with the film business and returned to the more conservative and economical pleasures of KC, where he practiced elder law with Hollywood laurels as his calling card.

The Kourys lived in a grand manor on KC's Rockhill Terrace that I was sometimes privileged to visit, and where I encountered Bill's beautiful sister Mary with whom I developed a Platonic relationship only out of sheer exuberance at being occasionally in her electrifying orbit. Like Uncle Anthony Prince, Phil Koury intrigued me. He too had an air of the world about him. I was careful never to admire anything of his out loud, though my eyes betrayed me when it came to his daughter. Their house was filled with rooms and passageways of all shapes and sizes, none out of range of the enchanting odor of Auntie Najeba's Lebanese bread.

Phil's mother, Najeba, was Tata's sister. She'd married Monsour Koury but moved to California when Monsour died and Phil and "Pum" (no one called his wife by her real name, Mary) moved to Hollywood. Tata's other sister, Essie, married Joe Kelly and gave birth to two penguins (what we called nuns in those days), Sister Mary Albina and Sister Mary Philomena. Mom always told us to "act normal" when the penguins came to visit, but that was hard considering the hard-nosed nunnish regime we were schooled under at St. Francis Xavier. I would stare at them from the corner of the room, wondering what it meant that my blood cousins had donned the holy robes.

Once landed in La-La Land, I and the kids regularly visited Auntie Najeba in her tiny white frame house on West Hobart

Boulevard, a neighborhood now known as Thai Town. "Would you like me to make you grape leaves," she asked, "or chili?"

"Yes," I answered. She was famous for both, and it's highly probable that Jede's chili con carne recipe traced back to hers.

Auntie Najeba never disappointed me, and always made both, with plenty left over to take home. I had to listen every time to the story of how the Virgin Mary saved her house from destruction during the last earthquake. Auntie had emerged from her bedroom to find that the statue on the living room mantelpiece had turned around to face the mirror! What more conclusive proof could any good Catholic ask? She evacuated the house immediately, moments before the quake struck.

When Phil and Pum moved back to KC to complete their children's education, Najeba had refused to leave miraculous Southern California.

I later came to see LA as Circe's island, where men could be turned into savage boars in the pursuit of dreams, pleasure, and fame. "If worse comes to worse," as a struggling actress friend once told me, "I'm happy now!" No wonder California was called "the Golden State."

Had the blur of my job-hunt turned into a physical fog? I wondered, that hot afternoon in late July 1970, when we passed a highway sign on the 10 that read, "Los Angeles 16." No. No, *this* blur was "smog." My heart sank. What had I brought my children to?

Although I'd driven from New Haven across country with sister Andrea and son Vincent, daughter Rosemary had flown ahead to Kansas City with her mother to visit my family before making the final leap to the Pacific coast. So I broke the road trip in the Heart of America, to reassemble my gang before embracing newspaper editor Horace Greeley's exhortation: "Go west, young man."

_____

Aunt Najeba's Chili

Ingredients:

4 lbs. ground round (sometimes I make it half & half with ground pork)

2 8-ounce cans Contadina tomato sauce

2-4 15-ounce cans of Goya black beans (or any good brand)— number based on how much you like beans in your chili

olive oil

jalapenos

2 large yellow onions, chopped

8 cloves garlic, chopped

chopped spicy red peppers (or you can use red pepper flakes)

1/3 cup black pepper

8 teaspoons paprika

6 teaspoons cumin

4 teaspoons cayenne

4 teaspoons chili powder

2 teaspoons salt

Tabasco sauce

16 ounces water or broth

Into the hot olive oil that fills your wrought-iron skillet at least to ½ inch, sauté onion and garlic until clarified—about five minutes.

Add your ground meat: cook, stirring and chopping, until the meat loses its red color.

Drain the fat well. Add remaining ingredients, the water or broth, and the beans, including the water they're packed in.

Bring to a boil; reduce heat, and simmer, covered, for at least an hour.

Occidental College

Occidental College, in Eagle Rock, was the next island I visited on my way to my earthly Ithaka (the West Side of Los Angeles)—after my childhood, alternating between the dread Cyclops' island of KC and Calypso's fondly mythic island of South Louisiana; my adolescence at Rockhurst High School, my Paris Island driven by Jesuit discipline; the Elysian fields of Georgetown; the lunar island of AT&T, and the Lotos Eaters' Island of Yale.

This new academic island, tucked between conservative Pasadena and midwestern-like Glendale, eight miles north of downtown LA, was an Alhambra of harmonious Spanish architecture and rose gardens guarded by stately and solemn eucalyptus—truly a grove of academe worthy of any artist's canvas. I would hold office hours on the quad, dragging my inquiring or petitioning or complaining or despairing student visitors on daily constitutionals among the roses—and wondering if Aristotle's peripatetic teaching was as rose-scented as mine.

On my ongoing quest for meaningful existence I'd moved to Oxy. During my seventeen years as a faculty member, I taught and challenged students and tilted with curriculum committees and faculty politics. Quickly I subscribed to Bernard Shaw's view: "If I should die, I would not like to attend any more meetings." To keep the spirit alive, I also followed Mark Twain's advice: "I never let my schooling interfere with my education." I continued to review books regularly, now for *The Los Angeles Times*, lectured on screen- and novel-writing at UCLA's Writers Program and at California State Los Angeles' graduate program where my course on research techniques was called "Shakespeare's 10 Worst Plays," founded and edited two academic journals, and started my own literary consulting firm. To occupy my summers with subsidized educational activities, I applied for and won grants from the Mellon Foundation, the National Endowment for the Arts, the National Endowment for the Humanities, The Graves Award; and published dozens of scholarly articles, hundreds of book and play reviews, and a half dozen scholarly books.

What I Know about Basketball arrived from Reynolds Bindery in the mail about a month after I broke my left femur playing a faculty pickup game at the Oxy gym. In the acoustically perfect gym, the break sounded like a loud firecracker going off. As I awaited the arrival of Doctor DeJohn and his morphine, "Just drag me off," I said to my team, "so you can go on with the game." "That's okay," Norman Cohen replied (professor of history specializing in Marxism and creator of the board game *Class Struggle*). "We'll move to the other court." So my basketball career ended abruptly, already comical because of my lack of height. My way was cleared for tennis.

Tennis: Partners

Something else I learned from tennis through the years. Switching from a partner with a strong will to win to one who says, "It's just a sport," I would not only lose, but start expressing negative body language when he blew his shots. I start blowing mine, too, no matter how hard I fight against it. Plus, he can tell from my body language that I am disheartened. I was depending on him; now he's letting me down. We generally lose.

Then one day not so long ago, I figured it out:

When dealing with a weaker partner, what can you do? Two things:

1) Take responsibility for winning upon your own shoulders and make your every shot count. Who knows, it may even inspire?

2) Support the losing partner when he or she does something right. Even when he/she loses a point, congratulate him for trying! That's why the pros do their hand-slaps, win or lose the point.

If neither strategy works and the partnership keeps losing regularly, it may be time to move on to a different partner.

Ya'ha'crut

Jede gave me a world history book in Arabic and had promised to teach me Arabic the next summer. But he passed away before next summer came, so I ended up learning only the few stray words I'd heard around his house: *teezak*, ass; *majdoube*, moron; *sa'tanyah*, keep eating; *zabr*, prick; *ya-habibi*, babe; and *Ya-ha'crut*.

I was clueless on that last word, until one day in Briarcliff Manor, at Cousin Bruce Prince-Joseph's house upon-Hudson. I'd been invited to another gathering of Hunter College professors, UN diplomats, and Bruce's fellow members of the New York Philharmonic where my distant cousin was first organist and second pianist; and where he and I collaborated on our choral symphony, *In Praise of Love*, that premiered in 1974.

Cousin Bruce introduced me to the Lebanese Ambassador to the United States.

The dapper diplomat asked me in Arabic if I spoke Arabic.

I shook my head and told him I wish Jede had lived long enough to teach it to me; but as it was, I knew only those five words.

At *Ya-ha'crut*, the ambassador's face froze, and Bruce's turned red with embarrassment. Then the ambassador let out a belly laugh that shook the room.

Bruce translated for me.

"Shithead." Not exactly a word for diplomatic parlors, though no doubt employed freely enough behind the scenes.

Recalling all those times I heard Jede mutter *Ya-ha'crut!* As he slammed down his phone, I vowed to learn Arabic someday—but never made it past Homeric Greek, Latin, French, Spanish, Attic Greek, *ein bisschen* German, Italian, Provençal, and household Japanese. I think it was a few weeks of Russian classes at Yale that did me in on Russian. After mastering the Greek alphabet, Cyrillic was one bridge too far—and I knew that I'd never make it through Arabic.

Defining Event Number Four:
Humming *In Praise of Love*

I was hanging out with Bruce Prince-Joseph quite a bit in those days, starting when I received a call from him out of the blue while I was studying theater history at Yale. He'd identified me as a long-lost cousin—who had also matriculated at Yale—and invited me to his stately frame house on a wooded hill east of the Hudson in Briarcliff Manor, nestled among the estates of Astors, Rockefellers, and Vanderbilts.

Bruce's name had been bandied about the Atchity household for years, mysteriously. No one seemed quite sure how he was related to us, though I think his mother Adele Prince was sister to Aunt Mary Prince, Uncle Anthony Prince's wife. Since Aunt Mary was Jede's cousin that made Adele his cousin too—or something like that.

One gorgeous spring day I made my way over to Briarcliff Manor, bringing Vincent and Rosemary with me because Bruce insisted he wanted to meet them. While they frolicked with us in his backyard pool, I learned that Bruce was a performing member of the New York Philharmonic. My imposter syndrome perked up its ears. Was this, like Georgetown and Yale, another opportunity for involvement over my head? Sure enough, Bruce told me that he'd always wanted to create something with a family member to celebrate Arab-Americans' contribution to American culture.

Until that moment I hadn't thought about being an Arab-American, didn't even know the category existed. Bruce showed me an Arab-American newspaper that suggested the opposite; and at subsequent parties introduced me to diplomats from the Levant. I pinched myself to be in such heady circles.

At one of Bruce's Sunday soirees, a distinguished guest bumped into a Ming vase in his living room. The whole party watched in horror as it toppled, then shattered on the floor. Without hesitating, Bruce elbowed the matching vase, which followed its twin to shards. "Don't worry about it," he assured the speechless guest. "I never really cared for those vases." Horrified gasps, followed by hearty laughs of relief, swept the room.

I loved him immediately.

Because we were both steeped in human expressions of love, we decided to collaborate on a choral symphony that I named *In Praise of Love*, combining my background in comparative literature and his in music. I would translate and compile the greatest literature about love from the beginning of time to the present, and he would set the book to music and make his conducting debut at Lincoln Center. I was too awestruck by the sudden appearance of a previously unknown Male Authority Figure in my life to think anything at all about the music. I mean, how often does a member of the New York Philharmonic offer to collaborate with you? I went to work on the book, translating, among others, an ancient Egyptian inscription and one of Pushkin's most romantic lyrics:

> *I loved you, and love, perhaps, has still*
> *Not wholly flickered out within me. But let it trouble you no*
> *more. I don't want to bother you at all.*
> *I loved you wordlessly, hopelessly,*

Consumed with shyness and with jealousy.
I loved you so honestly, so tenderly—
May God grant you be so loved by someone else.

I couldn't neglect Dante Alighieri, and included his little poem to Cino da Pistoia, in my translation from the Italian:

Love has been a friend of mine
Since I was a boy of nine.
I know how he pulls and pricks,
Making groans and laughter mix.

With him, Reason will prevail
No more than one voice in a gale
Can make cloud collisions cease
Or cause thunder to decrease.

So within Love's wide domain
Man's will is anything but free
And common sense is quite in vain.

I know he'll get the best of me
In the very next new lover's lane—
By now I'm far too weak to flee.

For the night of the premiere at Avery Fisher Hall, I'd invited Mom to fly out from KC to witness the excitement of it all. She and second-wife Circe wore gowns, I a tuxedo and 1960s academic beard. I performed my role as "Narrator" flawlessly, then proceeded to listen in growing consternation as the music unfolded. Bruce had asked that I *not* listen to it before the night itself and I, awestruck by my good fortune, complied.

Even though I'd relished my hours with *Washington Post* music critic Paul Hume, when I took his "Introduction to Classical Music" in the revered Healy Salon at Georgetown, I was no means a connoisseur. I just knew what I liked: all of Beethoven, a sprinkling of Mozart and Brahms, the most dramatic pieces from Wagner, Orff's *Carmina Burana* (because its stridency reminded me of my fanatic Catholic upbringing), Bach's Brandenburgs, Handel's *Messiah*, anything hopelessly romantic from Brahms to Rachmaninoff and Tchaikovsky, and most of all Stravinsky's *Petrouchka* and *Rite of Spring*.

Bruce's music wasn't anything like any of the above.

Maybe I just wasn't experienced enough to know how to judge it?

As I escorted my mother to our waiting limousine, I asked, "So, Mom, what'd you think?"

She gave me that look. "Do you honestly want to know?"

I nodded, half-heartedly.

"Let's get into the car first." When she was seated across from me, she whispered so as not to embarrass me in front of the driver: "Don't get involved with music you can't hum when you leave the theater."

She got that right.

Defining Event Number Four.

Her comment haunted me throughout my academic career, reappearing most strongly the day I lectured at the International Comparative Literature Association Annual Conference in Innsbruck, Austria, on "Narrative Strategies in the *Quixote*." And noticed that of the six young professors in attendance in the dimly lit classroom, one of them was sleeping and two others looked like they might nod off at any minute. I think it was that moment, coupled with the earlier non-hummable event, that made me realize it might be time to reconsider my career.

But that night in Manhattan we followed the Broadway ritual of waiting at Sardi's for the first edition of the newspapers to come in. *The New York Times* panned the evening mercilessly.

Mom gave me the wink.

My Cold Turkey

When I was twenty-eight, I stopped smoking cigarettes abruptly, overnight. I was in Florence, Italy, writing about Dante's *Divine Comedy* on a National Endowment for the Humanities grant.

The trip began in Rome, where, by chance, I met Yale *maestro* Tom Bergin at the Café Greco. Tom regaled me with stories of the writers he'd met there—from Ernest Hemingway to Dino Buzzati. But my favorite moment was with a total stranger at a trattoria near Stazione Termini, the day I took the Settebello to Firenze. I asked the waiter to bring me more bread even though I'd finished the last scrap of my *pasta fagioli*. He brought it without question, watched as I used the bread to scoop the remaining salsa from the plate. "*Fare la scarpetta,*" he nodded his approval with the ultimate accolade you can win from a Roman, imparting a tiny piece of wisdom, history, or advice to welcome me to the inner circle. I learned that *scarpetta*, the Italian word for "little shoe," colloquially meant "scoop" or "mop." The practice of eating with bread instead of utensils is pretty much universal in the Mediterranean.

A few hours later, I was on the train staring in awe at the ageless countryside dotted with vigilant cypress trees and ancient silver-leaved olives. I was sitting across from an Italian family, who looked nervous about something. Their daughter kept staring at me with her huge dark eyes and tried a smile. I smiled back. The father pulled her back, scolding, "Rosa Maria, *Lascia in pace l'uomo simpatico*, leave the nice man alone."

"*Ho una figlia di nome Rosa Maria*, I have a daughter named Rosemary," I said.

Their nervousness disappeared. They'd been trying to figure out if I spoke Italian. Once that was settled, we became best of friends. I shared heartily in their ample picnic—provolone, carpaccio, and scrumptious bread—and learned that they were from Lucca.

"Bonagiunta da Lucca," I nodded. I added that I was from Los Angeles.

Their eyes nearly popped out of their heads.

"You know Bonagiunta?" the man asked.

I nodded again. In Tom Bergin's Provençal class at Yale, I'd studied, along with Cino da Pistoia, Bonagiunta Orbicciani da Luca, he whose lyric prowess automatically enrolled him in what Dante called the *dolce stil novo*, "the sweet new style." I recited a few lines of Bonagiunta's, and they nearly fainted with joy. When I told them I was heading for Florence to study Dante Alighieri, their amazed expression rose to another level. "Why?" they wanted to know.

"Because," I said, "Dante is the most famous Italian poet in the world, *poeta l'italiano più famoso nel mondo*."

"Even more famous than Manzoni?" the man asked, astonished.

I nodded again and toasted him with the cup of Chianti he offered.

Exhilarated by the encounter, I rolled into Florence's Stazione Santa Maria Novella on cloud nine and bid them a fond farewell.

Walking out into the bright June air of the city of the Medici was a near-mystical experience. I inhaled the sharp smell of pines and espresso and felt like I'd returned to my birthplace. Years later, to my utter surprise, ancestry.com would tell me that I was 39% Italian and only 37% Lebanese, but that was nothing I knew that day in 1972 at the age of twenty-eight. Nonetheless, I *felt* I'd come home.

A week later I was fully acclimated to this enchanting city, the heart of the Italian Renaissance—the Renaissance which began, I liked to tell my Occidental classes, on the morning in 1321 when Dante died. Thanks to the two packs of Tareytons I was smoking every day, I was hard at work on the scholarly article, "*Inferno 7: The Idea of Order*," for which I'd received the grant, and which was later published in *Italian Quarterly.*

But, in this glorious city whose summer breeze dispelled all clouds of urban toxicity, I was tired of waking up every morning with a splitting headache and staring at the overflowing orangish brown crystal ashtray that Dad allowed me to take to college with me.

I walked down Via Galileo to the Ponte Vecchio to have a morning *semelle* and pick up my daily copy of the *International Herald Tribune.* The first thing that caught my eye was Russell Baker's column (I had reviewed his recent book for *The Los Angeles*

Times, which earned me a lunch with him at the New York City Yale Club). That day his column, entitled "I'm Back!" was about how he'd attempted to stop smoking and came down with writer's block.

That's it, I decided as I climbed the high staircase from the Arno to Via Galileo. *No more smoking for me!* Back at the studio on Costa di San Giorgio—two blocks from where Galileo lived—I picked up my favorite ashtray and the gold-plated alligator-skin cigarette lighter I'd bought in Bermuda on my honeymoon, trotted them down to the river, and unceremoniously tossed them in (*pace* my later-evolved eco-PC consciousness!).

I haven't smoked a single cigarette since. And I never stopped writing, by the way. Dad finally quit tobacco, too, though too late to save his life—that had literally gone up in smoke.

Willpower had not fallen far from the tree.

I didn't even evoke St. Jude. I simply said to myself, *If tobacco is my Muse, I don't need to be a writer anymore.*

Like that could happen.

You improve your habits by tricking your brain.

I *knew* that I could do it, as I later did with sleeping pills as well, because I saw my father do it with alcohol. Thank you, Dad.

My life as a professor was jam-packed with intensity and exploration, at least for the first sixteen years or so. I saw students as challenges and set out to make them live up to their potential. "I'm not teaching you," I declared. "I'm teaching your *best* you." I was notorious for giving Ds and Fs on the first midterm of a course, which got them front and center into my office with full attention. Each syllabus I presented to a new class started with my favorite quote from Oscar Wilde: "Education is an admirable thing, but it is well to remember from time to time that nothing worth learning can be taught." I made students grade themselves, reserving veto power. Putting them face to face with themselves this way I never had to exercise the veto. My favorite academic accolade would come only years later when I'd encounter them at graduations or alumni gatherings: "You woke me up more than any of my other profs. I hated you at the time, but I'm here to say I appreciate what you did for me."

During my teaching years I also won not one, but two Fulbright professorships. First, I was granted the award to teach in Zagreb, Yugoslavia, and began working on the rationalizations that would require. But before I could construct them, I was granted another Fulbright to teach American literature and culture at the ancient University of Bologna, founded in 1088, the oldest university in Europe if not the world. There was no hesitation over which to choose, and I was off to Italy again at the end of the next school year.

I landed in Bologna to discover a new island, of urban smugness, culinary pride, and *gente perbene*, "upright folk." Bogs, as I soon learned to refer to the northern Italian city, was more positively called *grassa e dotta*, "the fat and learned," since its cuisine was as famous as its educational history. I could walk nearly the entire twenty blocks from my apartment on Via Pietralata to the Facoltà di Magistero beneath the Renaissance *portici*, "galleries," that protected pedestrians from all-too-frequent rain. I showed up for the first time at the Facoltà di Magistero in September, assuming the school year would start when it did in Los Angeles. *Che scherzo!* "What a joke!" The *bidello*, the Italian equivalent of the "super" in Manhattan apartment life, told me, as

I stared at the empty classrooms and hallways, to "come back *più tardi*, 'later.'"

By the time October was about to end, and I'd shown up three more laters, the *bidello* and I had become quite friendly. He explained to me that the Italian school year consisted of six months, the months of two weeks, the weeks of two days, and the days of two hours. It was early November before I actually met my first class.

My office was next to that of master semiologist and bestselling novelist Umberto Eco, whose *The Name of the Rose* I would one day review for *The Los Angeles Times*. Umberto later wrote me that mine was the best review he'd read of the international phenomenon (Sean Connery would star in the film, after wearing a friar's wardrobe to his audition, as director Jean-Jacques Annaud told me in my interview with him for an LA arts paper). Meeting Eco was one of the highlights of a wonderful year, where I spent much more time on the piazza than in the classroom.

On Valentine's Day of that year, I arrived back to my modest marble-paved apartment on Via Pietralata from an exquisite dinner at Il Pappagallo. I'd compensated for my penurious Italian professor's salary by becoming a restaurant critic for *Bologna Incontri*, thereby earning free meals. I discovered a telegram awaiting me, from William Gerberding, Occidental College's Dean of the Faculty, advising me succinctly that I had been granted tenure, and promotion to Associate Professor.

I was thirty years old and didn't quite know what to make of it. Was I now to be defined permanently as "professor?" Is *that* who I really was?

On one hand, I knew I should celebrate and be grateful, and celebrating was never a thing I avoided. On the other, I felt a little weird because I'd never aimed at being locked in a golden cage.

For the last few years I'd organized and been an active participant in an organization called UFAT, "Untenured Faculty Against Tenure." Partly on principle and partly from observing many of our tenured colleagues' behavior and resumes, we UFATS believed that tenure destroyed incentive. By that time, I'd published more books, magazines, articles, and reviews than the entire faculty combined; I had no fear of competition.

But what's a man to do? Married, with two children from my first marriage, I could hardly turn tenure down.

Within days I was sinking into a nearly year-long depression that only at year's end, as I was emerging from it, did I trace to that telegram. I was married to a former graduate student, my second wife, Circe, and teaching a course called "Literature and Death," reflecting my mood that I was somehow feeling on the brink of death. Dying from suffocation again, I realized this time it was the suffocation of being covered by an academic security blanket of my own quilting. It was just another version of my childhood quilt that I had not set out consciously to need or desire.

I had learned that security was my father's highest value, but I'd come to understand that it was *not* mine. *Mine* was freedom, the freedom to test myself to the limit, the freedom to fail that my grandfather had considered America's greatest treasure. I knew even then that freedom is an *illusion*. But so is security—a fact borne out when academic institutions began laying off tenured faculty some years later.

I started, restlessly, to look around.

As my good luck would have it, I'd invited another MAF I hugely respected to speak in my "Death" seminar. His name was Norman Cousins, former editor of my favorite book review magazine *Saturday Review* and currently visiting professor of humanities at UCLA school of medicine. Class was at eleven a.m., and we were scheduled to lunch together at the Occidental Faculty Club after.

Norman sat around with my graduate seminar in a circle, commenting on humanity's love-hate relationship with death as expressed in my required reading: Carlos Fuentes' *The Death of Artemio Cruz,* Leo Tolstoy's "The Death of Ivan Ilyich," Ernest Hemingway's "The Short Happy Life of Francis Macomber," etc.— you get the gist. I was inspired by Norman's observations—based on his bestseller, *Anatomy of an Illness,* in which he'd reported how he'd taken charge of his own rehabilitation and used Charlie Chaplin and Three Stooges' films to heal himself of an intractable disease—with laughter. Norman wrapped up his remarks with a quote from an obscure Spanish philosopher that left me breathless with the excitement that only destined serendipity brings. I asked him if he'd mind stopping at my office on the way to the club.

There I showed him the same quote, which I'd framed and hung above my desk, from a footnote in José Ortega y Gasset's *On Love: It is immoral for a being not to live every instant of its life with the utmost intensity.*

Now fully bonded, Norman and I proceeded to a memorable lunch which ended with my preposterously begging him to let me visit him someday soon to ask him what "I should do when I grow up." He laughed gently, grinned, then asked me, "Do you play tennis?"

Do I play tennis!? I told him I was an avid organizer of the faculty's BBBTA, "Beer, Bread, and Bad Tennis Association."

Some years later I would film Norman and golf pro Jan Stephenson on his tennis court in Brentwood, for a sports pilot I created called, *BreakThrough!* about cutting-edge athletic achievement.

A few weeks passed, and I thought he'd forgotten my self-invitation. Then, one Saturday, Norman called to invite me to a doubles game at Bea Arthur's home in Mandeville Canyon—and to join him for brunch at his home afterwards. During the game, he, a recent Southern California transplant, marveled at the variegated forest surrounding her secluded court. "Are there any deciduous trees here?" he asked.

"A few, but most of them are still deciding."

My fortunate ad lib apparently cemented our bond—that and his immediate addiction to my then-printed (now internet) eclectic newsletter, "Door to Door," which he termed "an enormous ball of wax that goes around the world gathering up everything interesting." He dug my explanation of the newsletter's genesis: I was posting tidbits of wit and wisdom on my office door. When the door became covered completely, I took them all down and created the next instalment; then started with a fresh door. The true origin of "Door to Door," you might guess, was my high school Blue Book.

At Norman's hilltop brunch, I laid out what I'd done with my life until then and what I thought and dreamed I *could* do. He nodded with understanding when I reported how Paul Chance, editor of *Psychology Today*, had scolded me when I submitted our *DreamWorks Journal*, "dedicated to the relationship between dreams and the arts," for publication by his company. Chance's reaction to my co-editor Marsha Kinder's and my attempt to bring together the arts with psychological and medical studies of dreaming: "Find your niche, young man, find your niche!" One more authority figure, like Dean Ryf and President Gilman, who seemed frightened by my unbridled energy and refusal to *focus.*

Marsha Kinder, my *DreamWorks* co-founder, scoffed at Chance's response. After receiving her fourth or fifth edition of "Door to Door," Marsha dubbed me a *bricoleur,* an artist who develops his aesthetic from the bits and pieces of story he comes across. Later my first book editor and mentor, novelist John Gardner, would tell me I was "just plain nuts" to leave the security of the academic world—like Professor John Freccero, of Yale's Italian Department, calling me "crazy" for not jumping on the job offer from Cornell.

Defining Event Number Five

But Norman Cousins had a completely different, and delightful, reaction to my confession of my wide-angle profile: "Whatever you do," he said, "don't ever let go of your diversity. It's your defining characteristic." He thought of it as a positive. I loved that! It didn't intimidate him or make him "frightened." Just when I'd been getting used to considering my eclecticism one of the skeletons in my closet.

You can't imagine how great that made me feel.

He told me to consider entering the world of entertainment.

I laughed. I knew nothing about Hollywood. He rose and took a book from his well-stocked shelves, William Goldman's *Adventures in the Screen Trade*. He opened it to a dog-eared page and handed it to me. I read the words "Nobody knows anything..." The die was cast.

If entertainment was a level playing field, I was ready to play. Suddenly I faced my future with exhilaration instead of dread. My restlessness and inclination toward professional storytelling—instead of academic story analyzing—began to increase at an accelerated pace.

Gathering Moss

With the exception of that post-tenure depression, it shouldn't surprise that my depths of despair opened widest around money. Growing up Atchity-American meant that existential identity was mostly defined in monetary terms. My father's familiar refrain, "He ain't got a pot to piss in," was the ultimate indictment of failure.

It wasn't until years later that I realized that, no more than *security*, pissing into a pot was definitely *not* an aspiration of mine. Where I pissed was never as important as where I *wrote*. And, like Gilroy, I learned to write everywhere.

Not to mention the proverb that usually followed: "He's been living too high on the hog." Living high on the hog, at least in Mom's South Louisiana, meant dining on the most expensive upper parts of the pig. I realized I was safe in my love for bacon, which is *not* an upper part for sure. I didn't quite understand why anyone would want to live hog high.

Any more than I understood what Dad told me a few years later when I returned from that year's leave of absence from Occidental when I'd taught for a year in Italy for a fraction of my normal professor's salary.

"Are you back for a while now?" he asked.

"Yes, Dad."

"Do you think you got that out of your system?"

"Got what out of my system?"

"Foreign travel."

"I suppose so," by then figuring out the answer the retired Cyclops wanted to hear and focusing on curtailing the conversation.

"A rolling stone gathers no moss," he concluded.

"Hunh," I said thoughtfully, not knowing what else to say. Maybe Jede's fear of traveling to the Old Country had been imprinted in my father, whose only experience of Europe had been the Great War.

I ran the proverb back and forth through my mind. Was gathering moss, in this metaphor, a *good* thing? As in, if this Odysseus stopped rolling, that's what I'd do? Gather moss? Was I over-thinking this? It seemed to me that rolling was good, that being moss-free was my ideal, though apparently not his.

There was no moss on that rock Sisyphus kept rolling back up the hill. His determination didn't give it time to grow.

But now I understand that, in the logarithm of Dad's mind, "moss" was "money." Gathering money was a good thing. The more money, the happier and more successful. It was that simple: Keep a cash cushion against "a rainy day."

But Mom never let me buy into that equation. Because of her constant litanies that began with, "All he cares about is money," I learned to create my values in other directions—travel, creativity, publication, production, storytelling, and, yes, self-realization. Plus, I always loved standing out in the rain. Plus, it "never rains in southern California." I never had an emotional crisis over any of these alternatives; they were just challenges to overcome along the way. Ironically, and more or less unconsciously, my mother was molding me to do what she could not bring herself to do because of her Depression-child's anxieties over money.

Then I realized, by living long enough and paying more attention—with the added objectivity of distance (I was either on the east coast or the west coast, and as a frequent flyer knew full well that the repeated admonition, "Why don't you stop in Kansas City on your way," was a meaningless mantra; airline routes being what they are)—that my dear mother didn't distance herself from money at all. After all, she'd left her simple country roots to marry an Atchity and live in the big city. And, as years passed, and Freddy, Jr. became more and more financially successful, I noticed that Mom's visits to California were heavily weighted in his direction. Who wouldn't rather stay in his Hancock Park or La Quinta mansions than in my more modest penthouse apartment?

Finally I realized the strangest thing of all: She'd stuck with Dad all those years. They were a few years from their fiftieth anniversary when he died. If she hated him and his attachment to money so much, why did she hang around?

As for me, the espresso grinds had spoken clearly: I would shape my life with creative achievement, projects completed, rather than money in the bank. In fact, as long as I could keep a few hundred bucks, crumpled or not, in my pocket, I'd walk away from the ATM whistling a line from a Jingle-Jangle-Jingle Tex Ritter song I heard as a kid, "A dollar worth of beans, a new pair of jeans." By now I trust you know whose beans I thought of when I sang.

My head was so full of the next dream to be made real that I saw money only as the means to my creative ends and didn't need the security that money ultimately represented for my father's family.

Or so I thought until I realized finally that having a little financial security was okay. Nor was there a rule that said I wasn't entitled to it as much as my brother. In fact, I learned that partly from my brother.

Freddy's oft-proclaimed vision was that he wanted to have enough money to live in a mansion on a hill with a ten-foot wall around it and the words "Fuck you!" inscribed on the outside of the wall.

Nice, Freddy!

Freddy didn't like rejection. That's what money does to you?

My vision was different. I wanted enough cushion so that I could, at any given moment, escape the pressure of my own energy and take a nap. By the age of sixty I'd finally learned to nap, simply by waiting until I was dead tired and then reciting Am's mantra, "I love to sleep, sleep is my friend..."

Let Your Father Win

On that stop in KC to hook up with the kids en route to LA, I came up with a way of communicating with my father that was brilliant in its obviousness:

Instead of talking, which had never gone well, I'd invite him to listen to music (as we did when we drove from Las Vegas to KC) or play cards. It worked beautifully, father-son bonding without any attempt or need to go beneath the surface. Or any need to communicate more than an occasional grunt.

Remember that gaming was the safest way of communicating in my family. Ritualized competition, quips permitted, but no serious exchange of views or feelings—all masked in the humor of bluff and bravado.

The two of us were sitting in the breakfast room on 75th Street playing gin rummy, and all was hunky dory. As I went through the motions of the game, I noted, for the umpteenth time, how absent-minded Dad was—a characteristic I've inherited to some degree. I prefer to call it "preoccupied."

The phone rang. It was one of his tenants, calling about a plumbing problem in the duplex he rented on Lister Avenue. Dad was concentrating on the phone call. I had nothing to do but shuffle the cards.

I decided to conduct an experiment. Without attempting to hide my actions, I stacked the deck. Perfectly. So that, when he hung up and I said, "Cut," handed him the cards, and finessed the cut before his eyes, I dealt my father a perfect gin hand.

I casually arranged my cards; he quickly arranged his. That familiar perplexed look glazed his eyes for a moment—I could hear the cogs turning—before he looked at me and said, "Gin!"

"You've *got* to be kidding me. No way."

He laid his cards down. "No, I'm serious. See for yourself."

I started laughing.

He didn't get it.

"Dad, I stacked the cards," I said.

"You did not," he said.

"I did—right before your eyes."

Excited by his good fortune, he refused to believe me. I decided not to deprive him of the triumph I'd covertly arranged and took the loss.

Let your father win?

Fortunately, we were playing our usual "tenth of a cent a point" (as opposed to my brother's ten cents a point game). The reverse con game ended with Dad making an annotation of what I owed him in his little black book.

Immoral Producer

By 1987, when I left my tenured position at Occidental College, I was living in an enchanting 1930s Spanish colonial house on Escarpa Drive, overlooking the campus—with a view of the entire skyline of Los Angeles. Owned by a dear colleague in Religious Studies. The kind professor had followed *his* bliss and transplanted himself to Japan, so needed someone to take care of his LA homestead. Always in awe of his house with its arboreal and horticultural splendor, I was thrilled at the opportunity.

I thought of the house on Escarpa Drive as my Circe's island, because my second wife introduced me to the place and presided over it on the distaff side. Two cypresses flanked the front door like sentinels, and a rambunctious gang of beavertail cactus guarded the street entrance. Despite its terraced and fern-lush gardens, and trees of every species from palm to pine that thrived in our prolific subtropical climate, the wife I lived with there was an enchantress whose spells were not, God bless her, reserved only for me. But before I knew all that, my farmer's green thumb ever eager for use, I planted gardenias near the bedroom patio, honeysuckle on the flat-stone walls, and neon-purple bougainvillea to greet me every morning west of my sprawling office whose picture windows framed the Downtown LA view. I added to the eighty or so trees my own choices—apricot, tangerine, lemon, kumquat, and lime.

"Are you sure?" Mom asked me on a visit to what was now my bachelor quarters. I'd just broken the news to her that Circe had been banished. We were getting divorced. My mother repeated the question three times, like the Sanhedrin grilling St. Peter.

"Yes," I told her.

"Then this is the best thing you've done in ten years," she declared. Apparently, no love had been lost between them.

Circe exiled, I hosted a farewell party for myself before leaving for the unknown islands of my new career in entertainment. I invited the entire Occidental faculty of 113. Most of them came— even Dean Robert Ryf, who I'll never forget because he reviewed my ten-page annual report one year and asked me to his office to tell me, "You scare me to death. How long can you maintain this energy?"

"I have no idea," I said. "Why?"

Amid the merriment one of my Occidental "best friends," History prof John Rodes, approached me after a drink or two to demand, "So, how does it feel to be an immoral producer?"

"Gee, John..." I wish I'd said, "pretty much the way it felt to be an immoral professor."

Besides, of course, I didn't feel like a producer at all. I was just a guy trying to get something done in an environment where "nobody knows anything" and achievement takes on ethereal dimensions of nebulousness.

John admitted that his question came from seeing a headline in Friday's *Hollywood Reporter*: "Occidental Professor Announces Romance Film Series." He asked me, "Is that really true?" and I responded that the announcement was true, that I did hope and plan to produce a romance series. He looked me in the eye and asked accusingly, "Was this article legitimate or did you arrange it?" Sounded like a trick question to me, so I remained silent. "So you've become one of those people who mistake hope for reality?" he concluded and turned to head back to the bar.

I think I was supposed to feel bad about that, but the following Monday, I received an offer from Lorimar Home Video to finance my "contemporary romance" project—my proposed eight films, which would evolve into an additional eight. In my mind, the publicity I planted led to the deal. Dreams become reality because dreamers insist on it. That's how it works. I would come to realize that the difference between a con man and a visionary in Hollywood is simply success.

But how to explain all that to an academic colleague? If you have to explain it, you can't. I was learning to accept that not everyone is blessed with the entrepreneurial mindset.

In the past twenty years, I'd learned to look askance at the academic world for its fear of expanding horizons. I was beginning to experience that all-too-familiar feeling of suffocation. Occidental had become my career quilt. No wonder President Gilman called me to his office to discuss the complaint that I was running an off-campus poetry magazine, reviewing for the *Los Angeles Times*, and consulting at the Pasadena School Unified District—and accused me of being "entrepreneurial."

With my father-brother back-myth and my entrepreneurial Lebanese grandfather, seeing business as the Promised Land might have seemed inevitable at some point.

Speaking of the Promised Land, a few years before resigning from Occidental, I opened my own consulting office in Glendale, up a flight of stairs, like Dad's erstwhile income tax office, and called it L/A House, a "full-service literary firm" that offered editing, research, translation, and publishing services, with clients that included the Getty Museum and the United States Postal Service. I loved our palm tree/setting sun logo, designed by brother-in-law Rick McKeown, Andrea's husband. Rick always said, "Your dreams begin as stationery." I'd nod and add, "And die as scrap paper."

Working at my L/A House office one evening, I received an extraordinary call—from the State Department in Washington. A Middle Eastern diplomat was in the states wishing to visit with "an American of Middle Eastern descent who was involved in both business and the arts." Someone, in those pre-Google days, found me—publishing a poetry quarterly (*CQ: Poetry and Art*), an arts rag in Pasadena, and a literary journal about dreams and the arts (*DreamWorks*), all while teaching full time and running my little entrepreneurial literary clearinghouse on the side.

A few days later, the cultural attaché from Jordan showed up at my office in a black Lincoln town car with government tags, and a Diplomatic Security Service driver/bodyguard. We spent a pleasant hour or so together as he asked me questions and I explained what I was up to. At the end of our visit, he concluded: "You are following in the footsteps of your Phoenician ancestors. You're a story merchant."

I was thrilled. Here was another Male Authority Figure sent from the Levant, a bona fide Wise Man from the East, to not only

THE STORY MERCHANT

approve of what I was doing but also to give it a name. The Phoenicians, among the west's first traders, also brought with them, in their fast ships, the alphabet—making it easier to trade stories along with their other wares. Much later I adopted this ancestral motif as the first logo of my Story Merchant company. The letters on the sail aren't, as one would-be client concluded, "Masonic runes." They're the first and last letters of the Phoenician alphabet—which influenced both the Hebrew and Greek alphabets. Later, the logo got simplified.

As the academic world persisted in oppressing my irrepressibly free-lance mentality, I looked around one day and realized I couldn't identify anyone among the sixty-year-olds on the Occidental faculty that I wanted to be like when I grew up. I told myself I wasn't cut out to remain on campus all my life. I was the accidental academic.

A big fish in a small pond doesn't die of suffocation.

It dies of ennui.

But for now it was either receive tenure or resign, and at the age of thirty-one with two young children, I wasn't prepared to resign yet. After all, I actually taught only six hours a week, thirty weeks a "year," giving me plenty of time, including entire summers, to do "something else." For as long as the telephone would allow me, I kept one foot in academia, the other out the door.

Sic Transit

My transition from the orderly gardens of Occidental College to the jungle wilderness of the entertainment business was one of the scariest rollercoaster rides I've ever experienced. The twelve months that followed the article in *Variety* were exactly the nightmare my dreams had brought on me. Warner Brothers/Lorimar offered me a fifty percent guarantee for *eight* movies in the series I called "Shades of Love." All I had to do was to find the other fifty percent financing within six months (after

233

which they would withdraw their offer). Aye, there was the rub. I came close to succeeding three times, but each time the deal fell through. I was over-extended and freaked out month after month, but boy was I alive.

My brother bailed out on his investment in L/A Romances but brought in his partner Bernie to recoup him. When I asked Bernie's advice on how to get out of the mess I'd gotten myself into, he studied the situation carefully and concluded: "Ken, let's put it this way. At this point, continuing is your only option." Stay in the nightmare, he was saying, until you wake up to a happy ending.

A week later, which was a week before my six months with Warner was up and, believing that my ship was about to sink, I got a phone call from a distributor in Montreal named Stephen Greenberg. His father Harold was head of Astral Bellevue Pathe. "I heard about your romance series," he began.

I was too stunned to respond.

"Is your guarantee from Warner still in place?" he asked.

I nodded. Then I had the presence of mind to actually answer. "Yes," I said, "although it's about to expire."

"We'd like to partner with you," he said. "And provide the balance of the financing."

When? I wanted to say, wondering how much longer I could hold out but feeling the morsel of hope he was offering knew I could hold out as long as I needed to.

As though he could hear my thoughts, Stephen said. "Can you catch a flight up here tomorrow?"

Running on Empty

I've always pushed the envelope, whether by seeing how long the hydrangeas would last between waterings (and losing a few along the way) or seeing how far I could drive on "empty."

My uncanny success karma was in full manifestation on my first visit to Montreal in this last-ditch attempt to save the *Shades of Love* project. The gods of credit were smiling on me though seven of my eight credit cards were already maxed out. By maxing out my last American Express, I was able not only to fly to Montreal, but even to make a reservation at the elegant and prestigious Four Seasons on Sherbrooke. *After all*, I thought, *I can't have Mr. Greenberg calling me at a Motel 6!* Fake it till you make it, right? I was running full speed on Experian fumes.

After a restless night, I grabbed a taxi at eight-thirty in the morning to the Montreal industrial suburbs. As we pulled up in front of Astral headquarters, I had a sudden sickening realization. My billfold was not in my pocket. I was indeed at the end of my financial resources! Asking the driver to wait a sec for the eighteen Canadian dollars plus tip that I owed him, I walked through the glass doors of Astral literally dead broke. There I found a heavy-set and jolly woman at the reception desk. The Astral gatekeeper was the Fat Lady!

"I'm here for a nine o'clock meeting with Stephen and Harold," I explained. "But I'm embarrassed to say I left my billfold in my hotel room." (I certainly hoped I'd left it there—and that no one would come to clean the room before I got back). "So I have no money for the taxi."

She smiled and, without batting an eye, handed me a $20 note with Queen Elizabeth smiling serenely at me.

"Thank you," I stammered. "You are a lifesaver! I will pay you back later today! What's your name?"

Her name was Edith. "Don't worry about it," she said. *I've now heard the Fat Lady sing*, I thought.

Turns out her name was Edith *Greenberg*. She was Harold's wife.

Two hours later, I was shaking hands with the legendary Harold Greenberg to seal the deal, not forgetting to include in it a provision that Astral would also cover the $28,000 legal bill I'd amassed in the hair-raising past twelve months. Stephen walked me to the door, then said, with a wink, "I'll give you a ride back to your hotel."

Thank God! I was still flat broke.

I found the billfold under my bed—money lost, money returned—and sent Edith a bouquet of flowers with the $20 dollar bill and my profuse thanks.

We were heading for production of eight movies born from my dream that Professor Rodes had scoffed at as not "legitimate." I would be making $250,000 a year, more than four times what I'd received on my highest-paid year as a professor. No risk, no gain!

A few weeks later I was closing the L/A House Romances development office on Victory Avenue in Burbank and turning the key in the front door of my Escarpa Drive home. I felt like Atlas having Earth lifted from his shoulders. My stay on Circe's island was ended, and my flying carpet was waiting to take me to my next horizon.

Returning in Triumph

As I looked out the porthole of Air Canada business-class to Montreal (charged to someone else's credit card!), the lines from Christopher Marlowe's *Tamburlaine* sounded in my brain—as though Professor Wagner were himself reciting them:

...and ride in triumph to Persepolis...

On that second flight to Montreal, I allowed myself to breathe deeply the elation I was feeling. *A Writer's Time*, my first book on writing (still in print 35 years later), had just been published and I felt I was walking across a bridge between careers. Walking down Sherbrooke to my production vehicle a few days later, I dropped a wad of money on the sidewalk and a passerby had to alert me. I chuckled as I picked it up. In my driving focus on making dreams real, money could come and go.

But I did enjoy the performance of Astral's astute head of business affairs when Sam Berliner allowed me to sit in his office while he "settled" with my big LA law firm, warning me with a finger to his lips to remain silent while he worked on the hapless accountant at the other end of the line. The $28,000 bill was reduced to $12,000 and Sam winked at me.

The same morning, Tracy, my loyal assistant who I'd sent to Montreal ahead, and I faced an empty field while camera assistants measured its length and width. "What are they doing?" Tracy asked.

"I have no earthly idea," I said. "But let's use silence to cover anything we don't understand until we figure it out."

Which we did. They were measuring the field to determine how long it would take the horses to gallop across it so they could set the cameras correctly. Two months and two finished movies later, we felt like veterans as we handled every question thrown at us by various members of the crew. I was watching the dream become a reality. Plus, I would get to play a bit part in all the films—a bartender in *Make Mine Chartreuse,* a priest on a motorcycle in *The Emerald Tear,* a homeless person the leading lady greets in *The Garnet Princess.*

When the fourth film went into production, *Sincerely, Violet* (starring the aristocratic Simon MacCorkindale), I was to play a professor of graphology visited by the leading lady to determine if she should entertain his courtship. But a crisis occurred in the production office that day, and I had to phone the director to shoot the scene without me. He reported that he already had.

Two things had occurred that made me realize I'd reached a turning point. So happy were they with the rough cut of the first two films we'd shot, *Lilac Dreams* and *The Rose Café,* that Lorimar renewed our series. We were to shoot another eight films *next* year. Which led me to request a second year's leave of absence from Occidental. Which led Oxy's president to write me that the extension was granted but I had to decide whether I would for sure be coming back to my faculty position or would release it so the Comparative Literature department could plan accordingly.

"You can't even be a *pretend* professor," assistant Tracy pointed out when I missed my "call" on *Violet.* I realized it was time to resign my tenure at Occidental to pursue the least secure profession I could imagine, working in the commercial story marketplace of books and films.

I was evolving into the Story Merchant.

In the late eighties, the US economy was faltering. I rationalized that the "security" of tenure might be an illusion anyway. I reasoned that "freedom" might very well be an illusion as well, but it was, in the final analysis, the illusion I personally preferred. Freedom was *my* illusion. Mine were the very opposite of my father's values and, I would later realize, of my mother's as well.

My daughter Rosemary, whose final year at Columbia might have been affected by my leaving the Occidental faculty (one of my benefits was full tuition for my children), was very clear when I consulted her opinion. "Go for it!" echoing my mother's long-familiar mantra.

A few years later, after the *New York Times* article appeared, popular psychologist Dr. Joyce Brothers interviewed me for her television show. She thought it was unusual to hear that a tenured professor had given up security for an uncertain future. The segment ran, and I was fascinated to see that I looked and talked like I was much more focused than I felt. What *did* impress me was a seventy-year-old businessman who'd enrolled at Loyola law school at the age of sixty-five and was now practicing law. When he was standing in the registration line at law school, a youngster behind him tapped him on the shoulder, and asked, "Sir, are you sure you're not standing in the wrong line?"

"What line should I be standing in?" he asked the young man.

Relativity

After the grave fears he'd expressed when I declared a classics major at Georgetown, Dad had grown used to his oldest child being a tenured professor at Occidental College. Though he never admitted it to me, he expressed his pride to others, like Bill Reynolds, who loyally reported it when I visited him on trips back to KC.

My father had grown used to the idea that I would receive a regular paycheck until I retired, and then would receive pension checks for the rest of my life afterwards. No doubt that comforted him, even though those checks would never be astronomical. (They were, I realized later, larger than any checks he'd received from his jobs, but somehow that never came up—maybe because he, like me, always had income "on the side.").

Then, ironically, the same scenario repeated itself.

Calling from Montreal, I told him I'd given up my tenured position on the Occidental faculty. I was making movies, liked it, and decided, with a little pressure from the College to make up my mind, to commit myself to the least secure life imaginable, a life in publishing and entertainment with no guarantees or retirement plans.

"What are you going to do for a living?" was the way he put it on that call from Montreal.

But then he came up for that visit to the shoot, saw the two hundred+ people milling around making *my* movie—got to be one of them—and must have changed his mind.

"Your dad was proud of you," Bill Reynolds reported, at Dad's funeral. "Keep producing movies. He approved."

Dad just had a hard time saying that directly to me. Maybe it never occurred to him that a father should tell his son he's proud of him.

Dad's Camera Call

The day before we started shooting *The Rose Café*, I got a rare call from my brother, the first one in over a year. "I thought you were an executive producer," was his skip-the-small-talk greeting.

"I am," I answered hesitantly, alarmed that maybe he knew something I didn't.

"What kind of an executive producer are you?"

"What do you mean?" I asked, immediately on the defensive only he could put me on. Did he know I didn't have my name stenciled on my parking place yet?

"You're up there producing movies and you haven't even invited your father to come up and appear in one."

"I don't think Dad approves of my career change," I answered petulantly.

"Don't be stupid," Freddy replied. "He's proud of you."

"Anyway, you have no idea what a hassle that would be. AFTRA (American Federation of Radio & Television Artists) is strict, and it's already bad enough that *I'm* an American in this purportedly Canadian production."

"What's an aftra? As I said, what kind of an executive producer are you?"

He hung up.

A week or so later, Dad and Mom, along with my cousin Tony's widow Pedia, flew up to join me in Montreal for a few days.

They loved visiting the lakeside location of *The Rose Café*; then the downtown urban setting of *Champagne for Two* in downtown Montreal which was doubling for New York.

The night before Dad's appearance as an extra in *Champagne*, Mom and Pedia were asleep in the guest bedroom and my father and I were in the living room—he watching television, I talking on the phone with the production office about the ominous weather forecast for the next day.

It was after midnight. My father stayed up late; I did so only under the duress of being producer. Between my hang up and the next insistent ring of the phone, Dad said, "Where's the script?"

"What script?" I asked.

"The script for the movie I'm appearing in tomorrow." He looked at me like I was insane.

"Dad, you don't have to read the script. You're just *appearing*. You're not *saying* anything. There's nothing to prepare."

Pulling Canadian strings and arranging for waivers, I'd managed to set it up with director Lewis Furey that Dad would play "the bagel salesman" in front of whose stand the leading lady and her girlfriend were to pause after they exited their office in the Montreal Stock Exchange.

Maybe because I winced growing up each time Dad used "jew" as a transitive verb, I savored the irony of him appearing as the Jewish street food salesman in front of a building filled with money.

"I still think I should read the script," he said, sounding every bit like every would-be Hollywood actor.

But he was my father. What could I do? I called the production office, open 24/7, and asked them to messenger the latest script over, by snowshoe if necessary, ignoring the blizzard that had announced its arrival with a sudden dump of snow (This was Montreal, what else was new?). The script arrived in a few minutes.

As I telephoned into the wee hours, Dad sat on the couch, smoked, drank coffee, and read. Finally, I saw him close the script.

He looked a little sheepish. "Well?" I asked. "What do you think?"

"I think I should have some lines," he said. "At least one line. I don't have any lines."

"Of course, you don't have lines, Dad. You're not an AFTRA-enrolled actor. You're on a courtesy waiver. You can't have spoken lines. It presents a whole new level of problems for the production."

"I still think I should have at least one line," he said, shuffling off to his bedroom.

Θ

By the next morning I thought I'd mollified his artistic ego. I drove him, Mom, and the lovely Pedia to the set and watched them deploy into the fringes of the crowd to watch the action.

Next thing I knew I could see my father wearing a tacky baseball cap and tending an authentic-looking concession stand. I didn't see the scene being shot, distracted by director Lewis coming over to suggest I walk my mother across the street during the preliminary "establishing shot," where we "establish" the Stock Exchange before the leading lady exits to the bagel stand. I followed the director's orders, so Mom and I are there for all to see jousting with fake traffic ("picture cars") for a few brief seconds.

The next morning, my father had nothing to say about the experience, other than a "thanks for having us up" as I drove them to Dorval for the return trip to KC.

But several weeks later, after the movie was wrapped and we were in postproduction, I received a call from the director. "You might want to come to the editing room today," Lewis said. "We're editing your father's scene."

I laughed, and said I'd bring some bagels. Imagine my surprise when I watched on the editor's monitor as the actresses approached the bagel stand and started speaking to the bagel salesman. "We'd like one bagel each," the leading lady said.

"Onion or garlic?" Dad the bagel salesman replied.

I looked at Lewis. He smiled back. "I thought your father should have a line," he said.

When I asked him whether my father had put him up to this, like a true French-Canadian gentleman he refused to disclose the details of the transaction that led to my father's one and only motion picture speaking role.

In this unexpected way, my wacky life had led me to create my own father-son video. More on that to come.

Θ

Shades of Love was the most unrealistic introduction to the entertainment business fate could ever have designed, because it made me think this kind of thing was the norm.

It wasn't. After producing sixteen romance movies, two years later I closed up the house on Escarpa I returned to LA to face a Writer's Guild strike on the heels of a stock market crash. I was too naïve about it all to comprehend what the impact on business as usual would be. But my bank account understood and finally drilled it through my thick head. I'd been spending confidently, building L/A House, planning new romance series. Taking loans when necessary. Making promises.

Then revenues slowed to a trickle. And things got worse. I became a private career consultant and writing teacher. I held classes in my living room, worried about the rent and the debts I'd blithely contracted. I scraped by.

Things went from worse to hopeless.

That's when Dad surprised me. He had just, deftly, pumped enough answers out of me to assess my situation. "I don't understand why you don't declare bankruptcy," he declared.

I was thunderstruck. My accountant father, the rock of business propriety, was suggesting an option I thought he considered abhorrent.

"I'm serious," he continued. "I hate to see you under this kind of pressure. That's what bankruptcy is for."

In retrospect, I'm sure my father wished he'd had the nerve to go bankrupt when he lost his job at the brewery. It might have avoided his nervous breakdown.

I told him I truly appreciated his saying that. His permission made me feel like a mountain had been removed from my shoulders. He had given me a pin big enough to unravel my suffocating quilt. I told myself I would do what he suggested if I was unable, one way or another, to maintain my payments, keep my creditors at bay, and rebuild my cash flow. As it turned out, I managed to pay off all but one of my creditors or investors off in the next five years—that last one took ten.

And never had to go for the big B.

I've always preferred, and managed, to pay for my dreams, in fair exchange for a life modeled on my imagination. The deeper the hole, the greater the relief at having filled it.

But it was a real eye-opener that my father condoned it. And that he was that concerned about his estranged son.

Patience and Escape

"You're the most patient man I know," someone tells me at least once a week. "Patience is my middle name," I reply. "It's also my first name and my last name." The biblical Job was a piker compared to me.

I've often sold books I developed into movies after ten years of trying, sometimes even longer. *The Meg*, which grossed over half a billion dollars worldwide in 2018, made it to the screen twenty-two years after I started developing and selling it. *Angels in the Snow* took twenty years before the cameras rolled, *The Lost Valentine* twelve.

I've sold books to publishers years after even their own authors forgot about them.

I learned that patience is the root of accomplishment. It can be a bitter root unless you turn it sweet. People who aren't particularly effective often lack patience; they simply can't wait around long enough to see a beleaguered merchant ship come in. With patience, the quest for accomplishment can end only in success. Without patience, it almost inevitably ends in failure—which requires escape and disentanglement: another undoing of the quilt.

What can make patience bitter is the energy spent agonizing while you wait, begging for that "envelope in the mail," the "Greenlight!" phone call, that good news email, watching the horizon for arriving guests, over-nagging your prospective buyer to decide.

What turns patience sweet is finding something else to do while you're waiting.

So, I patiently saved my two dollars a week, spent the weeks productively studying, working at the grocery store, perfecting my altar, fighting with Freddy, avoiding Dad, trying to figure out girls— and before I knew it, it was May again— and I could head off to Louisiana.

Patience, work, reward. Definitely a life pattern. I had to laugh when I first ran across James Joyce's diary notation: "Silence, exile, cunning."

When the tennis ball comes to you, get it into the other person's court. That's all you must do to keep the game going. Do something else until the ball comes back to you.

Sooner or later some of those "something else's" become successful and you've created a win-win scenario. You don't have to be a perfect player to play a good game.

Brotherly Bonding

Freddy and I had our ups and downs over the years, bound and separated, attracted and repelled, by the curse of not only being siblings but siblings set at odds.

The trip we took to Mexico City together was the high point of our bonding, at least on Freddy's terms. Across my office I can see today a faded photo of us, framed in Mexican silver, looking like banditos with massive sombreros, waving to our wives from one of Xochimilco's flower-bedecked floating restaurants.

Though I usually maintain Aristotelian moderation when it comes to my evening martinis (was it Aristotle—or Dorothy Parker—who likened martinis to "breasts—one is too few, three is too many"?), I humored Freddy one night in a Zona Rosa nightclub by accepting his dare to match him drink for drink.

We alternated vodka tonics with shots of tequila.

By the fourth or fifth shot I noticed something odd: The tequila glasses seemed to be shattering as we placed them back on the table. I pointed the phenomenon out to Freddy. His were shattering too. The surface of our table and the floor beneath and around it was carpeted with broken glass.

Another shot or two and the management rescued us by escorting us gently but firmly to the door. Freddy did somersaults down the hall of our hotel, called me a few minutes later from his room. He was unable to speak actual words, but I listened to him laughing hysterically at the other end of the line until I too was weak from laughter and had to hang up. Tequila is a happy drunk.

The next morning was redeemed by the only hangover solution that's ever worked for me: a giant cheeseburger.

It had only been a few days before that evening that we'd stopped at a Bustamante sculpture shop in the Zona Rosa. Freddy fell in love with the famous sculptor's reclining camel made of bronze plates. He haggled with the shopkeeper, finally offering him three thousand dollars "including shipping." The owner, who was asking for six thousand laughed at him. "*De ninguna manera,*" "No way," he summarized his position.

As we headed for the door, the owner asked him where he was staying and what his name was. Freddy told him. We left, camel-less.

Out on the street, Freddy, while Jan looked embarrassed and I looked away, haggled with the teenage puppet seller on the corner and got him down from ten dollars to four dollars, grinning as he won his price, and then giving the purchased puppet back to the seller. "I don't need it," he shrugged. "You can sell it again." The larcenous looks they exchanged needed no translation.

Phoenician through and through, Freddy loved haggling.

We were packing our bags to depart the hotel when the phone rang in Freddy's room. Freddy appeared at my door to inform me that he'd meet us at the airport. He had to go back to the Bustamante shop, where the owner had agreed to his offer. The camel was his.

The year I came back from Montreal for a holiday in LA, 1988 I think, we invited Parker Stephenson and Kirstie Alley to join us at the festivities at Freddy's mansion in Hancock Park. Parker had starred in my *Rose Café* film, and he and Kirstie had become a Hollywood item. Grandpa Stephenson was in town, and I insisted they bring him along. Parker's grandfather loved the Bustamante camel, and promptly perched on it—until Freddy spotted him and unseated him.

For the rest of its life the Bustamante camel would sport a "Stephenson dent"—and I'd get hell every time I visited. Once Freddy got an angle on you, he never failed to work it. Kayoko's normally unflappable father, Keisaku, came to shun my brother because he never failed to ask Papa-san if he bought new golf shoes since the day they first played golf together and Freddy noticed a small hole in Papa-san's shoes—he'd packed the wrong ones. Freddy whose face grimaced at the mere mention of sushi—"Raw fish!"—was the living antithesis of Japanese propriety.

The dented Bustamante was finally exiled to *outside* Freddy's La Quinta house, alongside the life-size camel statue he named "Clyde" that nearly got my brother expelled from his country club (or was it because Freddy painted Clyde's lips with red nail polish?); and ended up in a trash heap from being too weathered to save.

Festive Livers

Chopped chicken livers in lemon was another staple of Atchity Lebanese heritage and formed the centerpiece of every holiday brunch.

You start with a pint of whole chicken livers. Drain the livers and toss them into a wrought-iron skillet. As you sauté them, add the fresh-squeezed juice of ten lemons. Chicken livers that would win my family's unqualified approval—especially Freddy's—have to be as lemony as a lemon tree.

I know something about lemon trees, by the way. On my trip to the Ecuadorian Amazon for HBO, I met Randy Borman, chief of the Cofánes. Among the tribe's favorite delicacies were "lemon ants." The dish was so named because this particular species of ant lay in wait for the final setting of the lemon blossoms, then swarmed the tree to gorge themselves on the sweetness. The Cofánes lurked at the foot of tree and captured the lemon-stuffed ants for their evening feast.

Now that the chicken livers are simmering in the juice, chop them up with whatever implement you can find that works. You want the result to be just short of being a paste, so take the time you need to accomplish this task. Once the livers are fully chopped, add a generous dose of black pepper, enough to coat the top of the mixture; and a couple shakes of salt. Then add one chopped up white onion and as many lightly roasted pine nuts as you like.

When the dish is fully cooked, spread on a serving platter, and serve with chunks of white onions and plenty of Lebanese bread or, if you can't find it, Lavash, flour tortillas (said to be introduced to Mexico by the Lebanese), or the thinnest pita you can get, for scooping. Yum!

Defining Event Number Six

After so many years holding onto my interpretation of my relationship with Dad as that of his misnamed and therefore mistreated older son, I tried my best to get past "Defining Event Number Two," the Foghorn Incident, by telling myself it was a false memory; that Mom had made up his disaffection for me. That I had imagined the rest.

In 1963, while I was a junior at Georgetown, Dad mailed me a blank calendar book for the year 1964, leather-bound 7 ¾ x 5 ¼ inches—and stamped on the front cover: "Fred J. Atchity." Because it was such an overt sign that he had made a conscious choice to send it to me instead of my brother, whose name after all was the same as his, I received it with reverent responsibility and proceeded to record my entire life in it every day until the calendars ceased coming from him in 1977 and I traveled afield to find calendars that reflected my newly-discovered infatuation with Italy.

Later I learned he'd offered the book to Freddy first—who turned it down in favor of a more expensive version he preferred. *Le droit de seigneur* passed to the first son from the second like a leftover meat pie.

It took a real mental wrenching to wean myself from written calendars a few years ago and convert to a calendar that synched with my computer and cell phone. Part of the wrenching had to do with the loss of this written accounting that certainly shaped my character. Thanks, Dad. And I mean that sincerely.

In 1987, after Dad was diagnosed with terminal lung cancer, he decided to spend the next year getting his office in order for his successor. And then retire. The Electricians' Union, I.B.E.W., whose Health & Welfare Fund he administered, threw Dad a roast. It was a surprise to him, one that the entire family was in on. Except me.

No one even mentioned it to me, all assuming I'd be unable to attend from 1800 miles away in California.

They sent me the video instead.

The head of the Union, as reported in the *Electrogram of Local Union 124, International Brotherhood of Electrical Workers,* presented Dad with a "beautiful engraved IBEW watch" and "an honorary membership in the Local 124 IBEW." Then the boss read this to the assembly:

> *Resolution*
>
> **Resolved,** *that we the undersigned officers and business agents of Local Union No. 124 International Brotherhood of Electrical Workers, with great humility and pride, at the regular monthly Local Union meeting, on this Thirteenth Day of January 1988, install our administrator and great friend, Frederick John Atchity Sr., to honorary membership in Local Union 124 International Brotherhood of Electrical Workers.*
>
> **Fred, we are proud to call you our friend and our Brother.**

The Resolution was signed by Zorn and Sullivan, Van Camp and Robinson, Womack and Barbieri, Owens and Nichols—the entire litany of management who would a year later attend Dad's funeral.

Θ

The video revealed that when the roasting was over, and the last laugh laughed, Dad, in his floppy cancer wig, approached the podium to receive his life-time service award. He gave a speech that was unremarkable for its humility—par for the course for him—but quite remarkable for its eloquence and sense of humor—giving me yet another pause in my ongoing reassessment.

At the end of his speech, the organizers pulled off one more surprise for him:

My mother and sisters marched in from the back of the hall where they'd been listening unannounced.

Greetings were exchanged all around, and then Dad turned, unselfconsciously, to the camera, and said: "I only wish my son could be here to see this. Hello, Fred, wish you could be here."

I got it on tape!

Sixth Defining Event Come Home to Roost

Delighted with his retirement event at the Union, my father sent copies of the video to everyone. This time even I was included in the subconsciously indiscriminate distribution. Was he telling me something, or just being his often-oblivious self?

I sat stunned as I watched my VHS.

My dad, in grainy color, turned to the camera—looking straight into my eagle-watchful eyes—and made the "my son Fred" speech.

I was stunned for reasons it took me awhile to sort out:

To begin with, here was concrete evidence that I was not, in fact, at least in my father's mind, his son. No hesitation, no flickering reference to passing age and memory, could be detected in his blatant statement of solo paternity. "I wish my son could have been here too."

Instead of being devastated, I felt oddly euphoric.

It was an extremely complicated feeling. Have you ever believed something so long, so needfully, that at a certain point you told yourself that it didn't *matter* whether it was true or not—you would go on believing it anyway because you've based your entire life on it?

Myths are more powerful than facts. They are stories we embrace, stories we love, stories we need. Stories we swear by and live by. Stories we, some way or another, create.

That's how I felt about believing all those years that my father was really not my father; that he was my brother's father. And that I needed to get the hell off his island as soon and as often and as permanently as possible. To that end, I'd thrown the bulk of my adolescent energy into my studies, wrangling an Ignatian Scholarship to Georgetown University that, with the intervention of my Rockhurst High School Religion teacher, Stanley Kalamaja, SJ, took me 1,200 miles away from my certified father and empowered me to establish with him, Mom, and the rest of my extended family in KC, that I'd never ever return there to live; allowed me to establish the exact distance necessary to loving them, and to processing their roles in a life I needed to reconstruct and define for myself.

Father Kalamaja was required to intervene because, in my usual over-achieving way, I'd also won several other scholarships, including one to Creighton University. My father wanted me to go to KU or UMKC or Rockhurst College. But Dad finally opted to throw his weight behind Creighton because he recognized the inevitability of my determination to move away from KC and was probably on some level relieved by it. The first of my eighteen first cousins to go to college, I wasn't about to stay anywhere near the Kansas-Missouri border. Creighton was up in Omaha, Nebraska. Though distant by KC standards, Nebraska was at least relatable to Dad—still solidly Mid-West, its 180 miles easily within a day's driving distance.

Against the combination of my determination and my Jesuit defender's eloquence, my father finally folded. For one thing, the pressure brought to bear could be presented in terms of opportunity and dream and challenge and ambition and family pride. *Per aspera ad astra* (through difficulties, to the stars) was a Georgetown motto. Later Dad would brag to his BFF Bill Reynolds about how proud he was that his son was at Georgetown; never mentioning thereafter that it had been, nearly, over his dead body.

My Brother, the Godfather

In my absence Freddy got used to playing godfather to our entire immediate family.

You think *I* was confused? Imagine *his* situation, being the Designated Son but having to deal with the Shadow Elder Brother who showed up just often enough to make him have to acknowledge that all those academic degrees, awards, and publications with my name on them were for real.

How, then, to determine the alpha male?

Freddy was one happy camper when I headed away or back to college, to Yale, or to Occidental, his Shadow retreating to long distance. As long as I wasn't physically around, he was left to occupy solo the position of elder son, king of the hill, and had come to relish that role much as I relished that I was my mother's, but not my father's, son.

Sometimes my brother even transposed his memories with mine. I overheard him at his daughter Sara's wedding at the Los Angeles Cathedral regaling everyone with the story of how he wore an Aunt Jemima costume one Halloween. I started to correct him but quickly realized that his fervent conviction couldn't be corrected. Yet the simple truth is, *I* was the one dressed as Aunt Jemima—reenacting my cross-dressing fetish, right? The photographic proof: Freddy appears behind the front porch balcony as Mom was taking the picture of me on the steps.

In the days of Uncle Ben (the Rice King) and Aunt Jemima (the Pancake Syrup) plastic salt and pepper shakers, not to mention Sambo's restaurant chain and the radio- turned-television-show *Amos 'n Andy*, racism was often disguised as "all good fun," though today we see it more clearly for what it is.

The little kid watching me askance as I posed in drag on the front steps of 3637 Benton Boulevard was the same little kid who crouched under the seat next to mine at the Ball Theater on Indiana Avenue—so terrified of *Creature from the Black*  *Lagoon* and the other black & white horror movies that occupied our entire Saturday afternoons that intermittent whispered reports from his older brother had to suffice. That was the only time Freddy voluntarily assumed a weaker position.

My brother's godfather pretension expanded with his affluence—boosted, conveniently, by his ongoing lip-service to Roman Catholicism, which I had abandoned both by choice (although I bought the morality of it, the institutionalism didn't make sense to me) and perforce—as a divorced person in those days, I was automatically cut off from the sacraments.

So, it made a sense I couldn't argue with that Freddy would be the brother our cousins most often chose to be the registered godfather of their kids. My disaffection with my father and KC had excluded me, the east-coast educated-California-academic-Hollywood maverick, from ascending the family hierarchy. Plus, I avoided bonds that would bring me back to KC more than what was absolutely necessary to keep the line open to my mother and sisters.

Freddy made sure he sat at the head of the table.

When people addressed him as the oldest, he never demurred.

Before or after every family dinner, he proposed the toast.

Nature abhors a vacuum.

Even though I lectured for a living, and was applauded for it, at the KC homestead I never spoke the words forming eloquently on the tip of my tongue, still obeying the childhood mandate, "Let your brother win."

What difference did it make, after all? I rationalized. It made Freddy happy, and everyone else seemed relieved with that. That made me as happy as I needed to be.

He was, after all, the Mr. Moneybags they all lived with on a daily basis—his favorite comic book scene, Scrooge McDuck singing happily as he takes a bath in his bathtub filled with dollar bills.

Whether it was in Prairie Village, Kansas, or Hancock Park, Los Angeles, going to Freddy's home became, progressively, more and more like attending the organized madness of street theater. You were always in for a surprise, as in "Mr. Toad's Wild Ride" at Disneyland. One year on Jan's birthday Fred hired a marching band to surprise her. He staged it perfectly; bringing her out the door and having the rest of us—command audience—lurk in the garage that he would open with the remote control at the first sound of music.

The Twenty-third Street Marching Cobras Band turned the corner of the otherwise quiet suburban neighborhood and marched toward her, playing an unforgettably brassy version of "Happy Birthday."

Neighbors' complaints he finessed by inviting all of them for a drink.

Christmas dinners at Freddy's house began with everyone around the table singing "The Twelve Days of Christmas" from Jan's matched set of water glasses that bore the lyrics for each part. For the first few times the glasses were introduced I participated reluctantly; but I must admit the fun of it all got to me, too, and I came to miss it when I wasn't with his family for Christmas.

Every single year, he repeated the story of the Christmas morning Mom and I conspired against him on 75th Street where he and I shared an upstairs bedroom. I would stand at the one window facing the street and shout, "Oh my God, Freddy, wake up!" (Freddy had copied Dad's habit of being impossible to awaken, causing sister Laurie to burst into tears when she was given the assignment).

"There goes Santa Claus!"

He staggered out of bed, made it to the window—my cue to say, "You just missed him!"

What did Mom have to do with it? It was *her* idea.

Freddy's way of making sure he didn't ever miss Santa Claus again was *becoming* Santa Claus every year—delighting in having the ladies as well as their children sit on his knee. He hired a van every Yuletide season to ferry anyone and everyone around their Prairie Village neighborhood, caroling.

One year the two of us dressed up like the Blues Brothers and played tennis racket guitar to Rolling Stones' music DJ'd by nephew Mark.

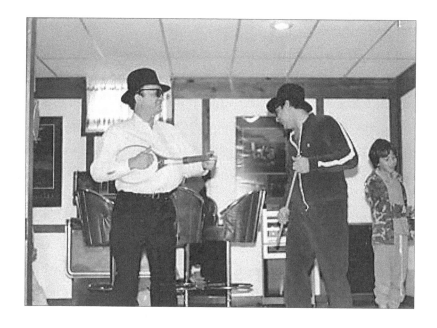

At his daughter Amy's first wedding at La Quinta Country Club, he drove her across the golf course toward the waiting clubhouse guests in an antique white Rolls Royce golf cart—then handed out a commemorative card with the bride and groom and the Santa Rosa mountains on one side, and himself as the Joker on the other. No one objected: After all, he was picking up the tab for the whole shindig. "It's my party, I joke if I want to."

Once he staked a 2,000-pound Black Angus in local radio personality Mike Murray's front yard. The police had it carted away because Mike's property was not licensed for animal husbandry.

Through it all Mom never stopped pressuring us both to get into business together. "With your creativity and his financial sense, you'd be unstoppable together."

We tried. It wasn't exactly a happy experience for either of us—too many family members around to foment the sibling rivalry. When we were operating from an office suite in Culver City once, Fred reduced an aspiring actress to tears of rage within the opening five seconds of a meeting I'd let him attend at his insistence (he was now "chairman of the board" after all). We met in L/A House's conference room adjacent to his company Stars to Go of America. The actress was thinking of working with my company to make a video.

"You know blondes like you are a dime a dozen," was the first thing he told her, by way of introduction—and before handshakes were even finished.

"What did you say?" her manager demanded as she broke into tears—revealing that he was her husband as well.

"I'm just saying every blonde in America shows up in this town."

"We won't take less than—" The husband brusquely stated their bottom line, while she nodded angrily through her tears.

Twenty minutes later we ushered them to the door, I apologizing for Freddy, though he'd managed to schmooze them down to earth and hugs in the last few minutes of the meeting.

"How'd I do?" he asked, smiling his naughty boy smile, as the door closed behind them.

"How did you do?" I shouted. "You alienated and insulted her beyond belief in the first sixty seconds. And embarrassed the shit out of me."

"I got them to the bottom line, didn't I—and saved us all a bunch of time?" He shook his head at my lack of appreciation.

But the closer I worked with my brother the more I had to admit that he had method to his madness. Freddy's most dramatic business ploy happened when he was brought in as partner by Bernie Horton for Stars to Go which was at the time located in Fresno, California.

Freddy moved up to that sizzling San Joaquin Valley outpost determined to do two things: to get the company relocated to civilization—Freddy's attitude toward Fresno was Dad's attitude toward Mom's Louisiana farm—and to undo the deal Bernie was about to close with Southland Corporation, owners of 7-Eleven.

Bernie told him it was too late to stop the deal, that it would bring them thousands of stores to distribute Stars to Go videotapes. Freddy told Bernie he was an idiot, and that their little company would be swallowed up by Southland. They were at an impasse. "I made the deal before you came on board, Fred. A deal is a deal."

Two young Southland execs flew to Fresno from Dallas on Carl Heller's private jet (no direct flights Fresno-Dallas). Freddy was silent as they and Bernie inked the deal. He had only one humble request: "I want to ride back with you guys to the airport."

Bernie started to include himself, but Freddy stopped him. "Just me and the guys," he said. "You got what you wanted."

Bernie backed off.

On the way to the airport in the white stretch limo Freddy had rented for the purpose he poured the two execs their drinks of choice. "I like you guys, and I want you to think of one thing when you get back to Dallas," he began.

"What?"

"You can always come work for me."

"What do you mean?"

"I can see you're good guys and mean well. I need guys like you to build this company."

Now they were sweating, and it wasn't just because of the blazing San Joaquin Valley sun. "Fred, what are you getting at?"

"Well," he said, "I'm afraid the shit is going to hit the fan when you get back and Southland realizes this deal isn't structured to work. All that money down is truly down the drain."

Now they were alarmed. "Explain yourself, goddamnit."

Freddy outlined his thoughts. Unless Southland had a strong ownership position in Stars to Go, they would quickly find it impossible to deal with the explosive growth the company was about to experience with him on board—including the competitive issues of needing to do business with Southland's chief rival, Circle K.

It was complicated, but for half an hour they listened to every word. "What can we do?" they finally asked in dismay, lamenting the signed paperwork safely tucked in their briefcases.

"I'll tell you what," Freddy said. "Because you're nice guys I'm willing to tear up the deal right now, on one condition."

"Name it," they said.

"I ride back to Dallas with you and meet one-on-one with Mr. Heller."

That's exactly what happened. They tore up the deal in the limousine, toasted on their private jet as Freddy rode down to Dallas with them—with the result that Southland bought into Freddy's new company, thereby providing stable financing.

Ө

Investing in my little romance-film company, L/A House, Freddy insisted that the elegant palm tree and setting sun logo designed by my Sister Andrea's husband Rick McKeown must now include a camel.

"Why?" I asked, afraid to hear his answer.

"Because we're Lebanese," he said. "Aren't you proud of that?"

This was the ever-adolescent Freddy who named his beige VW Beetle, which he drove from KC to Baton Rouge in his LSU years,

"Clyde the Camel." Ray Stevens' 1962 hit "Ahab, the A-rab" became his personal anthem. He hated his schoolmates calling him a camel-jockey (they all seemed to think Lebanon was full of camels too), so he figured he'd turn the negative into a proactive positive by embracing the image.

"Freddy, there are no camels in Lebanon," I replied patiently, for the umpteenth time. "It's stupid."

That didn't matter. The camel went into the logo—until, not being able to stand the agonizing wait for the deal to come together, he gave up on my company and withdrew his investment position—weeks before I finally snagged the financing at Astral-Bellevue-Pathe in Montreal.

I deleted the camel from the logo. I'm sorry, Freddy. It was too stupid.

But it did make me laugh.

Freddy, whose collection of camels eventually passed the three hundred mark, never stopped giving me a hard time about it.

And I did miss the dang thing. It never failed to provoke comment.

Atchity Brothers Entertainment, our final attempt at a company together, has a quill—and a camel—for its logo.

The final irony: at division of Freddy's estate, hundreds of camels stood idle. Freddy's daughters decided to distribute them at the family reunion in June. Even my kids and grandkids were delighted to get a "good luck camel." After some agonizing, I decided to attend the reunion with the camels. Even from beyond, Freddy commanded the center of attention. But, I figured, why the hell not? I could handle being one-upped one last time. Besides, I remembered my brother's governing philosophy: "*Fuck you if you can't take a joke.*" I owed it to his memory to take the joke.

When my seventy-fifth birthday rolled around, I signed us up to spend it among *elephants* in Thailand.

Θ

My prolonged silence about Freddy's infiltrations into my hierarchical status came to a rude end at the family poker game following sister Andrea's funeral—almost as if her spirit possessed me.

Atchitys take poker games dead seriously. Games are the normalcy bar that returns us to reality after traumatic upheavals like holidays, funerals, and weddings. After too many glasses of wine Freddy was once again disrupting the play, loudly bragging about the trip to Africa he'd financed for his whole family—exactly how much it cost, precisely how much it cost, really how much it cost, etc.

"Freddy, shut the fuck up," I couldn't believe I finally said.

266

The table fell quiet, Freddy included. I'd never erupted like that before.

Freddy stood up, reaching for his cigarettes, and headed for sister Mary's back porch.

The game resumed. No one said a word.

I felt like an asshole.

Freddy was absent for almost an hour, making me feel progressively worse about my unbrotherly sudden loss of control. I had *not* let my brother win. When he returned, quietly, and sat down, "Sorry I jumped on you," I began—

"Don't you dare be sorry," Cousin Matt Hake broke in. "He deserved it." Everyone chimed their agreement. I was startled they were supporting me, the Prodigal Son. But I'd stood up to the bully for them. I wish I could say it made me feel better.

Freddy ruefully accepted the deck of cards I offered him and dealt the next hand. The Liar's Poker game resumed and remained Africa-free. I felt a sharp bolt of guilt no doubt hurled at me by Mom's spirit somewhere in the great casino in the sky.

But I'd finally learned something important. Bullies need to be faced down. Years later, when we were working together on his dream for a movie about the Battle of New Orleans, his bullying got so bad my blood pressure went up the moment I saw it was him calling. I remembered the facedown at cards, and finally left him a clear message: "Freddy, don't call me anymore. Don't email me. Text me if there's a family emergency. I refuse to deal with any more bullying." I stuck to my word. We didn't speak for three weeks. But then I awoke one day to see he'd left a message. He told me he'd been at church, which I doubted, and that St. Jude had appeared to him and told him, "Be nice to your brother." And that he promised Dad's patron saint that he would. I had to laugh, wondering what fraction of the story was true. But he kept his faith with St. Jude and started talking to me differently.

A shrink I'd been consulting said, "Maybe he's just ready to acknowledge that he needs an older brother, and that your acting like an older brother instead of enabling him by backing down from the bullying—'letting him win'—has made him ready to acknowledge that you are indeed his older brother." Maybe the shrink got this one right. Mom's "let your brother win" mantra had not only suppressed me but had also *enabled* Freddy's bully gene, with which I believe he himself became progressively uneasy as he grew older.

Primal Myth Reinforced

The euphoria washing over me after watching the VHS of my father's retirement "roast" said this:

You were right all along.

Your father never internalized your filial relationship to him, never accepted it psychologically.

His paternal odometer, at your birth, never started ticking, frozen by Mom's telegram; did not begin clicking until brother Freddy—Dad's namesake—came along.

Only then did Dad's official life as a respected father begin.

Years later, at Grandfather Jede's funeral, I'd seen visual evidence that indicated how my personal nonentity plight got exacerbated, the simple tombstone at KC's St. Mary's Cemetery marked, "Atchity Baby." Going through Mom's medical records one day while she was still among us, I saw that she'd been pregnant between my and Freddy's births with a male son that was stillborn and never mentioned to any of us until we confronted her with the medical record. Then, with a shrug, she admitted it was true.

The miscarriage postponed my father's paternal status by another frustrating year, during which he had only Foghorn to ignore.

Θ

And the older son became usurper, while the actual usurper, my brother Freddy, became, at least between my rare appearances on the home front, the resident entitled one.

Combined with my peculiar euphoria was an overwhelming echo of loss. All these years I had let the loss dog my heels without having certified proof of its validity. That feeling of loss had even propelled me to leave home. The hollowness had become my constant companion, which dips into joyful female liaisons could only momentarily alleviate.

Now the loss was verified. It was real.

I had finally come of age.

Looking back over the myth that had guided my emotional view of my place in life until that moment, I now saw that it was not self-constructed after all. It was seated in the reality that the "father" listed on my birth certificate shared the paternal topography with my brother alone. I was absent from his mythic landscape, a sacrifice he made unwillingly to my mother's ego.

How did I feel about who I was?

I hadn't a clue.

Exceptions occurred from time to time, whenever something or someone confronted him with my provable physical existence: my mother, his friends, members of the family testing the myth on their own, a newspaper publication with my name in it, or even myself writing from the east or west coast or from abroad or calling on holidays to work my way through the awkward greetings before the phone was handed with an audible sigh of relief to my ever-voluble mother.

Oddly enough, verifying the loss through that fateful video not only made me feel relieved about my mind's ability to decipher reality and cope with it; it also marked the beginning of a long reassessment of my father, and particularly of his relationship with Mom, that led *his* mind to create such a myth to begin with. That event led to this book of reflection.

Evidence: my further discovery, after his death, that Dad kept a file of every single letter I'd ever sent him.

I, of course, kept a file of all he sent me—which was surprisingly voluminous though my Mom-centered consciousness had long given the contents short shrift.

What did that tell me?

Myth upon myth, sometimes recognized through a glass darkly, often examined, too often doubted—until the verification the videotape had now granted me clarity. The question was only, what was I going to make of it all?

Daddy Holding Me

While Dad was reassembling his mental equilibrium after his nervous breakdown, searching through family photos became my compulsion. I think I was searching for needles in the haystack of captured memories. After watching the Electricians Union VHS of my father's retirement roast, I paged again through the black and white photographs of my childhood mounted in my endless photo albums. One photo in particular stopped me short.

It was a shot of my father, wearing a 1950s business suit, crouched in what must have been the side yard of my grandparents' house on Wabash Avenue, holding me "on his knee." The photograph captivated me because I had told myself I couldn't recall a single time in my childhood where my father had displayed overt affection—much less a time when he held me on his lap. In the photo I, around age five or six, was looking either slightly or entirely nonplussed. Dad was directing his oddly bewildered squint at the camera, forced smile frozen on his lips.

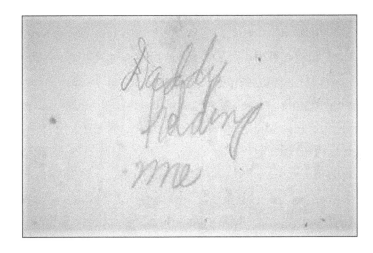

When I turned the snapshot over, I saw these words scrawled by the eleven-year-old me on the back: "Daddy holding me." There were three humps on the "m" in "me" instead of the Palmer-prescribed two. Me, seeking evidence that my mother's propaganda—that my father didn't love me, only *she* loved me—maybe wasn't quite accurate. I had, back then, somehow discovered what appeared to be an indication of my father's affection—and was so rattled by the discovery that I made that extra definitive hump.

It was in that same upset period I rediscovered the photo, around 1957—the year that Dad had his nervous breakdown—that I signed my name in prayer books, "Kennenth" instead of "Kenneth."

Rediscovering the "holding me" photo yet again, during the years between Dad's terminal diagnosis and his death, I studied it more carefully. Here's why I found the hand-written scrawl more revealing than the photo itself: When you look more carefully at the photo on this book's cover, it's clear he is *not* really holding me.

Dad's right knee sticking behind my right leg grounds the photo, for all the world to see, in witness to the maternal myth: I am actually standing, leaning against his knee. Both his large and competent hands are around me, to create the illusion I fell for. Holding me formally. Stiffly. Tentatively. No doubt only long enough for this photo to be snapped.

You believe not what you see but what you want to believe—what I wanted to believe at the age of eleven. As French philosopher Alphonse Bertillon puts it, "One can only see what one observes, one observes only things which are already in the mind."

But Dad's body language—and mine—speaks more loudly than my wishful scrawl on the back: two people frozen in time in a pose that neither is comfortable with, our heads very slightly tilted away from each other.

The year my father died I showed the photograph to dear artist friend Kathy Jacobi. At the time she was oiling her way through her haunting "family portrait" period— recreating childhood photos with the faces of adults in their strollers and highchairs and cradles.

It was eerie beyond words when she presented me with the oil she'd created from the "Daddy holding me" photograph.

Everyone who sees it thinks the larger face looming in the background is me as well. That is what we struggle with, isn't it? We try so hard, in the dialogue and myths we imagine and recount from ourselves to ourselves, to overcome our proximity to and affinity with the parents we are destined only to reflect. Gertrude Stein's *Making of Americans* got it right: *Once an angry man dragged his father along the ground through his own orchard. "Stop!" cried the groaning old man at last, "Stop!" I did not drag my father beyond this tree."*

Read on the Waters

When I was a twenty-something professor of comparative literature, after repeated pleas by ever-pressuring Mom, I'd signed up for several weeks one summer at the family's lakeside cabin at Lotawana "to get a book finished."

I arrived in my rental car from the airport around ten p.m., having been told Mom and Mary would be waiting there to greet me but then, they promised, would head back to town the next day to leave me in my requested solitude.

I drove up the driveway and turned off the motor, opening the door to the greeting of crickets and tree frogs and wondering, once again, why I couldn't accept how beautiful the state of Missouri could be instead of feeling like an earthling treading on an unfriendly planet. The serenity of Lotawana was captivating, though I'd almost drowned in this lake on a teenage outing (one of the several times I've come close to drowning in my life—liquid suffocation—that led me to respect Johnny Carson's definition of swimming as "staying alive in the water").

Although a light or two was on in the cabin, I heard no sign of life. I understood why when I reached the front door. "The key is under the mat," sister Mary's scrawled note said. "We have eaten ourselves into oblivion and gone to bed. Cherry pie in the fridge."

I laughed. That was my family. God bless them! Food and drink was our most trusted route to togetherness. Eating ourselves into oblivion. Aren't we all? It made me think how hard it was for us to understand that anyone wouldn't want to eat something. When you invited someone, "Would you like a piece of pie?" and they said no; then you asked them, "How about a slice of cake?" and they still said no, we would invariably say, "Well, then, how about a dirt sandwich?" It was the kind of people we were, as Richard Brautigan would say.

Andrea had baked me a cherry pie, sliding sweetly into dear late Aunt Selma's role. Mary and Mom had taken a piece each and left the rest for me.

Θ

I've written a bunch of books in my life, all of them snuck in between a chockfull schedule—none that I recall were completed from non-stop concentration like that I professed to contemplate this summer at the lake.

Apart from my 850-page Yale dissertation, "Homer's *Iliad*: The Song and Shield of Memory," which I wrote in two cold Connecticut winter months while holding down a waiter's job at Chuck's Steakhouse on the Boston Post Road. My burning desire to put graduate school behind me was fanned into flame by my being offered a full-time teaching position at Occidental College in rose-bedecked and sunny Los Angeles.

I picked up four handsome leather-bound copies of the thesis (eight volumes) from the New Haven binder, only to discover en route to my dissertation advisor Lowry Nelson's town house that their spines were stamped, in beautiful gold lettering against the Yale blue binding, "Homer's Illiad..."

OMG. I still cringe every time I see someone misspell the first and greatest epic of western civilization. Reluctantly I carried the two volumes he'd requested up the stairs to Lowry.

Lowry was thrilled. "Take them back," he said, "and demand that they change the binding by Monday. But I want to keep my set as is."

"Why?" I said.

"I adore literary curiosities," he said, and wouldn't change his mind.

The other volumes were duly re-stamped, including the one I'd promised to my Rockhurst High School pal Rusty Lusk as a swap for his University of Maryland PhD dissertation in theoretical mathematics.

Rusty's thesis was titled "Homeomorphic Embeddings in Topological Spheres." It was two pages, one page of which was an indecipherable drawing. On the narrative page, the only word I understood was "the."

I spun his unfathomable masterpiece into a love poem:

> *Suppose, dear—just suppose*
> *that M is a subset*
> *of Q°. Let Q be*
> *an n-cell, if you will;*
> *&, bear with me, please, my sweet,*
> *presume next S to be*
> *a topological sphere*
> *n-1. By now*
> *you understand, I trust,*
> *the neat necessity*
> *making my product, H,*
> *a homeomorphic em-*
> *bedding in your young*
> *S^{n-1} x*

I & S^n. Pardon
me, I beg you, if
my mean metaphor
is showing.

Rusty wrote me that he enjoyed my poem, framed it, didn't understand it. Touché.

Θ

I did everything *but* finish my book that summer at Lotawana: mowed the grass every week, painted, repaired, steam cleaned the dock, refueled the boats, and wrote a book review for *The Los Angeles Times Book Review.*

My father, in his sixties then, watched me reading the heavy tome, Joe McGinnis' *Final Vision*, a hair-raising study of Captain Jeffrey R. MacDonald's murder of his wife and children.

"Do you read every page?" he asked.

I jumped. But not because I knew someone someday would ask me that question but because I always jumped whenever Dad spoke to me, a hangover from childhood reaction to the Cyclops' unexpected rages that marred the course of my otherwise tranquil scholarly life, like those rabid Dobermans chasing my bicycle on winter mornings.

"Of course."

Dad nodded. As close as he got to communicating approval. Reading every page, in fact, is one of the reasons I finally stopped reviewing books, after twenty-nine years (my first review, Kenneth Tynan's *Bull Fever*—still one of the best books I've ever read every page of, appeared in the *Kansas City Star* when I was sixteen. Thorpe Menn, the crusty, nicotine-clouded, and beloved book editor, had no idea of my age because I handled all communication by correspondence. The flow of books never stopped for nearly three decades, from six different newspapers).

From the time I could read—at the age of four my mother used to claim—I had a disproportionate respect for the written world. Out of proportion because, after all, so much that's written is *not* worth reading—especially every page. As Sam Goldwyn once said when asked that question, in a Hollywood already forced to become jaded by the sheer mass of submissions (everyone in the known universe wants to be taken seriously in Hollywood): "I read part of it all the way through."

The real reason I respected books so much was the escape they provided me from the angst of making it through a day with Dad at Mom's throat and she fighting back; while I internalized my mother's sorrow. Reading *Heidi,* I was, instead, living vicariously in exile with my goatherd grandfather in an isolated mountain cottage, looking out from Heidi's point of view, transgenderly again, from my straw mattress in his loft at a sky filled with stars.

After my dozenth or so Kansas City Star review, I decided it was time to 'fess up, and replace my correspondence relationship with direct contact with this man Menn who was giving me a readership, and even paying me for reading books. Besides, my curiosity about the legendary Mr. Menn got the better of me and I couldn't resist a trip down Grand Avenue to the brick offices of the *Star & Times* (the "Star" came out in the evening, the "Times" in the morning). It was rumored that he'd been Ernest Hemingway's editor once upon a time.

I'll never forget the surprised look on Thorpe's face as I walked in and he realized my age. Nor will I forget the barely perceptible microsecond before he decided to ignore that entirely and treat me like the seasoned writer I, at the age of seventeen, now was—with two dozen published reviews under my belt.

That's when I recognized the power of writing, as something that reached outside myself. Gave me validity off island.

Another Male Authority Figure was approving of my writing, and perhaps therefore, by implication, approving me. An adult MAF was taking my foghorn, albeit safely modulated in written form not to exceed 1,000 words, seriously.

$$\Theta$$

"How much do they pay you for the review?" I'd gone to the stove to refill my coffee cup and Dad had picked up the book I was reading to see that it was nearly 800 pages.

"Around a thousand bucks."

He cringed. In his mind it was "dollars," never "bucks."

"How long does it take you to do it altogether?"

"Let's see. About twelve hours to read the book. Then another two to write the review, if I think about it before I start writing."

That bewildered look again. I could hear his brain calculating.

"Dad," I tried to intervene. "It's not like baking cookies. Where you first buy the eggs and flour and milk and nuts and sugar for an overall cost of five dollars, then mix and bake them, then sell the cookies one at a time for twenty-five dollars." He was nodding. I was talking Atchity language. My grandfather had canned chili and cabbage rolls. Dad was tracking. "It's part of being in the literary world, of building a reputation, of throwing bread upon the water."

"How much bread do you have to throw?" he asked.

Sometime after that—months, years, a decade or two, three or four hundred published reviews later—I made the decision to write no more reviews (unless I was begged by *The New Yorker* or the *New York Times*, of course ☺). By then I'd published enough of them, after all. I would miss the ego gratification of hearing someone over lunch at Michael's in Santa Monica or Michael's in Manhattan mention my recent review of Ursula Le Guin's latest novel or of David Hapgood's *The Murder of Napoleon*. I also loved what it did to my graduate school resume. But I didn't need the reviews anymore. Sources of stronger gratification abounded.

It was high time to wait for the bread to float back. If that's indeed what bread did.

Θ

The summer I spent at the Lake Lotawana cabin was when I started to realize there actually *was* an odd kind of love lurking beneath my parents' constant bickering and outright fighting—a love neither of them would ever admit out loud, or consciously display. Maybe they were loosening up as they aged, now that the kids were all out of the nest? A lifetime of fighting was being reduced before my eyes to nothing more than ritualistic scrapping, an almost-nostalgic bickering, as if they knew no other way of communicating. I've observed a lot of married folk act like that, behavior no doubt learned from their parents:

Dad was sitting at the breakfast table, grumbling.

Without looking up from my book I stopped to listen.

"You never do anything for me," he was complaining to my mother.

Mom was standing over him quietly peeling a peach and cutting it into pieces onto his plate. He liked his fruit sliced, as I do to this day.

She didn't reply. She kept slicing.

Maybe he was talking about something else?

Θ

I never shook off that Atchity Leveler, though—the immediate and constant monetization of every human activity. "I saw you produced *Joe Somebody*," my brother would remark at a holiday encounter. "How much did you make on it?" Not to mention, "How much did it make at the box office?"

Or "Did you like the Rombauer?" he'd ask after my first sip of Chardonnay. I would nod. "I got it for $49 a bottle," he'd say, "bought a case."

I grew more tolerant about habitual interrogation, especially after figuring out that I didn't have to answer a question I didn't want to answer.

AFI, Inc.

Patience is its own reward was another dictum I never quite figured out. Patience *does* reward the patient. I always say in Hollywood you *will know* everything you care to know, just not when it's useful to you. But hang around long enough, and you'll hear what really happened during that baffling falling apart of a deal.

Through the vicissitudes and accidents of my family's ongoing post-mortem housecleaning, Dad's spirit finally got me, his oldest son, to see the evidence of *his* official story fourteen years after he passed. Andrea, his closest daughter, had been going through Mom's things—Mom had eventually followed Dad heavenward on February 19, 2003, making her one-way trip to his plot at Mt. Olivet. Andrea found a few items Mom hadn't gotten around to distributing. One of them was a heavy-leather black binder with "AFI, Inc." embossed on its spine: "Atchity Family, Inc."—and, on its front: "Corporate Records."

My father's family was a corporation!

The binding that held it together for nearly thirty years was heavy metal, the end sheet a rich marbled red that underlined the seriousness of the contents. Andrea handed me the binder during her visit to Los Angeles for my third, but first fully conscious, wedding. "I thought you might want to have this, since you're sentimental." That was the official Atchity family word for people who remembered birthdays. The word was often used to distinguish me from Freddy the Multi-Millionaire, who was notorious for *not* being sentimental—actually, something of a bum rap, since my brother's bullying exterior hid a heart of chocolate lava cake beneath a relentlessly obnoxious bullying shtick cultivated to spare him onslaughts of unwanted solicitations.

I had heard of "AFI" off and on through the years, wondering what it stood for and, of course, wondering how much it was worth. Who wouldn't be intrigued by the concept of your family becoming a corporation? I knew nothing about it except the intrigue and mystique assigned by my mind: "Atchity Family, Incorporated." It sounded grand, so full of promise. I did think it odd that the stamped imprint was a bit redundant. Why need "Inc." if it was already built into "AFI"? Oh, well, I thought. They didn't consult me, the family editor and branding expert.

Θ

I opened the binder to discover the legal minutes and filings of the corporation. The first entry, the "Certificate of Incorporation" from the State of Missouri, was dated October 19, 1971, the last, "Minutes of the Annual Meeting of Board of Directors," April 12, 1988, a generation's life later, a year before my father passed away— and a year after he learned he was dying of lung cancer.

I suppose many folks would page through these dry, official, repetitious, and legalistic documents and be done with it. But because I am after all my father's son, I began to actually *read* page one—and, in installments over the next two weeks—every single page with the disciplined, compartmentalized, and highly-absorbed attention of a mystery fan glued to his latest book.

Folded and tucked into that black AFI binder before the first recorded minutes were two documents. One was the "Certificate of Incorporation," signed with a neat green signature stamp by James C. Kirkpatrick, "Secretary of State of the Great State of Missouri," on "this 19th day of October, 1971." The secretary of state "by virtue of the authority vested in him by law," certified and declared that "AFI, Inc." was henceforth "a body corporate, duly organized this day" and that, among other things, "its period of existence is"—and this word is typed in: "perpetual."

My familiarity with Latin served to remind me that by law what was happening at this momentous *incorporation* was a "word made flesh," as the opening of St. John's Gospel puts it: the company was declared by law and paper to be a *live being.* The "perpetual" existence of corporations struck me as magical, even when I learned years later that corporations hadn't *always* been perpetual. Roman law let corporations exist for five years only. If, at the end of that period, they could prove they had served the common good, they could be renewed for another five years. But that was that. The Romans feared corporations might become more powerful than people. Can you imagine? Modern capitalism is grounded in the perpetuity of corporations, paper fictions produced by human imagination to reshape reality.

Only their shareholders can put them out of existence.

What would happen with AFI? I had to keep reading to find out.

Ө

Aside from the word "perpetual" and the dates, the only other "personalized" typing on the gold-sparkling page was the "amount of its Authorized Shares": "ONE HUNDRED THOUSAND— Dollars."

That's what Dad and his siblings inherited from my grandfather's estate. My grandmother, Anna Fatall, born in Tripoli, Syria, on May 10, 1893, died in 1970, on April 4. With the resources he bequeathed her, she had lived comfortably, though a bit absent-mindedly, for her last eight years. The holy card issued at her funeral offered this Prayer:

*O gentle Heart of Jesus, ever present in the Blessed Sacrament,
ever consumed with burning love for the poor captive souls in
Purgatory, have mercy on the soul of Thy servant, Bring her from
the shadows of exile to the bright home in Heaven, where, we trust,
Thou and Thy Blessed Mother have woven for her a crown of
unfading bliss. Amen*

Though I knew it was the proper thing to say in a prayer, I
couldn't imagine my grandmother committing any sin that would
land her in Purgatory even for ten minutes. Though her girth
indicated a healthy appetite for her own food, I doubt it ever
crossed over into gluttony. Like the rest of us, she was just built
like an endomorph.

When it came time to do something with what Tata left
behind, her five sons and two daughters decided to keep the
money together. This was their interpretation of a well-known
Catholic slogan of the time blazoned on millions of holy cards:
"The family that prays together stays together." The Atchity
version: "The family that saves together stays together."

The "first meeting of the incorporators of AFI, INC." was held
on January 9, 1972, at the "office" in our home on 75th Street. The
first page of that first meeting was notable for the full complement
of signatures: "There were present all of the subscribers to the stock
of the corporation as evidenced by their signatures to the above
waiver of notice": Five brothers, two sisters, and all seven respective
spouses.

I can imagine them sitting at the dining room table: Fourteen
family members and Joe Lapin, Dad's attorney, there to make sure
all was executed properly. They must have had to scrunch extra

chairs at the end of the table on both sides, since it was, with leaves extended, comfortable enough only for twelve. One of those chairs—the armchair accorded the guest of honor—had once shattered under the ample weight of Father Z who, from the commencement of my Latin lessons till my departure for Georgetown and even after, was a regular at holiday celebrations. I remember how much redder his face became—not from pain or surprise, he explained when he'd been helped from the floor and shifted to a twice-tested chair, but from embarrassment. "Too much beer," he added, affably, holding out his wine glass for a refill.

As I read through the official minutes, like the literary analyst I'd been for years, I recognized that the narrative was a unique mixture of business and personal. Between presentation of stock transfers, investment purchases, and property sales, attempts at levity abounded:

> *Preliminary to the commencement of the official business to be brought before the meeting, the attention of all the Stockholders was directed to the physical condition of Carrie Atchity, by David Hake who stated that she was suffering from a broken toe. Inquiry was made as to the cause of the disability and Carrie replied that it had been caused by stumbling into a massive chair in an unlit room in the dead of night. Speculation was then made by various members whether it had been started by Anthony, made in hot pursuit, but it was quickly established that Anthony was engaged in a golfing tournament and in Florida at the time. A Resolution was quickly passed in which the company and all of its members offered their hopes and prayers for Carrie's quick, full and complete recovery.*

Another frequent entry:

> *The meeting ended with the President's announcement that "the*
> *company was providing all the Board members with a dinner*
> *and beverages... In acknowledgement for their services and*
> *attendance at the Special Meeting.*

Several such meetings were at Dad's lake cottage, where you could be sure the dinner was shish kebob, prepared by my father. Watching Dad carve a leg of lamb was to watch my grandfather's dream of an unbroken chain of grocery stores evaporate beneath the sharper blade of evolution. In his mind, Dad had been destined to be a butcher, intensely slicing and trimming behind the counter of an Atchity #5. Yet Jede must have experienced a sense of expanding horizons when his middle son chose to excel at numbers instead of cuts of pork.

Passages like these confirmed my dawning recognition of the true nature of the annual proceedings. In the guise of business, spouses joined together to celebrate their family relationship, bearing tribute to their parents and ancestors—and to the days when they'd met on Sundays at Jede and Tata's home to dine and discuss business together, then listen to Jede's oud and watch Aunt Lorraine dance with a scarf in the living room.

This was not a family to write autobiographies, much less novels and poems. They expressed themselves in minutes, recording the seriousness, the levity, the ups and downs, of this group predicament we refer to as life. The purpose of AFI was to continue these meetings, to hold on to as much of their parents' legacy as they could.

Hearing distant reports of various AFI meetings, having no idea what was at stake, I thought how wonderful it would be if AFI could live generation after generation. It was a noble dream—a worthy flame. In Dad's generation, every get-together had to be a "meeting." It's the way they were. Never: Dad just wanting to see his siblings and enjoy their company. Instead: Good business required that they meet more often. That is why solemn congratulations for a $1,350 report of capital gains to each member. *Not only are we getting together, but we're making good money doing it.*

A few months before brother Freddy died by falling off a curb in Ocean City, he called me. "Don't worry," he began. "I'm not calling to bug you about the film. It's not even business. I'm just calling to chat with my brother."

Dead silence at my end while I tried to process. I had never received such a call from him. "If you're serious," I finally said, "that's great. I'd love to just chat with my bro."

And then he was gone.

The minutes of AFI recorded one sibling after another passing on, Aunt Selma of the cherry pies from her rheumatoid arthritis, smiling Uncle Eddy from pancreatic cancer. My attitude toward death was annoyance and irritation. It irritated me that someone I loved was leaving the party. It made me angry, then hurt, then detached; in my utter self-centeredness, I felt betrayed. The lid of Uncle Eddy's piano was closed the final time I visited him. No one dared ask him if he would play something. We exchanged a lame joke or two to break the ice, but the ice in his eyes showed he knew that I knew that I wouldn't be seeing him again. When Mom sent me his obituary in *The Kansas City Star*, I was in far off Bologna.

Reading the minutes, I was reminded of Robert Frost's "The Census Taker":

The melancholy of having to count souls
When they diminish to none at all...

Aunt Selma had made it only to sixty-four, her last ten years in nearly constant pain. When I got that call from sister Mary, I lamented how many times I'd responded with a growl to Mom's, "You really *should* call Aunt Selma," then felt guilty as I took the first bite of her exquisite pie that she'd sent over because she knew I was coming to town.

Although my fondest farm memories were of Aguillard farms sprinkled across Prairie des Chiens (between Basile and Opelousas, Louisiana) the loss of *any* farm, even an Atchity farm, seemed an unbearable loss. I was sad to read the cut and dried manner in which the liquidation of my Lebanese grandfather's farm was treated by his sons, sold to the highest bidder.

One of my most treasured photographs shows both my grandfathers, James Atchity and Evan Aguillard, on Jede's farm (Jede in tank top) where Sunday picnics were held when the weather permitted. That's Tata in the picture, caught in a rare moment of relaxation. Nothing was *farmed* on Jede's farm. It was only a modest "country retreat" for family gatherings, nothing more than a ramshackle wood-frame house with a porch and tables and barbecue ovens outside. In the photo, the look on my Louisiana grandfather's face was bewilderment. A real farmer, whose life and the life of his children depended upon his ability to produce food from his ten acres and mule, he had no idea what to make of a "farm" that grew nothing except picnic tables.

At one of the Atchity family gatherings at the farm, Aunt Lorraine recounts, when she was a young girl, Jede horrified her by jumping up from the table and shooting a rabbit. Both my grandfathers were well-acquainted with guns. One of the family's favorite stories about that little-celebrated aspect of Jede's character was that when they lived downtown on Wabash Avenue, he used to take the streetcar to the southmost city limits to hunt—and was mightily unwelcome on the return tram the day he got on board with his rifle on one shoulder and a dead skunk over the other.

When Uncle Anthony announced that cancer was now nipping at his heels, it was a formal insert into the minutes, followed by the usual profitable buy-back of his shares:

> *I have greatly enjoyed my long association with AFI INC. as an officer and member of the Board of Directors and it is with great regret that this tender is made under circumstances beyond my control. Wishing the Company a prosperous future, I am,*

Sincerely and faithfully...

A meeting later Aunt Catherine tendered her resignation:

*Due to circumstances making the move necessary, I do want to
express that I have greatly enjoyed my association with AFI INC.
and wish a happy and prosperous future for the company and its
shareholders.*

The circumstances referred to her move to John Knox
Retirement Village, when she could no longer manage the big
house on West 69th Terrace where Uncle Eddy had lived and died
with her. She wanted to do something easier for herself in old age,
choosing a place where she could fish from the backyard of her
condo (my mother, who often joined her, had addicted her to
fishing) and play bridge with cronies on a daily basis—plus take a
one-mile daily walk around the periphery of the Village lake. In
2013, at the age of 97, she told me, with the same sweet smile she'd
been smiling for nearly a century, that following her routine was
the secret of her longevity. Twenty-five years passed after her
resignation from AFI. She lived just past 100.

Dad, who with Mom became the sole shareholders and he the
single director, would eventually no longer include them in the
waivers, notices, and minutes. The sixteenth meeting of AFI was
held on February 5, 1987, at my parents' final home on 104th Street
off Wornall. The waiver was signed only by Mom and Dad. I can
see Mom shrugging as he handed her the pen. Dad signed as
Chairman and president; Mom appeared as Secretary. The reading
of the minutes was dispensed with.

I couldn't help noticing, in Dad's final AFI spreadsheet, that $72,792.43 was *not* equal to $72,792.51. He could have gone back and corrected the discrepancy, but he didn't. He would have had to rewrite the entire spreadsheet. But there was no one left to report to anymore.

No one but me to witness the discrepancy; no one to care.

Act 3

Paradiso

In which a happier, wiser, less confused narrator bonds with Sisyphean rocks of his own choosing and commits himself to pushing them up steeper and steeper hills, then nudging them down again so he can return to the work he loves most—whistling joyful hymns of anxiety, sorrowful hymns of pure joy. Experiencing the world and facing every obstacle with the most creative spin possible, Odysseus story tells his way to the ultimate island, his Ithaka homeland, his own much-spinning mind. His home, where he rules as his own Renaissance Male Authority Figure, lies where his art is, and his art is storytelling—creating them, finding them, straightening them, publishing, and producing them.

"To burn always with this hard, gemlike flame, to maintain this ecstasy, is success in life."

—Walter Pater

Escape to Freedom

I was forty-three when I formally resigned from Occidental College to pursue my second profession editing, producing, and publishing—yet always, teaching. "The secret of a happy life," George Burns claimed, "is to fall in love with your future."

It wasn't until Georgetown, in Father Young, SJ's Attic Greek class, that I translated these words from Aristotle: "Happiness is not a plan."

I got it! I totally got it. It wasn't just the flippant falling in love with your future, it was an *arranged* marriage. It was *planning*.

You had to make a plan for your future, in general and in detail. Then stick to it, so that Hesiod's aphorism could bear truth: "If you put a little upon a little, soon it will become a lot."

Thanks to Jesuit indoctrination, from Rockhurst High School on, I not only planned each day but also planned it more or less minute by minute, including my "planning time," usually from 10:57-11:00 p.m. Those three minutes of planning were all it took.

Not only did I plan my days, I kept track of my successes or failures in forming the habits I intentionally cultivated.

Today my day planning is rudimentary by comparison:

This organizing note illustrates what I call my "rotation system," rotating from activity to activity in compartments of time.

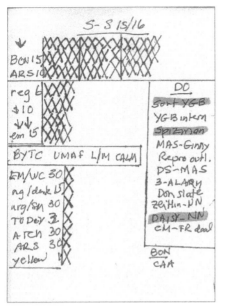

I like to compare the human mind to a revolving laser disc. The stylus reads the grooves on the disc of your mind as it skips from one to another, distributing the energy of each to all. That way my ADD doesn't get stuck in one groove to a point of non-productivity. If something starts feeling stale, I simply skip to the next rotation, the next groove in the disc.

Note the rectangular box with a bunch of capital letters in it. Those are my "affirmations" for the day, so ancient that I've reduced them to initials. UMAF = *You* are the Male Authority Figure. I began to realize that around the time my seventh decade commenced, and after decades of seeking a wise senior producer, magazine editor, retired Jesuit, trusted attorney, bearable therapist, or down-to-earth rabbi to tell me what the hell to do with "situations." No wonder it was getting harder and harder to find MAFS. I'll translate one other affirmation, BYTC = the Best is Yet to Come. I've lived by that optimistic rule all my life. It gets me through lots of worst.

Planning Your Life

I must have inherited the planning gene from Dad, though as but a warmup for the Jesuits who, after all, had indoctrinated him too (he had preceded me at Rockhurst). It was in one of my umpteen Greek classes at The Rock that I learned the Greeks not only planned their days, weeks, and years, but even planned their *lives*, seven years at a time. Ancient Hebrews had a word for that seven-year cycle, *shmita*. I *loved* that!

By the time I learned that little factoid, I'd already survived two relatively unplanned *shmita*. But from fifteen to twenty-one I determined I'd learn everything I came across that had to do with literature and communication—and sex (translating it all into my grandiosely recondite "Introduction to Conceptual Semantics," published in Georgetown's *Viewpoint*).

From twenty-one to twenty-eight I would bob and weave my way into adulthood. At nineteen I had been a schizoid KC–Louisiana virgin without a bachelor's degree; but at twenty-eight, I'd morphed into a travel-savvy A.T.&T. Communications Engineer in charge of the NASA desk in Washington DC, moving on to a Yale MPhil. in Theater History and PhD in comparative literature, married with two excellent children, and an Associate Professor at Occidental College in Los Angeles.

From twenty-eight to thirty-five I would find a way to "do something excellent," as *The Tao of Steve* puts it. Aside from winning American Council of Learned Societies, National Endowment for the Arts and Graves Foundation grants, I was honored with the Occidental Achievement Award for my prolific publication. I was also designated as "guest columnist" for *The Los Angeles Times Book Review* by editor and dear friend Art Seidenbaum. In addition to Brazilian novelist Jorge Amado, Israeli poet Yehuda Amichai, New York novelist Gilbert Sorrentino, and many others wrote to thank me for my reviews of their work.

8

Some of all this was planned, others the indirect result of planning—"planting seeds in the waiting room," as I now call it.

"Just because you made a good plan doesn't mean that's what's gonna happen," said Taylor Swift. Looking at what I accomplished in my ten *shmita*, I realize at least half of it wasn't what I planned. I guess I'm an opportunist who makes hay when the sun shines but follows plans whether it shines or not.

The Smith-Corona Letter

Two years before he died, when my father was diagnosed with inoperable lung cancer and given six months to live, after I rejected Mom's plan to meet them in Las Vegas, I flew from Los Angeles to spend some personal time with him in KC.

Looking for something constructive to suggest, I asked him if he'd thought about writing about his life. My father, who rarely wrote anything other than his gracefully elegant and identically articulated signature—usually beneath either minutes of a meeting or endless columns of numbers beneath a spreadsheet, each letter perfectly shaped—shook his head. "My typewriter is broken," he blurted out.

Then I remembered that he had, in fact, sent me typewritten letters through the first half of my life (when people still wrote letters). For some reason, no doubt connected with Mom's propaganda machine, I'd forgotten that.

I jumped in his car and drove over to Best Buy, where I bought him a portable electric typewriter. I was excited, knowing that my father's last experience with a keyboard was the old Royal non-electric on which I'd learned to type out tax forms without making a single mistake (he hated liquid paper—and don't even *breathe* the word "erasers" around him). Dad's no-error typing lessons made the BVM nuns of my grade school, and even the Jesuits of my high school and college, look like Romper Room attendants by comparison.

My father's eyes lit up when he saw the gift. I set it up near his desk, showed him how to switch it on, and watched him hunt and peck for a few minutes. Then I followed my nose upstairs to check in on my mother's progress with the fried chicken, pork roast and rice and gravy and potatoes. Maybe she could use a taster about now.

A half hour went by. I was sampling the first wing from the batch—Mom's peppery fried chicken, the best in the world—when Dad walked up from his basement den. He handed me a piece of paper, then sat down next to me while I read it.

It was the first, and last, product of the new typewriter. Mom said he never used it again, though he lived for nearly two more years. I was always lecturing apprentice writers on the importance of the actual mechanics of communication—making sure your instrument was what you needed it to be, to ensure that the flow could properly commence. Without thinking through the possibly negative ramifications, I'd provided Dad with the exact instrument he needed to communicate the closure that turned our relationship from one I'd regarded as pretty much dark and disturbing to one that, from that day forward, demanded massive re-thinking.

I, who keep everything on file, can't fathom how I lost track of that piece of typing paper. All I remember is that it said, "You have been a good son." Also, that he thanked me for that, and for the typewriter.

It was brief but typed perfectly with no mistakes—as I was trained to type, by him, even before I was old enough to escape to school. In those days—before I became the shining star of Mrs. Ann Molander's Touch Typing class at Rockhurst—I used the hunt and peck method on the old Royal that no one now recalls what happened to.

Dad put teenage me to work typing tax returns. Here's how he taught me to type perfectly: Every time I made a mistake, I should take the page out of the typewriter, ball it up, toss it, and began again. A few days of this discipline led first to constant grumbling and sighing, baskets full of paper, then, sure enough, to perfection. That night, before I turned in, I went to Dad's empty office downstairs and checked the wastebasket: It revealed five or six balled-up pages with typos—which he'd torn out.

On the phone the day before Dad died, when we last spoke, he said it again: "You've been a good son." It sounded almost like an afterthought, but I savored it because it was one of the final thoughts he expressed to me. I treasure that thought because though it came too late to affect the way I am it *was* the trophy I might have longed for in a part of my consciousness so ancient that I have no recollection of it at all.

I treasure that thought because anyone who had *not* experienced my father as I experienced him would think it something to be treasured. I treasure it because I didn't believe it was true. I may have made him proud, but I wasn't sure how good a son I was.

It led me to examine my filial conscience.

Fatherly Pride

"You've been a good son."

The odd thing is how those about-to-pass use the past-perfect tense for people they're leaving behind and who still *are* in the present. And how we about-to-be-left-behind accept that odd tense as our due—as though it was our secret handshake, to signify that we, after all, will eventually be part of the same moribund club. I once subscribed to Bernard Malamud's resolve: "The end of the world will occur when I die. After that, it's everyone for themselves."

I was thrilled to hear these fond paternal words from Dad again, because they came as confirmation to what he'd typed on the Smith-Corona two years earlier when I'd returned to KC after we first got word of his diagnosis.

Before that visit, over the years when I'd come home from whichever coast I happened to be adventuring in at the time, I'd listen eagerly but skeptically to my father's best friend, Bill Reynolds, tell me how "proud your father is of you."

"Funny he's never told me that," I would say.

"You know your father," he'd say.

I would lapse into silence. I thought I did know my father. He had been the angry Cyclops, the dark shadow over my early years.

Love Letters

The overwhelming evidence that Dad actually did love me as much as his own character—and Mom—allowed him to is (a) the sheaf of letters from me to him over the years, that he had filed away until handing it over to me while he was "putting his affairs in order"; (b) the much thicker file of letters—God help me, but I measured it: slightly more than two inches!—from him to me that I religiously filed away as though to consult it later and reassess my view of him; and (c) the stray letters from him that made their way to me after his funeral from Andrea, Laurie, and Mary—notably not from Mom.

Among the last was an age-browned envelope marked "Kenny Atchity," in a handwriting I don't recognize—maybe Uncle Anthony's or Tony's. It's a letter from Dad to Uncle Anthony and Aunt Carrie, looking forward "to the birth of the little one"—with a separate letter to Tony, Jr. ("Junie") appended—written from Paris on December 23, 1943—a month before I was born.

Although the bulk of (b) is comprised of letters to me after I arrived at Georgetown, letters to me during my Louisiana summers and after my first marriage are there too, showing he never lost the drive to communicate with his shadow son:

> *...We are all well and already miss you. Nothing exciting has happened since you left. I'll bet all the excitement was at your end.*

> *Hope you found all the folks well and especially Mamère. Give them all our love.*

> *Nobody is getting into your things—so don't worry about that or anything else.*

> *Hope you had a nice train ride.*

⊙

As I trudged to my one-room abode on P Street, or S Street, or T Street across the brick and cobblestone streets under the lowering skies of DC winter, I dreaded my father's letters as much as I delighted in those of Carrie Catherine or, later, of Dess.

I see why now.

I didn't love dealing with reality, even then; reality is where my father lived. I sympathized with Woody Allen: "I hate reality," he said, "but it's the only place you can get a decent chicken sandwich."

Dad's letters generally began with a painfully-realistic analysis of my financial state, or at least my reported financial state, with blunt advice about how to cut down:

> The enclosed $10.00 is for the fraternity pin [I had just been inducted into Eta Sigma Phi, the National Honors Society], and nothing else. I mean that we don't want you to use it for anything but that.

I hated the feeling of being remotely controlled:

> I think your financial thinking is O.K., except I don't possibly see how you can get by for $8.00 a week for food. If you eat out all three meals every day, it will cost you $2.00 per day even at the reasonable prices they are charging and which you mentioned. That is $14.00 per week. Take off one or two suppers a week that will be furnished perhaps by your friends, will still leave $12.00. $10.00 rent plus $12.00 food plus $5.00 laundry and incidentals adds up to $27.00 per week. Some weeks it will cost

you $30.00...I surely don't want you to worry about money, Ken, but you'll have to face the facts and skrimp...

"Scrimp" was high on his list of frequently-used words, along with "chintzy" and "dirt cheap." I faced the facts by restricting my food intake to one piece of cherry pie a day and boundless coffee; while buying books and books and books in irresistible Georgetown brick bookshops—and occasionally a little more pipe tobacco.

After my announcement, in the relative warmth of that street corner phone booth that rainy day, that I'd switched from pre-med to classics, Dad wrote me a letter saying he was truly "not shocked at such news," and went on to advise:

...You are only 17, almost 18, and only a freshman in college, but I want you to promise me that you will give a lot of thought this year to what occupation you would like to pursue in life, so that next year and thereafter you can devote your thoughts, ideas, and line of study towards that end. A person who has a definite goal, and who will direct himself determinedly, doggedly, and persistently towards that end will be a big success, regardless of what his occupation or profession be...

Dogged, persistent determination. That was my father's advice and, without attributing it to him, it became my MO as well. As Gandhi said, "Full effort is full victory."

As much as he was able, all too apparently Dad truly cared; truly did his best to be a good father even though, I'm sure, he was more comfortable with me at a distance than close by, where the dark atmosphere between him and Mom caused serious distortions in our communication. He even sent a telegram on February 27, 1963:

WE ARE ALL VERY PROUD OF YOUR ELECTION AS NEWS EDITOR OF THE HOYA. CONGRATULATIONS.

Yes, the letters reflect his preoccupation with money and keeping accounts straight. He was an accountant. What did I expect? What would anyone expect?

> *Congratulations! Wonderful, and exciting news upon your election. We are certainly proud and happy about it. You accomplish these things because you work hard for them and are persistent. It's not luck...*
> *...I was glad to make out your tax returns—after all—I should and will always be proud to do so.*

The letters are so detailed and voluminous that they tell an entirely different story from the Ken-Dad narrative I had been constructing, with Mom's help, since the Foghorn incident.

Never view another human being through someone else's eyes. It's not fair to him.

It's not fair to you.

Mom had taught me to read every word Dad wrote as an assault on my wellbeing, when clearly, many of his words were intended to be the very opposite. On my last visit to KC during his lifetime, Dad himself handed me a file he'd kept—"KENNY'S LETTERS," his neat printing called it. Seeing that hated diminutive in Dad's fine cursive made me stop hating it.

It included every letter I'd ever sent to him and Mom, including a letter I'd completely forgotten about but that witnesses my fascination with John Kennedy:

Christmas 1963
Dear Dad,

Merry Christmas! I hope this one will be a very happy one for you—you deserve it. I know I haven't been the best of sons in the past and for that I'm more sorry than I can ever say. I make it my most important New Year's resolution to look at myself and mind my ways along the good and straight lines you've laid down so consistently.

Thank you for everything, too. You've always given more than I've deserved. Someday I hope to be worth your faith in every way.

I hope you like your presents—the lamp is for reading at night. The portrait and the record are for something very great which we both have in common—a respect and love for a very great statesman, a great American, a great President, but most importantly—a great Man—in all the ways that we admire and would like to be.

It's very easy, on a college campus, to become critical of politicians when they fail, for whatever reason, to accomplish all the aims they stated in their desire to be elected. And, to some extent, I felt this way about Kennedy.

But there was always something about him that made him a magnetic personality for me. I'll miss him... [he was] a figure of hope. It was most inconceivable to me that he would leave the White House without proving to the world, his country, his party, and his opponents that he was indeed one of the few great men whose "task it is to safeguard freedom in her maximum hour of danger."

He embodied every quality the office of President of the United States could ask for–intelligence, compassion, wit, grace, and determination; his sense of history was an added element only shared by the great men of our history–Franklin, Jefferson, Lincoln...

The most beautiful epitaph I know was written by Homer about the death of Hektor, the great Trojan Hero, over four thousand years ago:

And when he fell in whirlwind, he went down

Like a mighty cedar, crashing

From its lofty throne on the mountainside:

Leaving a hollow emptiness against the sky.

I'd scribed the letter very carefully, using Jede's swirled black and beige fountain pen that I had inherited earlier that year when Tata slipped it to me from my grandfather's desk.

Even though Dad had served on General Eisenhower's staff during the war, it was Kennedy, not Ike, whose portrait hung on his office wall. No wonder I was so inspired to develop, sell, and produce Jerry Blaine and Lisa McCubbins' *The Kennedy Detail*–a New York Times bestseller and Discovery documentary nominated for an Emmy; then to work with Lisa and Jackie Kennedy's lead agent Clint Hill on his bestselling *Mrs. Kennedy and Me* and *Five Days in November*; and on turning Greg Lawrence's *Jackie as Editor* into a television series.

Dad's "Kenny" file is filled with pass books, loans taken and completed, notations of my won bets against the "Chiefs"

("Anybody who's disloyal to their home town doesn't deserve to win. Here's Fred Jr.'s 10.00 & my 5.00 Love Dad").

Reading through my letters to Dad over the years put my emotions through the shredder, revealing in black and white the discrepancy between how I recalled my feelings for him and what I wrote to him.

The Pot Thickens

"We have a problem." Mary's voice at the end of the line carried the edge that meant she didn't know how to handle something. That in itself, a rarity for my oldest sister, was a bad sign.

"What is it?"

"Having a problem," in our family, was not exactly unusual. It was February 2002. I'd departed KC and my mother's funeral only days before, where I did my best to maintain my most benign perspective toward the family whose suffocating intensity I could no longer handle, and ran away from, at the age of seventeen.

"Freddy wants the pot," was what I heard her saying.

My heart sank.

"You've *got* to be kidding. Freddy doesn't even know how to boil water!"

My brother was a self-fashioned throwback to an era where men and kitchens didn't mix.

I *lived* in the kitchen.

It was in the kitchen where Mom started every day with her indomitable morning optimism, singing made up words to

"Cielito Lindo" as she washed the breakfast dishes. "Ai-yi-yi," a Cajun lament, extended melodically to become "Ai-yi-yi-yi."

I was startled to discover on my first trip to Mexico that the actual song had lyrics that made actual sense.

When, as an adolescent, I wasn't deciphering Homeric Greek in my room I would migrate kitchenward to listen to the women gossip. Freddy and Dad didn't like gossip and walked away from it. To the women, and to me, gossip was the stuff of life, the nuclear cocktail of stories. The way the women taught me to look at life, if a tree fell in the forest with no one to talk about it, it just plain didn't fall.

The Freds focused on facts and bottom lines, not the confusion and pain that lies behind and beneath and around them. I loved to carry the sorrow around, as the women did. It made me feel close to Mom.

Too close, I saw, only in retrospect.

Θ

The pot that caused me this dismay was a four-gallon battered aluminum cauldron with a charred handle that I had acquisitioned, at Mom's insistence, a few months before she had her fatal stroke in front of the poker machine at Ameristar casino and died en route to North Kansas City Hospital.

The pot had belonged to my Lebanese grandmother, Anna Fatall Atchity, whose mother-in-law, my great grandmother, Sulimé, bought it from a door-to-door salesman in Pittsburgh for an outrageous twenty-five cents that got her in big trouble with my

311

great grandfather Antoine when he came home to discover it simmering on the stove filled with cabbage rolls.

"If you want a big family," she told him, no doubt flashing him those Lebanese eyes that stopped all retorts, "I need a big pot."

"Did you haggle for it?" he asked her, lighting his cigar, and walking away so he wouldn't hear her answer.

And that was the end of that.

In addition to Tata's beans and gumbo, I used the pot to make chili. Jede, remember, canned chili when he settled in KC, along with barbecue sauce and grape leaves. Years later someone in the family got confused and put barbecue sauce in their cabbage rolls. Ouch.

Θ

I asked Jede once why he'd never gone back to visit Lebanon (ancient Phoenicia) whence he emigrated at the age of fifteen to live in one room with three sisters and his father once he'd landed in America.

"Why would I want to do that, honey?" he asked, with the inarguable finality of the expatriate's logic.

None of his five sons and two daughters, or thirty-one grandchildren or forty-one great grandkids, ever went to Lebanon either—until the beautiful Christina Hake, Aunt Lorraine the Beauty's granddaughter, Cousin Mark and Vicki's daughter, made her first trip in 2013 and reported it all to us at the family reunion: "The food is great."

Θ

I'm convinced to this day that the pot itself was part of Tata's secret; why her beans surpassed all others'—as now, I humbly profess, do mine.

It cooks fast and distributes heat evenly.

The first two plates of the Sunday morning beans were served to my grandfather and me. We sat across from each other in silence and concentrated on the dish filled with bright red beans, which we shoveled into our mouths with the fresh-baked bread the aroma of which still filled the house.

The only side dish was wedges of sweet white onions, a sliver of which we would slip into each Lebanese-bread scoop of beans.

My mother liked to drive me crazy by chopping up the onions, claiming "that's the way Tata did."

Oh my God, Mom! Tata so did *not* chop them! She cut them in small wedges. Mom was a Cajun. Cajuns *chopped* onions. She did what she wanted to do and wasn't about to be bound by a Lebanese mother-in-law's way of doing things. I was furious because I *knew* what was going on with her and hated that she *lied* about it instead of simply fessing up that she *wanted* to do it that way and thought Tata's wedges were weird.

I enjoyed Tata's beans reverentially then, as I do to this day, and was so intent on the business of devouring what was on my plate that I noticed nothing else. Eating that first plate of beans, fresh from that pot, with the bread straight from the oven was to me like reading a good book. First, you turn the pages as fast as you can. Then, roughly halfway through the plate, you realize this will be the one and only time, therefore the last time, you will

313

"read" this particular plate—and you reverse gears, slowing down to savor every bite, like every page.

All of which unfailingly led me to be surprised when I would look up at a new familiar smell—and see that my grandfather was already lighting his Lucky Strike. Unburdened by the book-bean analogy, he was finished with his plate already, and I still had half my plate left.

Jede did everything fast, from driving his car to propagating five sons and two daughters. Nothing faster than eating. He grinned at me through the smoke and offered the Lebanese food-benediction: "*Sa'tanya*, honey," accompanied with a nod of approval.

Θ

When the rest of the family arrived and the weekly updates were finished (the uncles met with Jede in the living room while the aunts, Mom, Tata and I, milled around the kitchen hoping to be useful and sipping 7-Up, a luxury we never experienced at our house), we dug into the feast Tata had prepared, with me monitoring her every dash and pinch: *kibbeh nayeh*, with pine nuts browned in butter and sprinkled across the top, garnished with green onions and scooped with Tata's bread; baked kibbeh (leftovers of which made excellent sandwiches on Tastee bread slathered with mayonnaise); and sometimes *kusa* (zucchini or yellow squash) stuffed with rice and meat; and grape leaves.

Once, we in the kitchen overheard the subject of discussion in the men's living room meeting. The word *majdoube* (pronounced MOOSTOOFI), Arabic for "moron," was too loud not to be heard throughout the house—especially because Jede was repeating it emphatically.

Uncle Anthony, cigar and all, was under attack from his father.

That in itself was unusual because Jede had the closest paternal relationship with his oldest son. He and Tata played canasta with him and Aunt Carrie nearly every Saturday night into the wee hours of the morning, finishing with breakfast at the Muehlebach Hotel downtown. Jede called Carrie a "Bolshevik," and no one in the family had any idea why until someone repeated the word to Tata. "Bullshitter," she translated with a grunt of affirmation. "She was a bullshitter." Carrie never heard anything you said to her, interrupting instead to say in her husky smoker's voice, "You're a doll!"

"What did I hear about your buying a Cadillac?" Jede asked.

Eagle confessed that he had indeed bought a Cadillac, a blue one, and now brazenly invited his dad and brothers to come outside and see it.

"That's right, Dad," he said. "Business is good."

Jede was not amused. He made it clear that the purchase was a stupid business decision, made with Anthony's *zabr* rather than his brain. What would Anthony's customers think to see their grocer driving around in a Cadillac?

"They can kiss my big fat *teezak* if they don't like it," Anthony retorted.

Uncle Anthony's customers, at 48th & Main where he'd relocated his store from 41st and Wayne, were upscale folk who ordered Half 'n Half instead of milk for their coffee, Pepperidge Farm bread, and Wolferman's English muffins, for chrissakes. I knew because I pedaled the Broadmour Finest Foods black delivery bike to their posh apartments—the Casa Loma, the Locarno, the Biarritz, the Riviera—looking out across Brush Creek to the Country Club Plaza.

I couldn't picture any of these dignified old ladies kissing Eagle's ass.

LtoR: Uncles Jimmy, Vic, Dad, Eddy, Anthony; Aunt Selma, Jede, Tata, Aunt Lorraine

His son, Cousin Tony, though—he was different. Tony was a dashing, teasing lothario to them all. They would have kissed anything they could get to on him.

Jede may have been seething long before the Cadillac discovery. Anthony had brazenly called his new store, instead of

"Atchity's #4," "Broadmour Market." What was that all about, Jede wanted to know? He never got a straight answer.

For the rest of his life, Anthony bought one Cadillac after another, a new one each year, and drove it over to our house first to show it off. Dad shook his head, as Jede had, but secretly was admiring of his flamboyant oldest brother.

Though I joined the feast again when the yelling died down and Tata summoned us to the dining room table, my appetite had already been satisfied, on every level, by my privileged attendance at the moment of creation much earlier that day, where I felt like I was watching Hephaistos forging the mighty shield of Achilles.

The fragrant feast would draw to a close when coffee and *bet-lay-weh*, baklava—was served and someone would ask Jede to play his oud.

We all retreated to the living room, while he positioned himself in his little curved mahogany desk chair, moving it under the arch between living room and dining room. With his stoked cigarette holder dangling from his lips, he would hesitantly take the inlaid rosewood lute-shaped instrument from Uncle Jimmy who retrieved it from its mysterious sanctuary.

An aunt would hand him his ostrich feather plectrum, and Jede would begin to play.

Without further hesitation, Jede went from cranky head of business meeting to practiced impresario, whose smile inched across his face as the music resonated through the room. Sometimes my aunts and cousins would dance to the music, which alternated between eerie Middle Eastern strains of lonely intensity to the oddly-stirring stridency of Le Marseillaise.

Jede would sing the words in French—I know the militaristically demented lyrics by heart to this day—and beckon, with his eyes, my mother to join him. Mom would join him singing the words—that marked the reach of the French empire from Napoleon's Paris to the Middle East, where French had become the second language of Lebanon from the time of the Crusades, all the way to South Louisiana, where English had been made the official language of the state only as recently as 1915.

My grandfather had boarded the SS Pennsylvania for the New World, by way of Tripoli and Boulogne, at the age of fifteen; and gave up his past to build a future closer to his dreams and potential. The new world had been kind to him, and tears would form in my grandfather's eyes as he entertained his ample and prosperous family who honored him with their presence every Sunday.

They said he'd learned five languages from the Jesuits in Lebanon. He and Father Z set that bar for me. By the time I left Yale I had seven languages under my belt.

Θ

"Are you still there?" My sister's voice jarred me from my ruminations.

"Yeah," I said. "I just don't get it."

"Did you say pot?" she asked.

"What? Yeah... What did *you* say?"

"I said *plot*," she said, articulating. "Plot. P-l-o-t."

"What plot?" Had my brother become a writer and stolen one of my plots?

"You know, the extra plot Dad bought at Mt. Olivet."

Mt. Olivet is the cemetery in the outskirts of KC where many of the Atchity family liked to go to be buried.

"You've got to be kidding me," I said. "I thought you said 'pot.' You know I don't give a fig about plots! I don't even want to be buried," I assured her. "I'm not going to die." To me deciding where to be buried was the ultimate test of self-definition. I'd decided that, should I be mistaken about my physical immortality, cremation was the only way to avoid the ultimate self-sabotage. Did I want to be posthumously identified with KC, or with Louisiana where the little cemetery near Basile gave final abode to Mom's dad and mom, Mezille and Evan Aguillard, my "Cajun" grandparents?

"Don't talk like that," she said. "You know it's not right."

"Don't get me started."

"I told him I'd check with you to be sure you were okay with it. He'll buy another one, so he and Jan can be buried together near Mom and Dad."

I was relieved. "So, he doesn't want Tata's pot at all?"

"No," she said. "Honestly, he doesn't even know you have that pot. In fact, I remember Mom telling us not to say a word that she'd given it to you."

That sounded like Mom. She'd also given me the best spatula in the world, her old aluminum one, with a six-inch blade so thin and strong you could flip eggs "over easy" with masterful perfection. Only later did it come out, little by little, that she was sneaking things to each of us. Mary, of course, got the house; nothing sneakable about that. Andrea got Mom's zucchini-corer, one of the aluminum ones, hand-made by Jede. Laurie ended up with my favorite coffee table (I now have a duplicate in my den, discovered at a Temecula antique store).

I figured if Freddy knew about the pot, he'd pretend he wanted it, or that Mom had promised it to him.

I couldn't even *pretend* to want the cemetery plot.

Not only was I not interested in being buried, but I also definitely didn't want to be buried in KC, much as I grew to love the barbecue, the autumnal locust chants, and the Country Club Plaza at Christmas. I much prefer the ash route, mixed in a jar with Kayoko's and spread from a whale-watching boat across the Pacific, the ocean that joins my American with her Japanese origins. My "holding urn" awaits in my closet, arranged by the Neptune Society after Freddy's sudden demise made me realize this death thing could even happen to me.

Meanwhile, God be praised, the pot was mine for the duration. Thank you, Tata.

Dad's Happy List

One night a year before he died, I reached out to understand my father. We were returning to KC from the Lotawana lake cabin late. It was a cold winter's midnight, something like six below zero, as we drove through the woods in our accustomed father-son silence.

Looking out at the ice-wrapped trees, I realized something awful: If the car engine stopped, the two of us would freeze to death in minutes—without either having the slightest idea of who the other really was.

Before I could stop myself to think, I blurted the words out: "Dad, are you happy?"

Long silence.

What was I *thinking?*

I'd known better than to ask this kind of question from the time I was four years old. I regretted the words the moment they were spoken and couldn't believe I'd said them out loud. I'd never heard my father talk about happiness or about himself, and since both subjects, happiness, and self, were much on my relentlessly narcissistic mind, I was curious what he'd say.

We drove in silence through the stark winter woods for another few minutes. I wondered whether he'd maybe not heard me and started to breathe more deeply. Then he broke the silence. "Well, we sold the property on Lydia," he said, "and made a pretty good profit. So even though we just broke even on the 32nd Street place—it was condemned by the city, and we were lucky to sell it at all—I can't complain. My investments are in pretty good shape despite the market." He stopped.

I had heard his bottom line. He had reviewed the balance sheet and delivered his answer; the answer any persevering accountant would give to a query he had taken a few minutes to translate into the matrix of his personal world view. He left it to me, the accountant's somewhat son, to translate his answer back into my own peculiar sensitivity.

And I did translate it: Bottom line, my father was happy enough.

Like so many of his generation, my father didn't understand the process of asking yourself, "Am I happy?"—much less, "What is the meaning of life?" "Should I be doing something else?" "Who am I?" —and all such questions that spring up among those who have the leisure and psychological savvy to ask them.

My father's generation were warriors and builders, hunters and gatherers. They didn't study psychology or visit shrinks. They fought the wars they were asked to fight and then without fanfare returned to build families and homes and earn a living to support them.

For them, success was measured by three entirely tangible criteria: personal survival, a large family (evolution's extension of personal survival), and "a bigger, better home" (Dad's translation: "building equity"). A man was satisfied by serving his country, raising five children, educating them, and owning a respectable home for them.

I envied the simplicity of my father's criteria.

While my brother strove to emulate him, I strove to do the opposite of what Dad would do, following my mother's urging. He loved money and the bottom line. I loved words and the well told story.

Freddy joined the National Guard. I finessed the Vietnam draft by precociously having a family while still at Georgetown and Yale.

Freddy stopped short of matching Mom and Dad's five children—leaving out that first, unruly one, of five in another tacit erasure? He stopped at an even number: Matthew, Mark, Amy, and Sara. I not only stopped at the perfect son and perfect daughter, Vincent, and Rosemary; but again, as I did when I enrolled in college, broke all Atchity family precedent by divorcing. My lead in that distinction was soon followed by numerous cousins.

My brother hadn't approved of my second marriage, which a priggish English professor colleague called "the triumph of hope over experience." I kicked him out of our house on Campus Road one night when, deep in his cups, he told Circe, "I would never have chosen you as my brother's wife." Reenacting Dad's dismissal of Uncle Wib years ago, I watched Freddy pacing our front yard waiting for the taxi I'd called for him.

Freddy didn't approve of my divorce from her, either—thereby out-moralizing our parents, who were pleased by my decision and were happy for me that I was leaving an unhappy relationship, no doubt partly because they had themselves been unable to do the same. Years and years later, after forty-seven years of marriage, my brother divorced the long-suffering Jan (who the family did *not* divorce). Forty-seven years was how long my parents were married too, by the way. Dad's death precluded their making it to the Golden Anniversary that Jede and Tata had celebrated.

My father's relentless pursuit of a stable equity base moved us from Benton Boulevard to Virginia Avenue to East 75th Street to East 104th Street.

Freddy moved his family from Overland Park to Prairie Village then, in 1985, took the big leap over the Rockies to join me in California. He moved into a Hancock Park mansion that overshadowed in grandeur anything our father could have even aspired to.

Freddy measured happiness with his own version of "show and tell." Each new acquisition had no way of settling in his mind until he'd displayed it humbly, then, later, not so humbly—his way of expressing pride of accomplishment, as I do with words: a house with a stunning mountain view in La Quinta, another with an equally awesome view in Blaine, Washington, looking across the strait at Canada; BMWs, Jaguars, Bentleys galore; a golf cart with a camel hood ornament; the life-sized camel sculpture facing the golf course, an Art Deco condo across from Wilshire Country Club. For his second wedding, Freddy rode into the crowd on a camel and was assisted in the dismount by his oldest son Matthew.

Dad counted happiness in degrees of security caused by inching ahead on the profit-into-savings scale. He'd bought the

Benton Boulevard property for $2700 on a G.I. loan when he returned from the War to his fiercely independent wife and wrongly named son. He'd sold it for $34,000 when he moved to Virginia Avenue—the house he bought for $27,000 and sold for $54,000 en route to 75th Street. Etc.

I, on the other hand, had a psychologically hard time gathering any moss beyond what I needed to sustain my creative commitments to a "different" life. Until I bought a pied-à-terre on Manhattan's East Side in 1990, I'd never owned a home. As a professor, I'd been fortunate enough to live in one "faculty house" after another. But as a businessman, I was content with renting, an act my family equated with treason against the American way. It was enough for me to religiously take my maximum deduction from taxes for using my home as an office.

Normal Atchitys amassed money, home equity, and possessions. I, instead, accumulated creative accomplishments: poems, articles, books, movies written and/or published and/or produced and/or represented—whether or not substantial funds or any funds at all were attached. My resume replaced my bankbook.

I was the black sheep, at least in my own mind.

One thing my bro and I had in common: When I am anxiously trying to assess whether I'm happy or not, I draw up a list of things I've done and things I'm in the middle of doing. Not things that I own. Do, do, do was my mantra; I learned to prioritize *doing* over *thinking* and *feeling*. The listing of *dones* centered me. Through the good offices of my yogini wife, Kayoko, I would eventually discover that it was okay to just *be*—and *just being* I can be pretty danged happy.

I'm beginning to master my own game: to do and to be.

Do be do be do.

But it's not over till the Fat Lady sings. I've still got miles to go before I sleep. I feel the call of new adventure.

In a way, this book is *my* happy list.

Blowjobs on the Strip

Between the banishment of Circe and my departure to commence a new career in moviemaking in Montreal, Dad flew to LA to hang with me. We planned to drive to KC by way of Las Vegas, my least favorite city. Other than an occasional drive from Lake Lotawana back to E. 104th Street, I'd spent a lifetime avoiding being alone in a car with my father.

As we both grew older, I realized that I might have been missing an opportunity and arranged for this trip.

I recall no details of our drive from LA to Las Vegas except that we listened to music as we crossed the austerely serene and severe Mojave. I recognized the radio as a mechanism for avoiding those black holes of conversation that would throw me back into my childhood feelings of emptiness and loss: anything connected with money, with Mom, with KC.

In Vegas, we did the usual Atchity-family casino-hopping, pursuing the siren Lady Luck from one gaudy lair to another. At one point, we made the macho decision to walk along Las Vegas Boulevard from Caesar's Palace to the Silver Slipper.

Along our route, we passed two high-heeled and sequined ladies of the night heading in the opposite direction. At first, neither of us spoke. Then, out of the blue—and oblivious to what might have triggered such a thought, as was usual with Dad—he asked me. "They say that even nice girls these days give blowjobs."

I said nothing, my head churning to process this unexpected paternal comment.

He repeated the statement, but this time, making it clear from his intonation that it was a direct question.

"I wouldn't know, Dad," I answered testily. Of course, I knew perfectly well. But answering the question was tantamount to letting him invade my irrepressible libido, which I, after all, inherited from him. I lapsed into awkward silence, at the same time ruminating over a lifetime of lapsing into silence rather than engaging my father in the manly conversation he'd made an overture toward—just as his lakeside farts had challenged me in vain to join the league of soldierly men.

I didn't want to think what the question told me about his sex life.

Utah Awakening

That father-son trip to Las Vegas, a token attempt at belated male bonding, ended abruptly around seven p.m. on the second evening of our planned three-night outing in Sin City.

Dad, abandoning the craps tables, found me at my low-stakes blackjack table, my usual Vegas refuge from financial and psychological meltdown. I was usually able to keep $100 going for at least a few hours by carefully managing my bets and staving off utter boredom by reciting Latin epigrams in my mind (Martial LXVI):

> Et delator es et calumniator
> Et fraudator es et negotiator,
> Et fellator es et lanista, mirror
> Quare non habeas, Vacerra, nummos.

> Vacerra, you are a rat and a liar, a con-man
> And a fraud, a cocksucker, and troublemaker.
> I'm amazed you don't have more money.

"Are you ready to leave?" Dad asked, with his usual aversion to introductory small talk.

"Sure," I responded, with my usual aversion to involving him in unnecessarily probing chitchat.

"We can drive all night," he added cheerfully. My family loved driving all night, no matter *where* we were going or *how long* it took.

Ꝋ

A few hours later, we exited Nevada without further financial loss except what we pumped into the gasoline dispensers in direct exchange for escape. I could tell Dad was more relaxed as I pointed my black Pontiac toward the moon rising in the East to illuminate the prehistoric Utah seafloor with its magic lantern.

"Maybe I'll take a little nap," he said, asking my permission with his tone of voice.

"Good idea," I replied. "I'll stop so you can climb into the back seat to be more comfortable."

"Don't worry about it. I can crawl over." Atchitys hate unnecessary stops during road trips, as my sister Mary well knew when she left her purse behind at a gas station convenience store in Louisiana and only realized it 100 miles later. Dad's favorite driving mantra was, "We're making good time." It doesn't matter where we're going.

My father clambered over and around the headrests and made himself comfortable.

For the next two hours or so, I drove alone with my thoughts, mostly about how I'd survived being up close with Dad and even, a little, enjoyed it. That last thought came with more than a tinge of regret as I wondered how much I'd lost by not attempting the feat years ago. He wasn't a bad travel companion and, as long as I steered the conversation toward the routine banalities of travel—food, rest, relief, miles gone, and miles to go—I was feeling pretty much okay about it. Maybe he feared our conversation as much as I did.

Then, with his usual immediate alertness, I saw him sit up suddenly in the back seat and reach for his glasses parked on the rear window shelf. "I was thinking," he said. "If I lost what I just lost in Vegas every day for the rest of my life, and I lived to be 100, I'd still be okay."

"Do you want to turn around and go back?" I asked, pushing the envelope.

"No," he said. "I've had enough."

Θ

My father was the most risk-averse human being I've ever known— the living opposite of his father, my Jede.

Jede considered risk the gateway to success and fulfillment—as I do.

As Mom did.

Though he couldn't help occasionally toying with it at buddy poker games or at the proliferating casinos, Dad saw risk as the slippery slide into failure.

An Eagle Joke

A golfer was having a drink with an old friend.

"How was your game Sunday?" the friend asked.

"Well, it was a little rough because Charlie died on the eleventh hole."

"Omigod," the friend replied. "Charlie died? How awful. The poor guy. I can imagine. No wonder your game was ruined."

"Yeah," the golfer nodded. "For the last seven holes it was hit-the-ball, drag Charlie, hit-the-ball, drag Charlie."

Optimism

My father was a lifetime Optimist. He was also a member of the Salvation Army, the American Legion, and the V.F.W. (Veterans of Foreign Wars). He dragged us kids to their functions, all of us bewildered by the varied-colored bunting and symbolism we were too cool to ask for explanations of. Once a year, he would stand on downtown street corners in his business suit, selling fake poppies for the VFW. We were kind of embarrassed for him—for us all—without knowing exactly why. I think it had something to do with Mom's shrug.

Mom's natural chattiness didn't extend to business networking, being a farm girl whose idea of social organization was corralling three of her siblings to take bed sheets down from the clothesline and fold them, then go inside and bake pies.

But it was the Optimists Club that spoke most clearly to my father's soul. Its creed explains so much about him:

Promise Yourself
To be so strong that nothing can disturb your peace of mind.
To talk health, happiness and prosperity to every person you meet.
To make all your friends feel that there is something in them.
To look at the sunny side of everything and make your optimism come true.

To think only of the best, to work only for the best, and to expect only the best.

To be just as enthusiastic about the success of others as you are about your own.

To forget the mistakes of the past and press on to the greater achievements of the future.

To wear a cheerful countenance at all times and give every living creature you meet a smile.

To give so much time to the improvement of yourself that you have no time to criticize others.

To be too large for worry, too noble for anger, too strong for fear, and too happy to permit the presence of trouble.

If you judge the man by how perfectly he fulfilled these optimistic ideals, any man will come up wanting. Judge him by the standard he aspires to. How a man acts in public is likely to be quite different than how he acts in private, where his guard is relaxed, insecurities displayed, and his mask comes off. Dad was guilty of criticism, of anger, and of great tormenting fear—that came to a head when his secure gig at Lafferty & O'Gara Sales Company ended abruptly. The Lafferty brothers lost their Pabst Blue Ribbon beer distributorship, and Dad (and the rest of us) feared we were faced with being "out on the street."

I give my father credit for joining this club and adopting its creed as his own. I may have been slightly embarrassed that he belonged to such a corny organization, just as I was when he enlisted me to join him selling the red plastic "buddy poppies." But the adherence to optimism rubbed off on me. I start the day with a song, usually one of Mom's favorites, and I look forward to a happy evening no matter what the day throws in my path. If I can see any path leading to hope, that's all I need to keep pushing my rock up the hill. No one can travel farther on a half-pint of hope than an Atchity.

Optimism is the only logical philosophy for a human being to subscribe to for the simple reason that optimism may be wrong, but it's still a happier road to follow than pessimism, which is unhappy from beginning to end.

The time we were to drive together to Las Vegas, Dad arrived by air at my house on the hill in Southern California, with downtown Los Angeles as its glistening nighttime backdrop. A few years earlier, when I moved in, I'd taken pride in papering the half bathroom off the kitchen with rejection slips from the hundreds of poems and articles I'd submitted throughout my early writing career. One of my favorites was a jagged piece of scrap paper on which an overloaded poetry editor had hastily scribbled and returned to me with my submitted poem, a single word: "Nuts."

During the lull between courses on our first-night dinner celebrating his arrival, Dad excused himself to go the bathroom. When he returned, he looked at me and said, "I'm really proud of your persistence."

Tears came to my eyes. "Thank you."

Then he expelled a deep breath. "But God, that's depressing," he said. "I couldn't handle it," he added.

My father remained an optimist by not taking unnecessary risks that might depress him and make him pessimistic. From him, I learned to stay optimistic especially while taking risks.

Working Alone

Another sweet thing about work is that it's best done in solitude.

Growing up amid ever-expanding family chaos, being alone was sheer bliss. But I was always torn. I also hated to miss things. So, I often worked on the kitchen table, in the center of emotional maelstrom, our family's daily life.

I still love to work with people around: the student cafeteria, Rome's Campo di Fiori, the beach at Cabo San Lucas, LA's Farmer's Market, a 49th Street Manhattan café, my son Vincent's or daughter Rosemary's breakfast rooms, a crowded airplane. There you'll find me with my laptop open, happily working away as though I were alone.

Crowds make me focus.

Time pressures make me concentrate. As a professor, I did my best writing thirty minutes before a committee meeting; as a producer, in the back seat of a limo en route to the set or on the jitney to Long Island to meet a financier.

I love to concentrate, but first, you need the distraction.

My family provides me with a lifetime of happy distraction.

Mr. Lichtor Joke

A Jewish mother gives her son two ties for his birthday.

The next morning, to please her, he dresses up in his best suit, one of her ties, and picks her up to take her to breakfast.

"I knew it!" she says. "You didn't like the other one."

Bearing Gifts

I'm a sucker for strangely personalized presents, like the oversized chocolate bar friend and client Terry Stanfill gave me bearing the cover of my novel on its face, or the tap-dancing-balancing-pole world clock Mom gave me after her visit to Los Angeles to determine whether I was insane or not. The older I get, the less I like receiving *things*. My favorite gift to get is vodka (Stoli, Belvedere, or Smirnoff, please—or Mongolian Soyombo).

I must admit that personalized art is right up there. After I published my first book of poetry, *Sleeping with an Elephant*, Occidental College artist friend and Occidental colleague Linda Lyke painted me half naked in bed with a pachyderm. Dear friend Kathy Jacobi, who designed the logo of *DreamWorks* for Marsha Kinder and me, painted "Daddy Holding Me," which hangs in our foyer. A Yale crush, later girlfriend, did a watercolor that portrays my Hamlet persona, capturing a fleeting moment of indecision.

 My second wife created a signature rubber stamp when I was in my bearded phase. The phase was cured when sister Mary's husband Chester started calling me, "Uncle Beard." I shaved the beard off, but he never stopped calling me Uncle Beard.

The square bearded stamp made its way to L/A House matchbooks, and I'm holding one of those matchbooks in the pastel portrait Kathy Jacobi exhibited during the portrait period of her magnificent career.

Susan Hesse, GU classmate Steven's wife, even did several photo portraits of me as vegetables.

One of my favorite poet-students, Nan Wigington, touched me with this letter:

> 6/25/82
> Dear KJA,
>
> What a feather artist* you are sometimes. You can humanize others' desires and neutralize their doubts. As you did for me.
> I'll always worry about my writing, but not with the same intensity. I can't let the worry impede the writing. Nor can I let the anger or the hurt or the pride. Writing is a thing in itself, a sort of DING AN SICH experience....
> *SEE POEM ON BACK COVER

The back cover was a poem called "The Fancy Hat" about Amantecatl, "the feather artist":

> The good feather artist is skillful,
> is master of himself; it is his duty
> to humanize the desires of the people.

It made me happy when others thought I had it together more than I did.

Sharing my Jesuit past and classical training, my Brooklyn-born poet friend Mark McCloskey, now departed to a realm where he can finally express the full range of his sarcasm and disdain for students with impunity, wrote me this splendid, and accurate, poem for a birthday when he had no funds for vodka:

Ken

My calendar's a skating rink—
speed and curlicue and fall.
I talk in Greek and Provençal,
but litotes is how I think.

This is why I'm always broke:
my Dad's a church among the rich,
and I like lute and hemistich
and prose's oldest touch, the joke.

I think Picasso dreamed my eyes
when he was etching minotaurs;
my hooves wear out on streets and floors,
pants drag down my curly thighs.

My new wife, though, is like a flute:
She joggles me when I'm effete
to see I'm not as close to Crete
as wet New Orleans, dry Beirut.

And so I'll teach my kids trombone
and flying carpet—damn the cost!

The past composed on isn't lost,
surprise rescinds a monotone.

Never quite understoond that last line, but hugely preferred the verse even to vodka.

I wish my kids *had* learned trombone. Rosemary did play the sax.

I remember rescuing Mark from the broken beer bottle being wielded by none other than rival poet Charles Bukowski at an Easter dinner at my hillside apartment on Wildwood Drive. I marched Mark inside to the kitchen while Hank held unchallenged sway at the main table on the terrace. "I hate that sonofabitch," Mark muttered. I told him the story of taking my daughter, five-year-old Rosemary, to Bukowski's home in Silver Lake to look at his bust created by girlfriend Linda King. Rosemary walked in, looked around at the rolls of toilet paper and dirty breakfast dishes strewn all over the floor, and piped out: "This is the filthiest place I've ever seen!"

"Damned right," Bukowski grunted.

Another one of my favorite gifts was a handwritten tribute from an Occidental student, Gabriella Gutiérrez, whom I'd shaken into high performance by forcing her to confront some personal issues.

EL PEQUEÑO GRANDE

La primera vez que lo vi,
Pensé que era pequeño,
Pero ahora solo sus
Palabras lo dicen, alguna vez
Yo no lo veo,

Lo siento.
He olvidado que es pequeño
Para mi es grande,
muy grande.
El piensa que es pequeño,
si veera su grandeza
no estaria aqui.
Aqui es muy pequeño para el.
Dejesmoslo pensar
que es pequeño
Es un pequeño grande.

She was right about one thing: I never thought of myself as *pequeño*, surprised to this day when I see myself as the shortest in a candid shot with friends. Who *is* that guy? How did he get so *short?*

Between marriages, I traveled to Boston from New York one day after landing at JFK from Italy, to break up in person with an older woman I'd gotten involved with out of sheer infatuation with her prowess as a poet.

A few days after I'd landed back in California, I received her revenge, autographed at the bottom of the carefully typed sheet:

She and the Muse

Away he goes, the hour's delightful hero,
arrivederci: and his horse clatters
out of the courtyard, raising
a flurry of straw and scattering hens.

He turns in the saddle waving a plumed hat,
his saddlebags are filled with talismans,

mirrors, parchment histories, gifts and stones,
indecipherable clues to destiny.
He rides off in the dustcloud of his own
story, and when he has vanished she
who had stood firm to wave and watch
from the top step, goes in to the cool

flagstoned kitchen, clears honey and milk and bread
off the table, sweeps from the hearth
ashes of last night's fire, and climbs the stairs
to strip tumbled sheets from her wide bed.

Now the long-desired
visit is over. The heroine
is a scribe. Returned to solitude,
eagerly she reenters the third room,

the room hung with tapestries, scenes that change
whenever she looks away. Here is her lectern,
here her writing desk. She picks up a quill,
dips it, begins to write. But not of him.

I sensed a grand irony in this insightful tour-de-force—that it *is*, despite itself, "of him." And she catches me red-handed: a literary adventurer tilting through windmills of his own devising. I was indeed laden with present-filled saddlebags, always thinking of myself as a kind of Odysseus finding trouble in all directions whether I was looking for it or not—or a latter-day Phoenician trader loaded with stories. "Where are you going this time?" Andrea would ask from the KC end of the phone, hearing me packing and zipping as we talked. At least she didn't remind me that a rolling stone gathers no moss. We both knew I was just going to keep on rolling.

The poet's "plumed hat" and "tumbled sheets" are nice touches.

Caution: Shrinkage

I've visited a few psychotherapists in my life, hoping for clarity on all of the above. The sessions usually ended abruptly, though I did end up having an affair with one of them.

One time I was so grateful for the commentary one female psychologist offered me that I bought her a gift box of fancy soaps from Saks and delivered them on my first visit after Christmas.

Only to be castigated on the next visit because I had crossed her boundaries. She wanted to give the pretty box back.

I told her it was a gift, and you don't give gifts back. But that it was okay if she tossed it in the wastebasket.

Which she immediately did.

That was my last visit to her office.

Another time, during a crisis in my film production business, I found myself on the verge of bankruptcy with no other choice than to proceed full-bore in the direction I was already moving.

But I thought I'd use the opportunity to find out if some psychological block was holding me back. So, I went to another psychologist, this one in the San Fernando Valley, which to me, in LA parlance, was "GU" ("geographically undesirable"). After one session, I found myself rethinking what the good doctor told me as I drove over the hill to my pad in Mid-Wilshire.

I'd been telling him how I envisioned the future and how I rationalized all I was suffering to make it happen. I told him that the other day, after a meeting that went much better than I thought it would, I returned to my car to find a note under my windshield wiper: "*YOU ARE ON A ONE-WAY STREET.*" I smiled happily from the universe reinforcing my quest as I climbed into the car. But I turned the key, looked out at the traffic, and realized, instead, that I was *literally* facing the wrong-way on a one-way street. My obsessive optimism made me mis-read the note.

"You have the most amazing ability," he responded, "for self-delusion that I've ever encountered. You frighten me."

I took another look at him and realized he looked more like a fretting accountant than a supportive therapist. No wonder he was frightened. The Dean of the Faculty at Occidental College, after one of my annual faculty reviews in which he noted that I'd published more that year than the rest of the faculty combined, ended his assessment with a similar conclusion: "You frighten me." *What am I supposed to do about that?* I wanted to ask him. Instead, I stared him down until he glanced out the window. "Intimidating" is a word I heard a lot, and it puzzled me since it's the last thing in the world I felt.

But on the drive home that night, it occurred to me that Therapist #2 didn't mean his comment as a compliment. Which is what I'd taken it as. I thought he was applauding my imagination, as my mother usually did (when she wasn't warning me against it).

Instead, he was warning me that I was operating in a dangerous mode of self-delusion. Which I did not appreciate. More negativity I did not need.

I pulled out of that particular crisis and got the film in question done. But anyone who knows producers knows we *are* insane by most anyone's standards. If you're not self-deluding, you're not getting the job done.

The soaps-rejecting therapist made some useful contributions to my self-understanding. One time I told her I felt guilty about the fact that I sometimes had my dollar bills crumpled up in my pocket instead of neatly folded and ordered by denomination in a money clip.

She asked me to show her, so I pulled out the day's wad.

"How much is it?" she asked.

"Three hundred fifty-three dollars," I answered.

"So, let me ask you a question. Over the course of your life, as you crumpled money in your pocket, how much money do you think you've lost because of doing that?"

That *was* an interesting question.

"I'd say less than twenty dollars."

"So, what's the problem?" she asked. "Is there a God that tells you that you have to fold your money a certain way?"

I thought of my actor friend Alex Cord who, eschewing money clips, held his wad neatly together with a rubber band.

"No, I guess not," I said.

It's funny how carefully we shop for the advice we want to hear, instead of having the presence of mind to take it from ourselves.

Dad's *La-ha-mish-weh*

Once or twice a year, often at the lake once we had the cottage, Dad performed the ritual of proving that he *could* cook. The rest of the year he avoided any contact with kitchen implements, except during covert, usually late-night, construction of his Dagwood sandwiches, with no one around to witness him.

Making *La-ha-mish-weh* (Arabic for shish kebob) was the opposite: the more witnesses, the better. He was showing off.

The ritual began at the grocery store, where Dad could find a trustworthy butcher. Going to Anthony's Broadmour Market, of course, was a no-brainer. He knew his brother would give him the best possible leg of lamb, though it would cost him an arm.

Dad himself would bring the leg home and cut it clean from the bone. He would then cut the liberated meat into cubes no larger than two inches.

The rest of the preparation:

Cut green bell peppers into pierceable slices. In later times, one could get fancy by adding yellow or red peppers, though the green have the best taste.

Cut yellow onions into quarters or eighths (depending on the size of the onions).

That's it. Now for the part we kids were enlisted for: skewering the ingredients.

The family skewers were usually purchased from an old tinsmith Jede had discovered at the edge of town, who fashioned them from tin or steel. About fifteen inches long, they had handles formed from bending the metal at the end. We stored them reverently in the "skewer drawer."

Each skewering started with an onion, followed by a cube of lamb, followed by green pepper, and onward in the same pattern:

onion, lamb, pepper, lamb, onion, lamb, pepper, until the skewer was full.

It's important to pack them together just tightly enough for pleasing visual effect but not so close as to impede each piece's cooking.

Above a bed of charcoal, supplemented in Missouri with sweetly delicious chips of hickory wood, you place the skewers side by side across the grill. Turn them every five minutes so the cooking will be even.

At the end, the lamb will be crusted with burned edges, the onions soft and edge-blackened, and the green peppers slightly charred. The scent is heavenly. Use a piece of Lebanese bread to remove the *La-ha-mish-weh* from the skewers and onto each plate directly, or onto a central plate. Serve with Tata's beans and hummus.

Dad's face showed his pride, his absolute assumption that everyone would love it and thank him for it. They did.

Uncle Anthony Joke

An Italian couple holds their wedding in the groom's family home. All goes well until it's time to leave for their honeymoon when a terrible blizzard strikes the house and makes it impossible to go anywhere. So, they spend it in the guest room above the parents' room.

Downstairs the old couple is listening to the bedsprings doing their nastiest above their heads, and the old lady says, "Poppa, why don't we... you know, commemorate our wedding night?"

The old couple goes at it, and soon, the springs on both floors are squeaking in rhythm.

Then silence.

But a few minutes later, the noise upstairs begins again. Not to be outshone, the old woman climbs on top of her husband and goes at it—until both couples get the deed done.

After ten minutes of silence, though, the noise upstairs recommences, this time louder than before.

The old man crawls out of bed, reaches for his cane, and starts thumping on the bedroom ceiling. "Wassa wrong with you, Tony? You tryin' to kill your mother?"

Aging Tennis

On Saturday and Sunday mornings, when I found myself in Los Angeles, I played doubles organized by Hilton Idleman. Hilton was approaching ninety, wore a dress shirt and slacks, and sported a baseball cap that read: "Aging—The Ultimate Extreme Sport." He wore duct-taped tennis shoes way older than our youngest doubles partner.

But he rarely missed a ball that was headed his way and could sprint across the court like a gazelle with a leopard on its tail. He was a living model of how to age. Often late because he had an errand to do en route to Beverly Hills from the Valley, Hilton left promptly at ten to join his standing bridge game at his girlfriend's assisted-living home.

Hilton didn't need assisting.

Despite American culture's cold shoulder toward senior citizens and the burden the growing number of us place upon the economy, I hereby testify, in the words of Maurice Chevalier stolen cavalierly by President Reagan, that old age, "isn't that bad, when you consider the alternative." In fact, there's lots about it to be grateful for, on the court and off.

For one thing, you slowly but surely replace inexhaustible energy with accumulating experience. The two are twin pistons that work in tandem: starting, in youth, with the energy piston at its height of power and, moving, in mid-life to experience and energy more or less equal, until finally in your senior years where your experience piston is so vastly more powerful than your energy piston that you can often challenge much younger players—in the game of life as well as in the game of tennis.

You know from experience you don't need to go to the next Hollywood party because you'll find yourself among strangers whose only common ground with you is that they, too, are bored out of their minds. Instead of going anyway because you think you'll meet your fortune or experience nirvana at *this* one, you skip it and invite friends and family over for a home-cooked meal.

In such routine encounters, I'm pleased to have met and chattered with *American Psycho's* Brett Easton Ellis at Chateau Marmont a half dozen times, *Basic Instinct's* Sharon Stone at her friend's party in Coldwater Canyon where they served Kraft cheese and Ritz crackers, Bond girl Barbara Carrera at her home in the Hollywood Hills to talk about a book she wanted to write, TV host

Larry King at Nate & Al's in Beverly Hills, Freddy's friend and Pink Panther heroine Elke Sommer who cooked dinner for us one night at her Belair home, fitness guru Jack Lalanne at his home in Sherman Oaks filled with porcelain dolls. I swapped jokes and wrote scripts with *Airwolf's* Alex Cord, then toasted *Star Trek's* Bill Shatner over martinis in Burbank to discuss his directing our script *Liliane*. I bumped into *Hawaiian Eye's* Troy Donohue at the Beverly Hills Hotel where I stupidly said, "Weren't you Troy Donohue?" Comedian Steve Martin dined at the next table from ours with his extended family at one of our favorite Italian restaurants, Il Paradiso. I've had lunch a few times with irascible fellow Kansas Citian Ed Asner of *Mary Tyler Moore* fame on Ventura Boulevard, chatted with Woody Allen at the Carlisle in New York before he slept through a concert he was playing the clarinet in, and brushed elbows with *Brokeback Mountain's* Jake Gyllenhaal, Betty White on the set of *The Lost Valentine*, and Danny DeVito at the Polo Lounge. After hanging with her and her daughter during the filming of *Hysteria* in London, I bumped into Maggie Gyllenhaal and her husband *Dead Man Walking's* Peter Sarsgaard on Rome's Via Ripetta. Other than licensing me to name-drop, these weren't life-changing events.

I've learned life is a balance between the curiosity that makes me long to see places I've never seen, like Argentina or Viet Nam, or revisit my favorites like Italy and England and staying home and thriving from my routines. I remind myself that Kurt Vonnegut's observation, "Peculiar travel suggestions are dancing lessons from God," hangs on the word "peculiar." Which I'm the one who defines. The pleasures of staying home, or heading someplace else that *is* peculiar, can finesse the latest invitation. Since there's no inarguable proof that meaning exists except what we storytellers create, I've concluded that what drives us all is that balance between curiosity and familiarity.

Dark nights of the soul, especially around money, become fewer and farther between. Not that cash flow doesn't still get dodgy from time to time. But when it does, I remind myself that the world never came to an end because of money, and we're likely to get through one way or the other.

I savor that feeling.

I've always loved giving advice; only now I feel I mostly *do* know, from experience, what I'm talking about.

I occasionally hear a report that I'm recognized and respected in Hollywood and in New York publishing. Even though I'm aware that the rumor is based on my sheer longevity, it still feels good. But it doesn't exhilarate me, just as very little can truly depress me. As Bobby McFerrin sings, "Don't Worry, Be Happy."

My last shrink told me I have the least tolerance for relishing life's positive reinforcements than anyone he'd ever worked with.

I realize a lot of the wisdom you hear along the road either is just plain wrong or doesn't apply to me:

"You can't teach an old dog new tricks." Sure, you can! Ask me about "New Media."

"There are no free lunches." The last thing I need is a free lunch. I've never been in the remotest danger of starving.

An Alex Cord Joke

Lord Grundley awakens to the sound of his faithful butler James raising the shades and letting the bright sunlight flood his room.

"I see Master is sporting quite an excellent erection this morning," James says. "Shall I fetch the madam?"

"No, James," the old man wheezed. "Fetch me my baggy tweeds and bring the Austin around. I think I'll take this one into town."

Final Meeting of AFI

To an outsider who happened to be that day at the Greenhouse Restaurant on 85th Street in KC, the last meeting of AFI, Inc. would have looked for all the world like my Mom and Dad having lunch with an old friend—not the ontological watershed I judged it to be.

The lunch meeting was held on April 12, 1988, a few months after Dad learned of his inoperable lung cancer diagnosis.

The remaining two stockholders were there to sign the final entry: Fred J. Atchity, chairman (my father); and Myrza Atchity, secretary (my mother). The "old friend" was lawyer Joe Lapin, who duly witnessed the signing of the waiver notices.

As "Chairman of the Board of Directors and President of the Company," Dad "presided at the meeting." Mom and Dad signed the "call and waiver of notice" for the stockholders' meeting. Joe kept the minutes. Dad was moved to be sole director, with "nominations and elections" for that purpose waived. After ratifying all Dad's actions for the previous year, the stockholders' meeting was quickly adjourned, to give way to the directors' meeting.

My father's was the only signature. He presided as sole director and chairman of the meeting.

The meeting's business began with the reinstatement of Dad as chairman, president, and treasurer, and of Mom as vice-president and secretary.

Following a discussion of the company's financial status, the traditional one-dollar dividend was declared, with a total payout of $2487 authorized. The numbers $2846 appear in the typescript but are lined out and replaced with $2487—an error my father, molded by Jesuit standards of perfection that he, like my brother and I, inhaled at Rockhurst High, normally would never have permitted me, much less himself.

He was, God bless him, finally getting tired.

Dad, I want you to know I noticed. But I forgive you.

Then the history of AFI, Inc. came to an abrupt end:

> There then followed a general discussion pertaining to the future of the Company. Matters discussed among others was the advisability and feasibility of a dissolution and liquidation of the Company.

The meeting ended with the usual resolution that "all acts and conduct" of the corporation's officers were "ratified, approved and confirmed."

"The meeting was then lawfully adjourned."

And that's how AFI ended, not with a bang, but a lawful motion.

Cancelled Stock

Two folders were tucked inside the black AFI, Inc. binder.

One was a brown office folder with a heavy-duty clamp to keep the contents in order. It held an almost complete set of cancelled stock certificates, showing the gradual attrition of AFI shareholders, each signed by President Dad, who had written the repeated word "canceled" across the document.

As I looked through it, only one was missing: Mom and Dad's, which I knew had been the final cancellation.

Sure enough, I found it in the other, gray, folder called,

AFI, INC.
LIQUIDATION & DISSOLUTION
Effective-May 31, 1988

I don't know why we save things. Does staying in touch with the past prove we're alive? Who did it prove that *to*? Who did Dad think would be looking for this gray folder in his future?

Me?

Was he intentionally leaving me another piece to the jigsaw puzzle it would take my lifetime to put together?

The thin gray folder was the saddest of all. It was entitled "Certificate of Dissolution" and includes all the legal paperwork to evidence that the AFI corporation was fully and finally dissolved.

Dad's neat handwriting records the "applicable value" of the corporation's stock as $36,665.95 and signs the form for the last time as President.

Finally, he appends his four surrendered stock certificates to complete the record. Unlike all the others in the brown clamp-book, these stock certificates are not marred by Dad's repeated "Canceled."

He didn't have the heart to cancel himself.

Was it thumbing his nose at Mother Nature for taking care of that?

For the last of his remaining days, AFI would live in his memory, although he'd terminated the family corporation "for the record."

Dad's Funeral

St. Thomas More was standing room only at my father's funeral. The church was packed with Atchitys, Kourys, Laffertys, Decaros, Calegaris, Naumans, Owens, Kellys, Bonahans, Lapins, a few delegates from Mom's Louisiana family, and contingents of union folk who worked with Dad at IBEW-NECA including members of the late John Simms family.

Dad made it only to age seventy-one. I was forty-three at the time he passed. Kneeling at his funeral I asked myself, *Can I fill up another twenty-eight years?* On that day, I wasn't at all sure. Recently divorced from Circe, despite a parade of entertaining ladies who showed up to distract me I was kinda lonely. Not to have people around. Not to have a family in my house. It just didn't feel normal.

Not that I liked company all the time. But I realized my need to have something and someone to retreat from, a terrible thing to say but it's the core irony of my psyche: I go to KC to appreciate my exile. Still, like a kid I needed to come downstairs to get the nurture of being upset, so I could retreat upstairs to my Latin and Greek—until someone came to lure me back down with pie or cookies. I guess I love anxiety, love to be upset. Love to be smothered under quilts so I could keep threading my way out of the infinite labyrinth of my life. Was that true? Was there any way to break free of this pattern? Was there any reason to?

Maybe this pattern, this cycle between hurt and creativity, between pain and control, was my story.

I wondered whether this meant I was doomed to live alone. Or doomed to define living alone as a negative state. Most of the time, I see solitude as positive, *So, let's face it*, I told myself, *this, my father's funeral, is not one of those times. This is the time to take nurture from the presence of others.*

After the services, more than half the congregants, including elegantly black-dressed June, came to pay tribute to my father—and to Mom—at the family house on 104th Street, most bringing food and photographs.

Mom was in full funeral deployment, her own unlimited culinary largesse amplified by Atchity and Aguillard family's and friends' contributions. Nothing like having a half dozen veteran chefs in the kitchen.

After the guests had finally left, I walked down the basement steps, where my father's office occupied a prominent corner. A dark and work-serious cubbyhole, it was indeed a den. A family of industrious foxes would have been more than happy in its shadows.

At first, I didn't spot her: youngest sister Laurie, looking through Dad's file cabinet, her face a mask of anxiety. "What are you looking for?" I asked her, no doubt with authority in my voice that came more from age and random testosterone than from intention. Although I've been called "intimidating" all my life, I really don't see why, though I will readily admit to "intense." When I was visiting Cambridge, Massachusetts, to joust martinis at Chez Dreyfus with Homeric scholar Cedric Whitman during my graduate school years, I crossed paths with a secretary as I was marching across the Harvard Yard. "Smile, sir!" she admonished me. That did make me smile.

Θ

The martinis at Chez Dreyfus gave me the opportunity to explain my theory of Homeric origins to Professor Whitman, one of my most revered mentors because of his book *Homer and the Heroic Tradition*. Scholars said that the *Iliad* and the *Odyssey* were composed as early as 1200 BC. I had come to the unorthodox conclusion that they were composed, more or less in the version we have today, in the time of Pericles (494-429 BC) when the great poet-tragedian Aeschylus (525-425) was alive and thriving. Why did I conclude that? Two reasons: (1) Scholars argued that lines in Aeschylus' great plays, like *Oedipus the King* and *Antigone* were strongly reminiscent of lines from Homer's epics. Funny, I thought it made more sense that those Homeric hexameters sounded that way because they were penned by Aeschylus. (2) Depictions on Greek vases of Achilles's mighty shield, the centerpiece of *Iliad: 18*, changed radically during the period around 450 BC. Before that period, the subject matter of the depicted shields ranged from Centaurs' backsides to the Gorgon's head—at least a half dozen *different* motifs. But after that time, Achilles' shield was no longer shown frontally—or, if it was, only so highly glossed that nothing in particular could be made out on its surface. The high gloss, in fact, mirrored the lines from the *Iliad* about the sun reflecting from the shield so brightly the eyes of the Myrmidons were blinded. Through martini after martini, Cedric listened with the utmost attention and respect. Finally, he passed judgement: "Atchity," he said with all the gravitas a lifetime of professoring at Harvard allowed him, "do me a favor and don't publish any of this until after I'm gone." I respected his wishes. He didn't want to have to redo a lifetime of scholarship. Let your mentor win!

Θ

My sister Laurie looked at me like a deer in a poacher's light. "I don't know," she finally said, to my question, "What are you doing here?" in Dad's den after his funeral.

Later, I would figure it out. She was looking for love in all the remaining places—like me tracing my view of the patterns of it all by scribing these memories.

The deer beat a hasty retreat, high tailing it up the stairs.

I sat down at Dad's modest swivel chair and surveyed the cast-off sickly-blonde-wood desktop that had made the move with us from Virginia Avenue, then from 75th Street. I realized my father would never look up from this chair again with earthly eyes (though Andrea claimed his radio kept going off and on for weeks after his death). I always thought this laminated desk was hideously ugly, but someone had offered it to Dad at a price he couldn't resist.

It was neatly arrayed with the apparatus of his craft—which Laurie would later divide into five lots from which to create for each of her siblings a shadowbox displaying them. My shadow box contains one of Dad's business cards:

Fred J. Atchity

Administrative Manager

IBEW-NECA BENEFIT TRUST FUNDS

The card included the usual contact information, which, characteristically, also listed his "Res. Phone." Because Dad dealt with medical benefits, it was common for him to take phone calls at all hours of the day and night. I never saw him resent even one of those calls. Dad was happy to be needed.

The three centerpieces of Laurie's artistically arranged epitaph for our father were:

The first: A black & white photograph of a smiling Dad, hands crossed on his desk, then at the "new Health & Welfare Office at 4016 Washington Room 202...in March 1964"—when I was a junior at Georgetown. In the photo, Dad's desk is perfectly tidy and displays the wood block bearing his children's photographs. He's wearing, as usual, black-framed glasses—his oculistic style of choice, accentuating the prominent "Roman nose" that got my brother into deep trouble in one the funniest-awful moments of our tense adolescence.

The second: The little black book Dad controlled his—and our—lives from, including his address book, the blank first page inscribed in his handwriting: "Long distance Directory Assistance 1+Area Code+555-1212."

My father carried this book in his shirt pocket, whipped it out at the least sign of a financial transaction. "Dad, here's the $2 I owe you...Dad, can I borrow $5?" Nothing happened without a notation in the book.

Oddly enough—that is, odd to me, who regularly loses his glasses, keys, and billfold—Dad never once lost this book. Years later, I realized that it was because he never changed his routine, methodically gathering moss as he rotated from office to home to church to the bindery or one of his social clubs—without ever taking the myriad detours that have made my life so different from his.

The third was a list of expenses, torn from one of my father's countless ledger books, this one written seven years before he died, showing several mysterious twenty-dollar donations.

Thanks, Laurie, for reminding me of Dad every day.

Funny how we take the living for granted, even when we're aware of doing so. If Dad were still alive, I'd like to ask him what the unspecified "donations" listed in his black book were. More puzzling was one with the annotation "Political Donation" (which, I concluded, had to be to the Democratic Party, the only Party my father would consider supporting). If Mom were still with us, I'd ask her what the twenty-dollar donations were. She'd shrug and say, "to St. Elizabeth's Church," though I'd know that her credibility was close to zero since my mother never met a question she didn't have an immediate answer to, accurate or not.

Now that I think about it, they might have been gambling losses. He couldn't stand not recording them one way or the other.

Poker and betting minor amounts were Dad's venial sins, though my mother so surpassed him at one later point that he cut back drastically on his dalliances with Lady Luck. Not to mention Freddy, Jr., who thought nothing of winning or losing $60,000 in one night at the casino, turning his father's cautious footsteps into launch pads.

The longer they've been away from us, Mom and Dad, the more numerous the questions become—and the harder it is to accept that I'll never know the answers to them. What did my mother put in her pickled green peppers to make them taste that way? How did she make her peanut butter-lemon fish sauce exactly?

Another question occurred to me the day Kayoko and I were trying to reconstruct Mom's recipe for cabbage rolls: How did she get the leaves soggy enough to roll?

In the past, I'd simply dial Mom's number night or day, and know that she'd pick up and answer. That was a time when her answers about cooking could still be trusted.

Dad's list of expenses must have been written in spring or summer, with all that grass-cutting—I wondered how much of that money was paid to an Atchity cousin. My family has never been averse to working together, though there's hell, and gossip and ostracism to pay if someone doesn't show up on time and perform.

"Dock materials" had to be a reference to the cabin at Lake Lotawana, where Dad rebuilt the dock—to the delight of the wild ducks that persisted in landing there and leave behind their corrosive calling cards.

☉

Laurie's artistic processing of her emotional need—"the last leaf on
the tree gets the least sap," as catty commentator Betty Lafferty
once put it—was years in the future that funeral day as I sat there
in my father's utilitarian swivel chair.

The typewriter I bought him was silent now; had been, after
that single letter to me. I looked for the ruler with the J F K
memorial fifty-cent piece embedded in Lucite along with
companion penny, quarter, nickel, and dime. It's now on son
Vincent's desk.

I saw the NECA (National Electrical Contractors Association)
desktop calculator that never quite worked because it was solar-
powered, and this den was nowhere within reach of sunlight.

Θ

Dad's briar patch, I called it. He had a habit of escaping from
dinner or from social events where his presence wasn't absolutely
essential by saying, with a reluctant grumble in his voice, "I'm
afraid I have to get downstairs to work." I've used the same
approach for decades myself and know the exact feeling he
experienced when he sat down in the desk chair.

Relief.

Escape from the confusion of reality.

Competence.

A feeling of control.

A feeling of tangibility versus the ebb and flow of unproductive
conversation. A feeling of the meaningfulness of the passing
moment, easily lost amid too much small talk and laughter and

sorrow—none of which led directly to more security, more self-realization, more "money in the bank."

Only *doing* does that. Only working.

Finally, my gaze came to rest on a paperweight, that photo-decorated block of wood I'd seen without seeing for years and years. Five of its faces included photographs of his kids—mine the formal high school portrait I loathed because it made me look like a well-coiffed and powdered dandy.

Another surface held the "NECA" emblem, and another an inscription to Dad for his hard work for the organization—the IBEW ("International Brotherhood of Electrical Workers"), whose health & welfare funds he managed.

The final surface of the wooden Rubik-cube-like block displayed one of the several proverbs by which Dad pursued his life: "Risk Nothing, Lose Nothing." I pondered it with the dull-mindedness of someone staring at something that he'd stared at without understanding for a lifetime, awaiting a revelation.

Then, as though my father's spirit had broken through the ethereal-corporeal barrier, a light switched on in my brain. Throughout my life since high school, I'd taken this statement to mean, "Go for it." To gain, you must risk.

Dad had taken it, all his life, to mean the opposite: That if nothing is risked, there's no loss. My father was the epitome of the No-Risk mentality, explaining his reaction to my decision to major in classics rather than pre-med, become a professor instead of an account manager, become an independent producer instead of a tenured professor.

I wept for him, hoping that whatever afterlife his unaccountable virtues had earned would, at last, give him the exhilarating freedom that comes only from experiencing risk.

Freddy's Encomium for Dad

On the day of Dad's funeral, I listened in a kind of euphoric fog, sitting next to Mom in the first pew of St. Thomas More Church, to my godfather-brother's self-empowered eulogy. Freddy began with a statement none of his siblings believed for one second: *I have been asked to read this on behalf of the Atchity kids who feel that this is what they believe their dad would say to his family and friends.*

Ai-Yi-Yi, as Mom would say. No such empowering had occurred—no such "asking." None of us had authorized Freddy to take over.

Except, maybe Dad himself—in Freddy's mind.

But let that pass. No one stopped him either.

The longer Freddy went on, the more I understood my brother's vision of our family story, and the deeper we all peered into Freddy's many-chambered heart:

> *To My Dear Friends and Loving Family:*
>
> *It has always been hard for me to express my love for the people around me, and now I finally have the opportunity to share my thoughts with you.*
>
> *I can't tell you what a thrill it is to have seen all of you last night and today. It is wonderful for all of you to have come to tell me goodbye. My biggest dream in life was to have a lot of friends*

and to be loved by a lot of people. You have shown me with your presence today that I have fulfilled that dream in my lifetime.

I assure you I will always be thinking of you and will continue to love you and will be watching your progress in life as you face your various trials and tribulations. I will always be with you in spirit and would love to think you will always be carrying my encouragement with you. My fondest memories are all the problems we faced together and, most importantly, all of the happiness we experienced.

Because my dad taught me to make sure I took care of my family and help as many people as I could, my only regret in life is that because I was so busy, I could not spend more time with you and share my personal thoughts of the love I have for you...

...to Bill Reynolds, a special friend all of my life, thank you for your friendship, for the aggravation you gave me in letting me take care of your books, and all of the joy you have given me and my family....

...to my brothers still living, Anthony, Vic and Jimmy, and my sister, Lorraine, all of you have been successful, and I thank you for sharing your lives with me. We have done a good job in achieving the objectives that I believe our mom and dad set forth for us in this country. It was great to see all of you in recent weeks, and I appreciate all you did for me. To my big brother, Anthony, I can't tell you how much I appreciate all the gin games both at the house and in the hospital over the last few weeks. I guarantee that the first person I plan to see in heaven is Tony, Jr., so that I can bone up on my gin game and be ready for you when you get there. I also look forward to seeing my brother and sister, Eddie and Selma.

To my sister-in-law Catherine Atchity, you could not have done more for Myrza and me. I can't tell you how much it meant to both of us. I sure hope you and Myrza continue to enjoy good times together....

To my oldest son, Ken, I have been so proud of your becoming a Yale PhD and the educational accomplishments you have achieved in the last several years. I am even more proud of your achieving your dream of producing movies. However, I never expected you to put *me* in the movies. But, I wish you would have had me serving Lebanese food instead of those Jewish bagels. And, by the way, I forgive you for not meeting me and your mother in Las Vegas. That was a good decision.

To Fred, Jr., you have surprised me with your accomplishments. Keep on going since I know you can do it. It is no different than when you were little, and you played baseball. Keep trying for those homeruns...

To Mary, even though you and your beautiful family have been away for 12 years, I know you still have a soft spot for Kansas City. But, the sun shines just as brightly in Florida as it does here at home.

To Andrea, you have been a saint as has your husband, Rick. You both have given me more than I could expect from my children. Honey, your help at the lake and helping your mother with me over the last year and a half has been a great gift to both of us.

To Laurie, you have recently married and found a wonderful husband. It was a joy for me to be at your wedding and I am sure your future will be happier than you ever dreamed.

All of you have made me so proud with the lives you have established for yourselves. I could not have asked any of you to marry any better; and I really love Jan, Rick, Chester, and Marty as my own. The grandchildren you have given me, I know, will take the Atchity name forward and their accomplishments will reach new heights...

...I have left the most important person in my life for last, my loving wife, Myrza, we have gone through so much together, and achieved more than I dared dream. On our first date in New Orleans during World War II, I knew I had found a beautiful little Cajun girl, and I never stopped realizing what a diamond you really are. I accomplished so much in my life, which I could not have done without your love and support. Our friends love us, and we have raised wonderful children all of whom have been very successful.

We had stressful times in our lives because of my insecurity and sometimes paranoia of my not being able to provide properly for my family and in not being able to set aside enough for a rainy day. Honey, forgive me for those times, and thank you for staying with me when I did not deserve you. Thank you for understanding it was the stress of the times.

In the last few years while I have been sick, it was a renewed realization to me of how much you loved me. I feel so bad I could not eat all the wonderful meals you prepared for me.

I know I have left a good roadmap for you to follow. I have covered it with the kids and am sure you won't have any problems. I really loved you, Myrza, and I always will. 'You are my sunshine.'

I must close now since I hear my call. I can't wait to see my family and friends already in heaven. I have been told things are great up there and that I will have a wonderful time. I have to think God could use a little organizing, however, so I am prepared to do a little work besides.

I am a little worried that perhaps I could have done better on earth. So, please, say a little prayer that I have some insurance. Don't worry about me. Remember, I got out of the stock market at an all-time high, and I feel fine. Also remember, don't pay interest on your credit card accounts, buy wholesale and work hard. I will be with you every day in spirit.

This dying business isn't as tough as I thought it would be, and I really look forward to the good times we are going to have together in the future.

With all my love,
Fred

Ironically, due to the magic of "assumed first-person narrative," Freddy addresses our mother as though *he* were married to her, trumping me once and for all. But I wasn't quite petty enough to mind that.

For my part, I sincerely hoped that day that people in the grand counting house in the sky would laugh at Dad's jokes, that he wouldn't have to repeat himself, and that he would get lucky in cards; and, finally, I recognized the irony in "Dad's" public acknowledgment that I was the "oldest son"—channeled from my brother's brain and mouth.

Most of all, I appreciated Freddy's coherently rosy view of Dad's life and death, his version of our story so different from mine. If anyone was entitled to channel Dad, it was my brother, his namesake.

All in the church were in tears. I was in tears.

Freddy was his own creative genius who could spin a story with the best of us.

The euphoria I felt was a coming of age. I no longer feared my life. I no longer minded what happened. I was free at last.

The thing about family is that everyone's story is true.

Straight Arrow

It was imperative to Dad to leave no i undotted, nor t uncrossed; so, in a way, terminal cancer was exactly the exit visa the accountant ordered.

As painful as his suffering was, it allowed my father to make sure he'd balanced all his accounts, leaving precise instructions for Mom, a clear will for both of them, to be read to all of us, showing he'd provided for equal shares to be distributed upon her death (if she hadn't blown it all at the casino, we all thought, I half hoping that she'd do exactly that).

I would drive through a blizzard with him on a December Saturday night in KC so he could make his bank deposit *before* mailing his bill payments out the next day. "What difference does it make?" I asked him. "The snow is supposed to stop in the morning. You can go to the bank then."

"The money needs to be in the bank before I mail the checks." His look was not withering; it was that bewildered gleam in his eye he'd get when he had absolutely no comprehension of what he'd heard me say—kind of like his reaction to everyone else's reaction to his jokes. "The money needs to be in the bank before I mail the checks," he repeated.

Otherwise, I'm sure my father couldn't fall asleep. So, we drove to the bank first. He barged through a drift to get to the night deposit box. I'd offered to do him for it, but I guess my question made him decide he needed to do it himself.

Only then did we head for the post office to mail the checks.

Dad's Legacy

If one were not an optimist, one would conclude that life is a balancing act performed on a tightrope across which we are destined to crawl or race or stagger toward death. On the one hand, we search for meaning, for clues to overcoming the underlying structural weaknesses in our character. On the other hand, those very weaknesses rush us toward the same dying that is, after all, our destiny.

What did Dad leave us?

He left us with the lesson that the happiness we taste in life is structured through intensity, the intensity of will—of knowing you can make a decision and implement it, whether it's to quit drinking or smoking or drugs. Or to work on, regardless of your moods, health, or crises surrounding you.

That's all there is to courage, isn't it? All you have to do is persist, no matter how you feel, no matter the grief others are giving you; just *do*.

He left us with the certainty that it's *thinking*—the constant, mostly idle, gossip of the mind—that screws us up, that *doing* is what matters the most.

He left us with the most important lesson, perhaps life's hardest lesson of all, also the hardest both to learn and accept—a truth my father rarely lost sight of: That endurance might be its best part of it.

That all we're asked to do, in return for the privilege of living on this whacky planet in this zany universe, is continue doing what we do, with as much joy and good nature as we can muster. Chop wood, carry water.

The corollary to Dad's lesson, as it governed him, was, Never stop to question who you are; there's no bottom line in it. That one didn't have to apply to me—did it?—since I never stopped questioning even while I went on doing.

Just *be*, feel it deeply, live it fully. Never forgetting the Sinatra vocals that my father hummed when he thought no one was watching: "Do be do be do."

Gather a little moss. Translation: Have a cash cushion so you can take naps.

The day before I left for Georgetown, Dad walked into my room, where I was busy packing everything except the *Mad* magazines I'd incinerated in a moment of patent insanity in the backyard barbecue to keep them from falling into the hands of my sisters.

I don't remember him *ever* being in my room. "I want you to remember something," Dad confided. "When I get tired, I go into the bathroom and wash my face with cold water."

I was floored. An overt piece of paternal advice. Unique. Completely unsolicited!

More consternated than touched, I don't recall how I responded.

In retrospect, the sheer practicality of this one piece of fatherly wisdom was perfection itself. Through the years, I would hold it as my ace up the sleeve—refusing to do the energizing face wash unless all else had failed.

When you get tired, wash your face.

For some reason, it took me until the age of seventy to realize that it's okay to be tired. Before that, I felt so overwhelmed by the speed of things happening that I thought I needed eight hours of sleep every single night or I wouldn't be able to deal with it all.

Dad spent most of his adult life being tired, his only antidote, aside from the 20+ cups of coffee, washing his face with cold water.

I finally realized I could be tired and still do things; it wasn't the end of the world to do what my father did.

And one more thing:

Dad left me my own AFI, Inc., the structure of this story.

Structure may be his greatest gift of all.

Two Last Tennis Breakthroughs

You'd think I'd learned all I was going to learn from tennis already. But one day, a new player to our game, in the middle of a progressively messier set that would have discouraged anyone else, muttered, "Every second the game starts again."

I loved that! It became my new mantra, cutting through all the self-examination and forthrightly telling me:

Keep doing whatever you're doing but do it *better*—and start doing it better *now!*

I finally learned to *give myself* positive reinforcement, by saying, *Good shot, Ken,* when I did something right—instead of beating myself up when I blew a shot. *Affirmation* feels great!

"Don't Forget Me"

The third thing my father told me before he passed away was, "Don't forget me."

For him to say that was a break in a lifetime of self-effacement. Dad's focus was on doing what needed to be done, believing, I suppose that if you concentrated on what needed to be done, whatever you were thinking about your own condition became unimportant.

A typical example happened ten years or so earlier. Dad had been rushed to the hospital in an ambulance. I heard about it from Freddy, who'd spoken to someone in my father's office minutes after it happened, and then called me. He didn't know which hospital they'd taken Dad to.

No one answered when I called home.

I assumed Mom had been notified and that she flew out of the house to meet him in some emergency room.

My sisters, normally hovering by the phone for any hint of bad news that could interrupt their workaday routine, were nowhere to be found either.

I imagined the worst: They were all at his bedside, he had minutes to live, etc.

After an hour of futile phoning and fretting, I called Dad's office, finally figuring out that they would surely know where they'd sent him.

"Electricians' Health and Welfare," Dad answered.

"Dad?!"

"Hi," he confirmed. His voice sounded perfectly normal.

"What are you doing at work?"

"What do you mean?" The usual tiny pause, then: "What do you mean?"

"I heard about your accident."

He confirmed the details: the "girls" in his office had asked him to change a light bulb, he'd climbed on the stepladder, the ladder gave away, he'd fallen face down on his glasses, been blinded by the blood.

They panicked; called the ambulance.

The ambulance rushed him to St. Luke's, where Mom met him.

They'd given him twelve stitches above the eye and put a big patch over it. His eye was a little numb, but otherwise, he felt fine.

"And you came back to work?"

"What else was I supposed to do, honey? Sit around the house all afternoon feeling sorry for myself? Your mother wanted me to stay home, but I told her I had too many things to do here."

"Why are you answering the office phone?"

"Oh, I sent the girls out to lunch on me. They were asking too many questions."

Θ

That was Dad: When life throws you a curve, or disappoints or overwhelms you, or even delights you—go back to work.

Work is what you do while waiting for life to get its act together, to reveal its hand. It's what keeps your mind off the messiness of it all, off the realization that life just plain refuses to live up to your image of what it should be.

☉

As printed in the gold-colored program for the "Funeral of Fred J. Atchity, Sr.," the "Gathering Song" was called "Be Not Afraid":

> *You shall cross the barren desert,*
> *But you shall not die of thirst,*
> *You shall wander far from safety,*
> *Though you do not know the way.*
> *You shall speak your words in foreign lands,*
> *And all will understand.*
> *You shall see the face of God and live.*
> *BE NOT AFRAID.*
> *I GO BEFORE YOU ALWAYS.*
> *COME, FOLLOW ME, AND I WILL GIVE YOU REST.*

After all I believed he put me through growing up, my primary feeling at my father's funeral was *relief*. I felt as though a mountain range had been lifted from my shoulders.

It wasn't until I started reading the AFI black binder that I came to terms with who he was and what he had done for me instead of to me.

The relief was not because I hated Dad, though I was convinced I did for the first eighteen years of my life; but because it had taken me the rest of his life to learn to deal with him—and I wasn't sure how long I could sustain it. I didn't even feel guilty from feeling this way, as though the guilt thing had also been lifted.

What was really lifted was something I need to define before life takes me to the next step, and that exact need was the inspiration for telling this story.

As I walked out of St. Thomas More that September day in 1989, daughter Rosemary at my side, I remember thinking that it might well be very easy to forget my father. After all, my adolescence had been a boot camp aimed at centering my mindfulness not on him but on my mother.

What was there to remember about Dad?

Rosemary confided in me that he played Michael Jackson songs for her when they rode alone in his car, his favorites "Beat It!" and "Billie Jean." He let her drive his speedboat at the lake.

God help me for tasting the fruit Mom had designated as forbidden: having a kind thought about my father.

But Dad worked hard. He stopped fretting when he was working.

He repeated things twice.

He repeated things twice.

For everyone in business and in the family as well, he never failed to come through. He never failed to call out right from wrong, even if it alienated some of his clients and in-laws.

He kept track of every financial transaction with his children, brothers, and nieces and nephews, in that little black book carried in his shirt pocket—along with his pens in a white plastic pocket protector. That protector looked so goofy to me that I've spent a lifetime throwing out ink-stained shirts instead of using one.

My Brother, the Living Dead

"You can fall off a curb and kill yourself if you don't know what you're doing."
—William Wharton, *Birdy*

I left my brother's ICU room in Maryland after pressing my hand against his cheek and promising to finish our *The Battle of New Orleans* movie no matter what, demanding his cooperation from the beyond. Freddy had fallen off a curb in Ocean City, Maryland, where the curbs are high because the tides can flood the streets. He had literally never seen it coming as he smashed the back of his head.

Kayoko and I happened to be in our Manhattan apartment when we got word the next morning. We rushed down by train and rental car. Though Freddy's heart was beating strongly as ever, partly due to regular injections of norepinephrine, he did not respond. Because he had been brain-dead, he was ruled DOA.

My brother resides now in my mind and heart, along with my other saints: Mom and Dad, Andrea, Uncle Wib and Bobbie, Bart Giamatti, Norman Cousins, John Gardner, Lowry Nelson, Tom Bergin, Uncles Eddy and Anthony, Cousin Tony. The older we get, the longer our Litany of Saints becomes.

Even though his five or six phone calls a day had been wearing on me, I now ordered Freddy to keep in touch from beyond.

I know he will. That's the thing about these saints we the living keep collecting. They don't let go. They are still here for us when we need them, or whether we need them or not.

Freddy remained lucky to the end. He never knew what hit him. The Fat Lady sang, and his party was over before her first note was out of her mouth. In the most final way of all, I let my brother win because I, not he, am left to feel the pain. The faux older brother beat me to the finish line, his repose trumping the paternal filial cards in my hand, as I, thinking of Tata's pot, watched him take command of his forced-inherited plot at Mt. Olivet.

The state of Maryland defines legal death as *brain death*. The hospital authorities took all day to reach the point of admitting my brother's brain was dead, though the paramedics who picked him up from the pavement in front of 7-Eleven the night before knew it from the dilation of his pupils when they found him. The nurse who valiantly attended his last day described the various tests and procedures to us. Freddy's daughter Amy and her husband Justin, his new wife Cheryl, Kayoko, and I watched the monitors stolidly display his heart rate and blood pressure. He was breathing only with the ventilator's insistence. Even when they raised his CO_2 level to the normally unbearable, Freddy's body wasn't troubled enough to respond. But they kept that ventilator going because they wanted his organs. It was a bit like *Twilight Zone,* a routine triumph of human generosity over the relentless progress of morbidity. When the doctor came in to say he was ready to make the pronouncement if we were ready to receive it, we nodded that we were. Business between us unfinished or not, it was time to let my brother go.

Kayoko and I drove the four hours back to Manhattan, texting his children and ours, our friends, my sisters, mending the quilt, reasserting the connections that would lead us all back to KC in the all-too-near future. Speculating about the preciousness of life, the sudden pulling out of the rug beneath our feet.

As we made our way back to LA to regroup before the funeral, my brother's body was still in the ICU room, warm, heart beating, being fed and cleansed for the health of the organs he'd donate to nameless recipients for whom the party was not yet over. Freddy still breathed but without the brain that made him my brother. He was now the living dead, living to bring hope to others.

We are all lined up on that precipice from which he fell suddenly and heavily into immediate oblivion. I read peace on his face, I hope a reflection of his final moments, of the last sunset he enjoyed. He'd told me a few days earlier, "I don't want this honeymoon to ever end." He wasn't eager to go back to La Quinta and figure out what he wanted to do when he grew up. Careful what you wish for.

Sorrow transcends words but is eclipsed by the joy of memory.

Back at St. Thomas More again, the true older brother would give the younger brother's eulogy. Instead of the euphoria I felt at my father's funeral, or the anger at Andrea's, now I was feeling nonplussed:

I always found Death irritating. Inconvenient. Aggravating. Rude. A betrayal. Thoughtless. Mean. Not to mention discouraging! It just plain sucks.

Turns out—it's actually LIFE that can be that way.

Life makes us fall in love with it: with sunrises and sunsets that light the skies over Kansas City or Lebanon, over La Quinta or Ocean City; with private "big picture" moments of contemplation and resolve, and feasts with family and friends— dances of celebration; with grape leaves and gumbo; with the satisfying THUMP of a well-caught baseball and the silent speed of a well-made car.

And then, when we're head over heels in love with it, Life pulls the rug out. That's the part that seems to suck.

Unless, just maybe, being alive means we need to somehow love that part too. We need to love death. That must be what Wallace Stevens meant when he wrote:

Death is the mother of beauty; hence from her,
Alone, shall come fulfillment to our dreams
And our desires...
Death is the mother of beauty, mystical,
Within whose burning bosom we devise
Our earthly mothers waiting, sleeplessly.

Until our own moment arrives, maybe, after all, it's just about how we play the game with all the odds stacked against us by the house—doing our best minute by minute with the cards we hold in our hands. Never knowing when the bell will ring, and the musical chairs stop.

Freddy's party down here is over, except in our memories. His eternal party is just beginning.

Anthony Bourdain, who proceeded Fred to that great casino in the sky where Mom and Dad and Andrea welcome him, said, "your body is not a temple; it's a carnival amusement ride. Ride it for all it's worth." My brother certainly rode that ride. I've never met *a human being with a greater capacity for play. He played his cards all-out, right to the end.*

By the way, he also managed to leave a few vital organs so others could continue their ride, live their dreams. That would make him smile–that Lebanese smile we've read all our lives on the faces of Jede and Dad, Tony, and Uncle Eddy, and Uncle Anthony–and Amy.

Like Mom at Ameristar casino, Freddy rode his luck to the end, cashing in his chips early while he was ahead. He believed in luck, and Lady Luck served him well.

But he had no patience for serious opera. When his Fat Lady sang, Freddy only had to listen to a single note before crossing the finish line into the blessed peace of no more hassles.

From now, dear great modern family, Freddy, carrying the baton, marches at the head of "our saints" who live, not in some distant Valhalla, but right here for easy access in the quiet clearings of our minds and hearts: Jede and Tata, Nanee, Mamère, Uncle Wib, Uncle Dave, Cousin Bobbie, Aunt Catherine, Kathy Coco, Aunt Selma and Uncle Bob, Aunt Leona and Uncle Vick, Bill and Connie Reynolds, Joe Lapin, the list marches on.

Nature creates a unique force field between siblings of the same sex, two forces pulling in opposite directions–

One force drives AWAY from each other, toward polar opposition: jovial vs serious, athlete vs scholar, Louisiana vs Missouri, extrovert vs introvert, monetary vs literary, great hair vs not so much. The other force pulls, not exactly TOWARD each other, but WITH each other so totally you can read your brother's

mind from a single glance, and sometimes without even the need
for that.

I feel blessed to report that after many years of pulling apart
to define our separate places in life we were able to come together
in the last few years, when Freddy brought me his dream to make
a movie, ANDREW JACKSON–BATTLE FOR NEW
ORLEANS–redefining nature's force field even stronger than it
had ever been on Benton Boulevard, Virginia Avenue, or 75ᵗʰ
Street.

Let's all continue, as Freddy did, to dream on. Let some of
Death's peace and perspective seep into how we treat one another.
Play on! Take the mysteries of life with a grain of salt but take the
game dead seriously in the moment. In the spirit of my dear
brother, let's party on–till we too reach the time to drop.

And thanks, Freddy, for teaching me–from whatever table you're
sitting at–the secret of gin rummy: Play to knock before your
opponent.

Among the many sympathy cards I received after his funeral
was an elegant one from Rockhurst, our high school. It read:

Dear Ken,

Please accept our condolences on the passing of your brother. We
were saddened upon hearing the news.
We will remember Ken in our masses and prayers...

So, wait a minute, Freddy, what are you up to here? Was this
only an honest typo, or did you intervene from beyond? You get to
be numbered among the living dead while I get to be the dead still
living? Leave it to those Jesuits to give us something to think about.

Does Sisyphus get bummed every time his rock rolls down the hill? I think not. Valiantly he trudges after it. Pushes it back up—with joy in his heart for having that rock.

My Happy List

I guess you never escape the original trauma, that old suffocating quilt. In a recent dream—really, what my client Dennis Palumbo refers to as a 'night terror'—I'm in an orange sector of a sphere, taking a test. I begin to read the question, which has to do with, "I am an alien god, that is devouring the whole sphere. You will watch me devour myself"—and suddenly, I feel a presence, in another sector, that is devouring the whole sphere. I will be consumed with it. I try to escape, try to leave the sphere, but I'm stuck. I can't move at all as the presence becomes noisier, getting closer and close. I cry out.

And Kayoko wakes me up. "Ken! What was it this time?"

Well, let me explain...

Whoa, I said to myself, *I need to make a map of my mind. I am doing too many things. Splitting it too many ways. In danger of destroying the whole shooting match.*

What could be clearer? But how to stop the dividing? How to eliminate the sectors? Or how to keep adding them without destroying the whole house of cards?

I guess, in the end, personal experience is incommunicable. You just have to be there.

Dad taught me to keep track of things. Genetically dosed with his OCD, I overcompensated. If he loaned us money, we repaid it with interest. Not that he needed it, you understand; it taught us "the value of money" and the folly of over-borrowing. No one wanted to be an unclosed item in his little book. Ha! (as Mom would say).

He stood at the hall doorway when the rest of us were in the dining room telling jokes, on the outside looking in. Dad carried that look on his face of a kid peering into a candy store or a room filled with naked women dancing, knowing he wasn't allowed.

That's how I felt about my father, on the outside looking in.

That's how I've felt about lots of things.

Including much of my life.

But, after all, isn't that what they call enlightenment? Looking at yourself from an outside vantage point? Dad found his happiness among the numbers. I found mine among letters. You find what you need where you look for it.

I hope my father is dancing naked in the sky with nice girls who give blowjobs.

I'd suffered all my life from what I learned was called "the imposter syndrome"—walking around like a phony in coat and tie at Georgetown, hobnobbing like a pretender at Yale with tweedy professors who were becoming my friends, encroaching on the rose-lined campuses of Occidental College and UCLA, faking my salesman's role in the word-musty halls of New York publishers, or playing producer on the crew-filled set of my first movies in Montreal, and now across the studio campuses of Sony, or Universal, or Paramount, or Warner Bros, or Disney, or Netflix, or Apple and the social clubs of Los Angeles and New York: California Club, Soho House, Jonathan Club; Colony Club, Lotos Club, Harvard Club, University Club, and my dear Yale Club.

As Dad listed his rental houses and stocks, I catalog my riches to convince myself that I'm happy. Only are *things*, like the gray '52 Hudson ("Horace"), with vacuum powered window washers that worked only when you stepped on the gas. I bought Horace from a little old lady living in a trailer park in Pasadena. The car had only 50,000 miles on it—because she wanted to buy a new Mustang.

But most of my happiest memories are of intense *moments*: Because of my New York coop I was able to meet Dominick Dunne who lived in the penthouse; and have lunch with Russell Baker and Gilbert Sorrentino, who both loved the reviews I'd done of their books (*Growing Up* and *Mulligan Stew*, respectively) for *The Los Angeles Times Book Review*. Randy Borman, chief of the Cofánes, cooked for me a bland white meat called *watsui* (which he begrudgingly translated as "weasel"). From a bush beside the chief's thatched hut, I picked a BB-sized pepper. Randy failed to stop me from popping it into my mouth. Within seconds, it nearly blew my head off with its fiery intensity. We became friends for life when I brought him a half-gallon bottle of vodka. I smuggled back a plastic film-tube filled with the peppers; they lasted us over a year.

After I'd praised Peter S. Feibleman's novel *Charley Boy* in *The Los Angeles Times Book Review*, Peter tracked me down and invited me to dinner at his home in the Hollywood Hills (which Pink Floyd had spray-painted neon pink when Peter rented him the house while he was in Europe). "I have a friend who wants to meet you," Peter added, after thanking me graciously for my review.

I was filled with curiosity that night as I arrived, wondering who the mysterious "friend" was. Peter's long-time friend and sometime companion, novelist Lillian Hellman (they'd written *Eating Together*), was among the guests and appeared to be staying with him during her sojourn in Los Angeles—as he stayed with her on Martha's Vineyard. Imagine my consternation when he insisted on seating her next to me at the dinner table (laden with delicacies of their mutual concoction).

Her opening words took my breath away: "Did you really write *Homer's Iliad: The Shield of Memory?*" she asked. I gasped. I'd tallied that maybe my first book on Homer had sold, to date, worldwide, sixty-four copies. "I love it," she added and proceeded to tell me that her favorite chapters were the ones on "Helen." When it comes to pinnacles of intellectual satisfaction, it doesn't get much pinnacler than that.

John Gardner, who wrote *The Life and Times of Chaucer* as well as *Sunlight Dialogues* and *Grendel*, cured me of academic writing when he edited my book on Homer, by telling me, "Atchity, if you can't say 'piss or go sit down,' instead of 'void the surfeit accumulation of your urinary reservoir or, alternately, circumambulate the camera and resume your former sedentary position,' then you shouldn't be writing in English."

I invited Lawrence Ferlinghetti (*A Coney Island of the Mind*) to read his iconoclastic poetry at the Occidental Poets Series then hosted him at a gumbo party at my humble faculty house on Campus Road. I invited LA's notorious poet Charles Bukowski as well as an arts reporter from *The Los Angeles Times* to join us The next day the *Times Calendar* section ran a headline: *ANCIENT ARMADILLO REARS ITS HOARY HEAD*—and Ferlinghetti never spoke to me again, other than writing me one pithy line on a mottled postcard: "I am *not* an ancient armadillo." (The *Times* had simply lifted the headline from one of his poems, that he read that night; but I suppose that didn't occur to him).

I enjoyed dinners and delightful conversations with Dominique Swain during the CBS *Madams Family* shoot in New Orleans. Later, Kayo and I enjoyed a home-cooked meal at Academy Award winner Ellen Burstyn's lovely home at Nyack-on-Hudson. Ellen co-starred with Dominique in *Madams*. Unfortunately, we screened the just-finished film for her that night—on her brand-new widescreen television, which she hadn't yet turned on. She was horrified. "Omigod," she wailed. "I look like I weigh 300 pounds!"

I ate oysters in Vancouver with "Buffy the Vampire-Slayer" Kristy Swanson in a break from filming *Angels in the Snow* and learned that her reticence between shots was just shyness.

I've watched Tim Allen, star of *Joe Somebody*, primping nervously in his trailer to meet my client Governor Jesse Ventura—whose bodyguard I played in the same film, and whose books, *I*

Ain't Got Time to Bleed and *Do I Stand Alone?* I helped turn into *New York Times* bestsellers. I stood with Angelina Jolie on the Seattle set of *Life or Something Like It,* wondering why she was hopping on one leg. "I have to pee so bad," she finally admitted. "Then why don't you?" I asked. "I hate to hold up shooting." I laughed and whispered to the first A.D., who gestured for her to escape while he continued orchestrating the gaffers and best boys.

I've delighted in hosting the flamboyantly articulate Bruno Tonioli of *Dancing with the Stars* over Kayo's exquisite home-made sushi several times at our Midwilshire home. His is one of the fastest minds and mouths I've ever encountered; I would have loved to introduce him to Lowry Nelson, my polymathic Yale mentor.

One day over cigars in his Minnesota ranch house, Governor Jesse Ventura dared me to take my receding hairline by the horns and shave it all off like he had his. I've been bald ever since—"Grass doesn't grow on a busy street!"—though, alas, Jesse reverted to a scraggly motorcycle ponytail. Later, after hearing Jim White, a wine connoisseur friend in Napa Valley, lament his own diminishing hairline, I carried on the tradition of initiation by supervising his first clean head-shave. He loved it!

Two of my favorite Hollywood moments were tied to the ongoing family drama going on inside my head. I invited Freddy to the *Joe Somebody* premiere in Westwood, and he told me afterward, over drinks, that he had to admit he was proud of me—and jealous. With all his monetary success, he really wanted to be producing movies, had seen how hard I struggled to stay in that game and wished he had the "balls" to do it. I told him it didn't take balls, just the Courtier's nonchalance, Lebanese wiles, and

Cajun stubbornness—plus persistence and having no alternative. A former partner of his, analyzing my financial situation at one moment of crisis or another, told me, "You have no choice. Going backward is impossible. You can't stay the way things are. So your *only* way to success is forward." Yeah, Bernie, I get to that every time I sit down to sort things out during those dark sleepless nights.

The other was the *Joe Somebody* premiere that I arranged at KC's Country Club Plaza. Walking in arm in arm with Mom, she in her red dress and winking to everyone she knew there, gave me a real feeling of deep-down satisfaction. Her wink said, "I take responsibility for this. I'm the one who told him, 'Go for it!'" And she was right. No one was prouder that night than Mom. Her favorite son had done something people could hum.

Once I turned my head at a wrap party in Montreal to accept an illicit puff of marijuana from someone elbowing me at the bar— to discover that the elbower was my son Vincent!

The riches I treasure the most, of course, are relationships.

I'm happily married to Kayoko, brilliant, no-nonsense, and huge-hearted Japanese lady, who tolerates my Sisyphean moods and supports my quixotic eccentricities—just as I support her vision, to express her gratitude for the gift of yoga by giving back to underserved women and children in India (YogaGivesBack.org). At our wedding, in the capacious living room of our penthouse, I recited these lines from Homer's *Odyssey* that had haunted me from the time on Cyclops Island when I first read them in ancient Greek all the way through both my troubled first and second marriages:

There is nothing more admirable than when two people who see eye to eye keep house as man and wife, confounding their enemies and delighting their friends.

On our honeymoon in Rio, we hang-glided and played beach volleyball. We travel to Italy (smuggling out limoncello and Umbrian and Sicilian wines), Japan (smuggling in pork roast, and returning with sake, real wasabi, and miso paste), England (Stilton, and mustards from Fortnum & Mason), France (preferably by bullet train from London), Costa Rica, Spain (smuggling out a wheel of manchego), London, India, Hong Kong, Ireland, Mexico, Thailand, Sedona, Sebastopol, and Colorado. We've visited Neverland as a guest of Miami artist Romero Britto, where we witnessed Los Angeles DJ Rick Dees face-pie the fastidious Michael Jackson.

I got to prepare my special *salsa cruda* (a recipe I learned from Giose Rimanelli, my co-editor of *Italian Literature: Roots & Branches* published by Yale University Press) in Jose Pimentel's luxurious Brazilian ambassador's residence in New Delhi where we were hosted for a splendid week; later, I named a character after the good ambassador in my novel *The Messiah Matrix*.

I've been blessed with two great children with solid careers, and five brilliant grandkids. Whenever we're together, son Vincent makes meat pies two of which I relish every day for breakfast. Daughter Rosemary shares life's frustrations with me with a bonhomie that warms my heart. Oldest grandchild, Meggie, during her college years at Marquette, served as an intern to a US Congressman; we took her to Japan one year, to Rome another (to the Rome Film Festival premiere of *Hysteria*). I brought her brother

Teddy with me on his first trip to his ancestral Ireland, where I spoke for the third time at Laurence O'Brien's Dublin Writers Conference and retraced with Teddy the route of James Joyce's main character Leopold Bloom's peregrinations around town (from *Ulysses*).

I keep in touch with Atchity cousins through a biennial family reunion and with my wonderful sisters.

Tolerant tennis partners who teach me tennis and life hacks.

And loyal friends, who we host, and who entertain us—and who haven't yet "killed me with an ax."

Thanks to my cell phone, that two-edged sword of bondage and freedom, I've closed book and film deals from the beach at Cabo, Piazza Santa Croce in Florence, and a Buddhist temple in Kyoto. No one on the other ends knows, or cares, where I am. One of the delights of my work is that I can do it anywhere. I've sold books to all the major publishing houses in New York, resulting in a goodly number of *New York Times* bestsellers. I have long-time trusted partners in film and television and the book business who give me feedback and support. In the days before Zoom, I went to meetings on one studio lot or another (my new "campuses") several times a month and developed films at all of them, and at most major and minor networks and cable companies.

More than once, I've bitten off more than I could chew but somehow survived. Having three films fall apart before my eyes was way up there with life-shaking lows.

What in the world was my problem? Why did I feel like an outsider, even in my own bed where I still sleep on the very edge— as though ready to fall at any second? What was I doing with my life? Until I figured that out, did I even have the right to sleep? Was that why Dad had trouble sleeping?

Was it, maybe, all right to be an outsider?

Why was I always beating myself up? "No one is holding a gun to your head except yourself," folks keep pointing out.

Why couldn't I get over my "troubles" and just let the good times roll? They say that's what you get for pushing the envelope.

The places I felt most perfectly comfortable and at home in, and in which my mind was not racing elsewhere, were podiums, movie sets, webinars, writing—and kitchens where I was doing the cooking. Someone said if everyone tossed their problems—like keys at a spouse-swapping party—on the table, we'd be scrambling to make sure we walk away with our own.

Wasn't it high time to put aside the things of a child, to feel that deep-down serenity all the time, no matter what was happening around me? Can I relegate the boxing dog of my torturing ego, however entertaining I can make it by report, to its final resting place in these pages? And simply enjoy the dust cloud of my own story.

En route to Vancouver to shoot *Angels in the Snow* for UP Channel, while finishing up the "Raptor" script based on my client Jock Miller's novel *Fossil River* with an empty two seats beside me on Air Canada, I looked out the window at the snowcapped Sierras and felt ecstatically happy. What a wonderful life I've fashioned, I say to myself when things all come together. Why couldn't it always be this way? There would be no struggle, no need for patience and endurance. As a shrink once told me, as I'm sure he would've told Sisyphus, "What you're doing is heroic."

I was being a producer and a writer and a literary manager and all at the same time. Juggling any number of rocks as I herded them up the hill.

I was being me.

And, for all that, Dad, I thank you. And thank you, Lowry, Norman, Bart, Tony, Uncle Wib, Bill, and all you others who egged me on.

Nothing to remember?

As that day of ceremonial departure recedes in time, remembering my father has gotten easier

St. Thomas More Church was full at Dad's funeral, as though everyone in KC felt they needed to appear to let my siblings and me know something they could not articulate other than by showing up.

"Your father loved you," we got from many, seeking to reassure us because they knew we needed reassurance. "He was a wonderful man."

"You could always count on Freddy," his contemporaries hastened to add. I was startled to hear that affectionate diminutive applied to my formidable father.

No way can I forget you, Dad.

Epilogue

"The first rule is becoming aware. And actually there is no second rule....
The rest is Attitude!"

—friend David Adashek

I read somewhere long ago that etymologically "Odysseus" means, "Here comes trouble."

I can relate.

Once upon a time I was going to write a book about *The Odyssey*, to follow up on my *Iliad* book. Instead, I chose to depart the academic world to go on an odyssey of my own. Under the aegis of my ancient hero, whose alleged island home of Ithaki I trudged across with my son Vincent years ago, I feel I've spent my lifetime going from one quilt of trouble to another—all of my own weaving:

It's a terrible thing," wrote Sophocles, "for a man to look upon his troubles and to recognize that he himself and no one else is the cause of them."

Complicate, uncomplicate.

I get things complicated.

The complications become overwhelming.

Then I dismantle the complication, one way or the other.

Almost always with the help of someone to talk it through with me. Odysseus had his private Athena to confide in. I found my mother- and father-substitutes on the shores or interiors of whatever island fate cast me.

To put it another way: I tied up the biggest ball of knots imaginable, pulled them tight—then I tried to unravel them, like my Uncle Pero endlessly unsnagging his fishing line on the dock in Cameron, Louisiana.

Like that suffocating quilt that I with only the "little needle" of my pen must unsew before it suffocates me.

I guess I did kinda figure it out:

Life is a ball of knots for us to undo best we can.

As fast as we can.

Before it chokes us.

It's one big fat joyful mess of our own creating.

Well, maybe not exactly entirely of our own creating. But that's another book, isn't it?

Hopefully, as we learn from our experiences, we undo the snarl faster and faster.

Maybe we learn to walk away from an oppressive knot that we finally conclude we can't unravel. Maybe we give up.

I know I have done that all too rarely, and not as nearly as often as I might have to lead a less stressful life.

Unknotting the quilt is my designated, and accepted, stress.

I've learned to love it.

When I used to ask myself why I was keeping track of all that stuff through the years I honestly didn't know the answer. But I think I know it now. I was keeping track because I didn't understand the pattern that was flying by me at the speed of life.

I was hoping that my keeping track would allow me, someday, to figure it out—to finally discern the pattern. That, I think, was the quest.

Communicate it. That was the purpose of the quest.

You live with uncertainty until you finally identify it—or you die with uncertainty before you do.

Identifying it—telling its story—is joyfully winning the game.

Dying before you get your story out is letting Brother Death win.

Exhausted strivers do that, but those whose masochism is as strong as we Catholics', keep on carrying that cross, rolling that rock, to the top of the hill.

By the way, it may not be possible for us to change our behavior. The quilt-like snarls, progressively more familiar the older we get, keep reappearing on every clean slate life allows us.

What we *can* change is our attitude.

We either bow before the weight, the sadness, the exhaustion of all the trauma we're given to face; or we keep our chins up, walking through the storm with our heads up high and singing that morning song at the kitchen sink or selling a red street-corner poppy and relishing our ability to unsnarl as bravely as we create our messes in the first place.

Albert Camus concluded, in that compelling lyric essay I first read at Georgetown: "One must imagine Sisyphus happy."

That is the only optimistic way to look at life's flamboyant absurdity, isn't it? Like the optimist halfway down from the Empire State Building.

If Dad was *my* stone, maybe I was his.

You either figure out the pattern while you're alive; or you don't.

If you do, I believe you win the game.

If you don't, well, at least you get to relax.

But winning brings a unique joy that I hope everyone in the Atchity clan gets to experience.

And you, dear reader, too.

Who am I?

I'm a story merchant. This is my story.

Acknowledgments

In a way, this whole book is an acknowledgment of those who've helped along the way. But its actual writing was much enhanced and inspired by my faithful editors, Annaliese Reid, Story Merchant exec vp Lisa Cerasoli, and longtime AEI partner Chi-Li Wong. My hat is off to my indefatigable son Vincent, who insisted I "take responsibility" for this narrative; and to my ever supportive daughter Rosemary. Norman Stephens and Lois de la Haba inspired me by telling me not to stop; and Margo McHugh for her careful proofing. A special thanks to sister Laurie for a last-minute fact and photo check.

For her constant support of my dreams, my dear wife Kayoko deserves my eternal gratitude.

Note that I've changed some non-family names to spare them any embarrassment.

About the Author

At the age of ten, Kenneth Atchity began instructions in the Latin language from a multilingual Jesuit mentor and went on to continue Latin, and commence studies in Homeric Greek and French, at the Jesuit high school, Rockhurst, in Kansas City, Missouri. He won an Ignatian Scholarship to Georgetown University in Washington, DC, and enrolled in the Honors Program as a classics major. He won the University's Virgilian Academy Silver Medal for his nationally tested knowledge of Virgil's *Aeneid*.

At Georgetown, he added to his four years of high school Homeric Greek with studies of Attic and koine Greek and further studies in Homer and four more years of Latin. He spent his junior year summer at King's College, Cambridge—mostly huddled by a schilling-room heater on Jesus Green, reading Lawrence Durrell's *Alexandrian Quartet* back-to-back.

Atchity earned an MPhil from Yale in Theater Studies and his PhD in Comparative Literature, after adding first Provençal, then Italian, as his sixth and seventh languages, focusing on the study of Dante under Harvard's Dante Della Terza and Yale's Thomas Bergin. Looking back, he would say, "I learned Greek to read Homer, Latin to read Virgil's *Aeneid*, French to read Rabelais' *Gargantua* and *Pantagruel*, Anglo-Saxon to read *Beowulf*, Italian to read Dante, Spanish to read *Don Quixote*." His dissertation, *Homer's Iliad: The Shield of Memory*, was awarded the Porter Prize, Yale Graduate School's highest academic honor. His mentors at Yale included Thomas Bergin, Adam Parry, Thomas Greene, A. Bartlett Giamatti, Richard Ellmann, Erich Segal, and Lowry Nelson, Jr.

He was professor of literature and classics at Occidental College in Los Angeles, 1970-87, served as chairman of its comparative literature department, and as Fulbright Professor to the University of Bologna. His academic career included books on Homer, Spenser, and Italian literature and dozens of scholarly articles and reviews. During his years at Occidental, Atchity was a frequent columnist for *The Los Angeles Times Book Review* and reviewed novels by Doris Lessing, Gabriel Garcia-Marquez, Carlos Fuentes, Paul Bowles, and many others.

In his second career he represented both fiction and nonfiction writers, accounting for numerous bestsellers like Steve Alten's *Meg*, Jesse Ventura's *I Ain't Got Time to Bleed*, Dacre Stoker's *Dracula: The Un-Dead*, James Pratt's *The Last Valentine*, and Lisa McCubbins' and Jerry Blaine's *The Kennedy Detail*. Movies he produced for both television and big screen include *The Amityville Horror–The Evil Escapes* (NBC), *The Lost Valentine* (Hallmark Hall of Fame), *The Madams Family* (CBS), *Angels in the Snow* (UP! Channel); *Joe Somebody* (Fox), *Life or Something Like It* (Fox), *Gospel Hill* (Fox), *Hysteria* (Sony), and *The Meg* (Warner Brothers). In the footsteps of Dominick Dunne, Sidney Sheldon, and Stephen J. Cannell, he drew on his professional experience with storytelling to complete William Diehl's *Seven Ways to Die* and his own thriller about the Jesuits, Jesus, and Caesar Augustus, *The Messiah Matrix*.

His editing, writing, managing, publishing, and producing companies can be found at www.storymerchant.com, www.storymerchantbooks.com, www.thewriterslifeline.com, and www.atchityproductions.com. Follow Ken's blog at www.kenatchity.blogspot.com and check out "Door to Door" at http://kenatchitydoortodoor.blogspot.com/.

Turn the page for a sneak peek of Volume II...

My Obit 2:
My Southern Belle

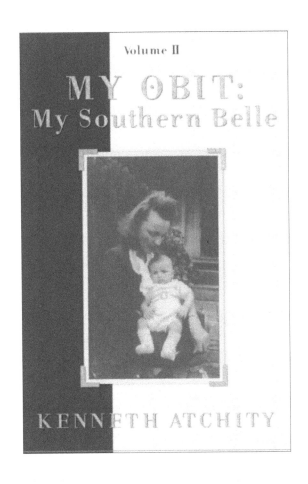

Kansas City Southern

If I flattened my nose against the window glass on a long enough curve, I could see the bullet-black locomotive elegantly leading me south on my annual escape from Kansas City. With its elegant red and yellow stripe, the black passenger liner was my chariot of the gods—carrying me, bump by click, from the misery of my under-bed existence in Yankee KC to the gumbo-fueled ecstasy of long hot summers in Louisiana. The land of mimosa and wisteria, Tasso and boudin and maque choux, hydrangea and fuchsia and satsuma and muscadine, was the place of my birth and of my mother's Aguillard family. Gas stations in Louisiana were selling food decades before branded food at branded gas stations became the nationwide norm. I remember passing one gas station outside Lafayette, whose sign proclaimed "BOUDIN BALLS," with "NO GAS" scribbled underneath.

Though the train ride south took more than twenty hours, I didn't sleep much because the opportunity curve—when I could actually see that powerful painted engine—came no more than twice on the trip at most. I could never remember exactly where it happened. I was too excited. To this day, I can't sleep on trains and planes.

I was grateful for the length of the trip. As much as I looked forward to arriving at my south Louisiana destination, my northern exposure to stress and unhappiness took some decompression before my brain felt safe enough to open itself to the southern comfort of my Cajun aunts and uncles. I admit my transitional cure was accelerated by multiple helpings from the brown paper bag packed with Mom's lovingly fried chicken, along with kibbeh and mayonnaise sandwiches on Tastee bread. Louisiana was, of course, Fried Chicken Central, and it quickly occurred to me that Mom always packed her superbly peppery fried chicken into my departure bag to remind me that she, too, knew how to prepare it and I needn't feared starving upon my return north.

Even if I was nodding off to the rhythm of the tracks, the moment my body sensed that we'd entered such a curve I would be instantly wide awake and flattening my nose, determined to see the colors of the magic carpet that was wafting me from the bondage of Cyclops' Island to the Promised Land. The "Southern Belle" (as the train was named) was the most beautiful sight in the world to me.

I boarded the train in KC's cavernously stately Union Station, which felt to me like the ultimate cathedral, whose doors shut out Hell and opened the way to Heaven. I was heading for the warmth and camaraderie my mother missed in KC, where my father's Atchity family just didn't understand the knack of "hanging out" day in and day out on the front porch shooting the breeze and swapping stories. Unlike KC, where every single action and thought were confessed and judged—by grandfather, uncles, aunts, and cousins; or by the nuns and Jesuit priests and scholastics who dominated my Missouri days—down in Louisiana talking seemed just for the sheer joy of it. At the north end of those magic tracks were icy KC winters and the unceasing warfare between Mom and Dad that left me biting my nails and crying myself to sleep. At the south end was the heartfelt welcome of my French-speaking grandmother, "Mamère," and aunts, uncles, and cousins all waiting for my annual arrival with Magnalite pots simmering at ready on stovetops, and pies and cakes in ovens baking their sweet defiance of the tropical heat.

I would eat my way eastward on Airline Highway, US 190, the northern route from Lake Charles (Nanee) to Kinder (Cousin Jackie) to Basile (Aunt Ophelia and "the Aguillard cemetery") to Eunice (Jonnie Ruppert, Hubert Martel, and Aunt Laurence and "the old Aguillard cemetery") to Opelousas (cracklins) to Krotz Springs and Melville (Uncle Ed Aguillard) to Port Allen (Cousin David) to Baton Rouge (Uncle Wib). Then I would return to Nanee's on the southern route (I-10 West) to Port Allen to Breaux Bridge (Mike Rees) to Lafayette to Iowa (for cracklins) to Lake Charles.

My stomach became a reservoir of fried chicken; roux made of sautéed onions, crawfish fat, parsley, bell peppers, red peppers, and onion tops; crawfish étouffée, or crawfish boiled or baked into pies; cracklins straight from the oven; sweet blackberries handpicked in the quiet of the woods; home-made biscuits; Aunt Laurence's baby limas; garden-fresh tomatoes, cucumbers, garlic, and spicy green peppers; peaches and pecans straight from the tree—with, all along the way, endless rice and gravy. In South Louisiana, a meal without rice doesn't count.

Sometimes I made my statewide trek by car, sometimes by Trailways bus after being delivered, jerkily, to the red and white rolling caravan by Uncle Pero in Lake Charles. Two hours later I would be picked up in Krotz Springs, the closest terminal to isolated little Melville, by my Uncle Ed Aguillard, Mom's oldest brother.

When I was old enough to drive and later had my own car and family, the familiar eating pressure cycle had not diminished. We'd leave breakfast in Baton Rouge, with, "Why are you leaving so early?" ringing in our ears—only to arrive at eleven-thirty at a Eunice homestead, to be greeted with, "Why you comin' so late?"—and immediately sitting down to a welcome "dinner," as we called the midday meal. Leaving that dinner as late as I dared, at three-thirty, I would drive as fast as I could safely or not (with more than a few tickets served by Highway Patrol along the way) — to arrive in Sugartown just in time for "supper" and the mournful complaint that I had waited too long to get there, so Cousin Danny "had to leave for work."

From feeling like a random number in KC as the third oldest male Atchity cousin, in Louisiana, I was the oldest of the Aguillard grandchildren and the undisputed prince returning to the kingdom. In KC, I had to adjust to the adults around me; in Louisiana, I was guaranteed to be the center of attention just by being myself. Mom's family wanted to know all about me, inside out. And I, the muted "Foghorn" in KC, became here a garrulous confessor of events and emotions.

The repasts waiting for me at each stop would haunt my dreams, and combat my night terrors, the rest of the year: roast and rice and gravy from Uncle Pero's wife and Mom's sister Aunt Bernice or "Nanee"; buttered and honeyed baby lima beans from her own garden from Aunt Laurence, my grandmother Mezille's sister; Aunt Mossy's steak and gravy; and the best fried chicken from Cousin Ida Belle Odom Ruppert, or Hubert Martel's wife, Aunt Viola—or both. Their chicken was so fresh you could detect its savor a mile away, that heavenly fragrance that issued only from home-grown and plucked-that-day chicken.

Planning my route in each direction forced me to make cold-hearted decisions about whose étouffée was the best (Aunt Ruby's), whose fried chicken (Viola's, in a tossup with Ida Belle's), whose roast (Nanee's)—or I'd find myself willy-nilly eating the same dish twice a day. How would I compare their fried chicken with Mom's? That question made me realize, from infancy, that some questions needn't be answered because they are *trick questions*.

A week into my two-month stay on Uncle Jonnie and Ida Belle's rice plantation near Iota, Ida Belle asked me what my favorite food in Louisiana was. "Your fried chicken," I said with all my heart.

"How often could you eat it?" she asked.

"I could eat it for breakfast, lunch, and dinner," I said.

She rose to the bait. "I'll tell you what. I'll fix it for you for breakfast, lunch, and dinner until you tell me you're tired of it."

"Yes!" I shouted.

"Long as you kill the chickens."

I'd never killed a chicken in my life, but that didn't stop me from accepting the challenge. I'd watched my grandmother do the deed often enough. Others would wring the chicken's neck and let it flap and flop around the yard, and even under the house. until its muscles and nerves fitfully conceded its life was over. But Mamère dispatched it with one swift motion of her butcher knife and hung the headless bird by its feet on the clothesline to bleed out and finally stop its flopping. I didn't like her method of execution—too bloody. Ida Belle showed me how to wring a chicken's neck with one sudden motion that ended with a definitive crack and virtually eliminated the post-mortem spasms. Once you grab a chicken by the head, there's no room for tentativeness. A merciful killer must be decisive.

Any Aguillard woman knew how to prepare the chicken from there. You immerse it in boiling water to soften the feathers, pluck out the feathers, then singe the carcass in a fire to sear off the pin feathers. The sharp acrid smell burns in my memory. Then, deftly, butcher the cleaned carcass to render traditional drumsticks, wings, thighs, breasts, back, and neck for the frying. Mamère always reserved the neck and back for herself, claiming they were her favorite pieces when I suspected it was only her adapting to her maternal fate; everyone else preferred breast, legs, wings, and thighs. My favorite: wings.

The morning after Ida Belle's gauntlet was thrown, I awoke to the smell of fried chicken and eggs for breakfast. Black housekeeper Mary had done the deed before I woke up. Dinner was fried chicken and fresh okra, and ham or pork chops for Uncle Jonnie, along with the ever-present salad that both my northern and southern families served, with Wishbone Italian dressing. Salads were made with crunchy iceberg lettuce in a world that had not even imagined Romaine, not to mention arugula, Batavia, Boston, or red Butterhead. A grocer's grandson, I always wondered if the claim that all those lettuces were "healthier for you than iceberg" was nothing but marketing.

Before supper rolled around, I marched out to the yard again and handed the victim to Mary to clean and Ida Belle to fry and accompany with purple hull field peas, rice, biscuits, and honey.

This happy cycle of life lasted me for over two weeks when, without warning, after an umpteenth fried chicken breakfast, Ida

Belle announced, "That's it. You win! I am not going to fry another chicken today—maybe even ever!" I couldn't believe my ears. This little run of paradise had ended, and we immediately reverted that day at dinner to fresh crawfish, *des écrevisses*, just harvested from Uncle Jonnie's rice fields. Everyone talked as though I had won, Ida Belle had lost—when as far as I was concerned, I hadn't won at all.

Thank God, Ida Belle went back to frying chicken once or twice a week, while the rest of the week we slogged our way valiantly through baked ham and gravy, crawfish creole, or pan-fried Gaspergou from the nearby canals and lakes; even, one day, sweetbreads that she told me were scrambled eggs until I looked more closely—by that time, firmly hooked on them. "Why are these eggs so delicious?" I'd asked. "Because they're not eggs," she said with a mother-like shrug.

The train ride always ended with me in my coach seat peering through the shadow-darkened glass at the platform in Alexandria, Louisiana, to see if I could spot Uncle Wib smoking his pipe as he waited. I never could, though my nose could identify his tobacco. Trickster from first to last, he knew our game too well and never lost. But each time when he emerged from behind his pillar, he looked whiter around the eyes than I'd remembered him.

To the Reader

Without you, writers are clouds in the wind. Readers are that wind, the wind that determines the storyteller's course. If you'd be so kind as to leave a review on amazon.com, I'd be most appreciative. And I'd love to hear from you at atchity@storymerchant.com.

My Obit 1